W[...]
U[...]

"If the present is unaware of the past it cannot shape the future. We now see the past beyond the constraints of prejudice and have the chance to recognize the wrongs that were committed."

> —Prof. Dr. Andreas Khol,
> Chairman of the Austrian National Assembly

"Brilliantly researched and perfectly crafted, Rammerstorfer's book offers a sensitive portrayal of a man whose memory stretches over the entire 20th century. Following decades of persecution, prejudice, and ridicule, Leopold Engleitner now receives belated recognition through this book which reaches far beyond the borders of his native Austria."

> —Prof. Dr. Walter Manoschek, political scientist,
> Institute for Political Science at the
> University of Vienna

"Leopold Engleitner's life story *Unbroken Will* describes an exceptional personality who took a courageous stand by refusing to serve in the German Wehrmacht. To say 'I won't serve in Hitler's army' was far more than just a statement; it was regarded as high treason and carried the death penalty. *Unbroken Will* is a dramatic portrayal of Mr. Engleitner's tremendous personal courage."

> —Leon Askin, actor and director
> author, *Quietude and Quest*

"It is widely known how important the testimony of survivors is for shedding light on persecution and resistance....The motives for refusing to fight in the war and the challenges arising from this decision become clear, as does the suffering that had to be borne in concentration camps. Leopold Engleitner stuck to his "No" and not even the SS succeeded in breaking his will. In his release from the concentration camp, we see the helplessness of his persecutors, who finally had to concede that they were dealing with a phenomenon, with people who were prepared to make any sacrifice for the sake of their faith....Leopold Engleitner's unwavering "No" would not have led to such suffering if there had been a 'No' from many more individuals."

— Dr. Detlef Garbe, author of
*Zwischen Widerstand und Martyrium:
Die Zeugen Jehovas im Dritten Reich*

UNBROKEN WILL

The Extraordinary Courage
of an Ordinary Man

Bernhard Rammerstorfer

Grammaton Press
New Orleans

PUBLISHED WITH THE SUPPORT OF THE AUSTRIAN
FEDERAL MINISTRY FOR EDUCATION, SCIENCE AND
CULTURE IN VIENNA

Federal Ministry

for Foreign Affairs

SUPPORTED BY THE AUSTRIAN FEDERAL MINISTRY
FOR FOREIGN AFFAIRS

Grammaton Press, LLC, New Orleans, LA 70130;
(504) 376-4592; books@grammatonpress.com.

Original title: *Nein statt Ja und Amen—Leopold Engleitner: Er ging
einen anderen Weg*

Published by Bernhard Rammerstorfer
Copyright © Bernhard Rammerstorfer 1999
Bernhard Rammerstorfer, Koth 34, 4175 Herzogsdorf, Austria,
Europe
Website: http://www.rammerstorfer.cc
E-mail: office@rammerstorfer.cc

Unbroken Will: The Extraordinary Courage of an Ordinary Man
Bernhard Rammerstorfer
Translated from the German by Neil Perkins

ISBN 0-9679366-8-3

CONTENTS

Preface

It would be easy to agree with those who say that Leopold Engleitner was an ordinary man whom history forced to behave in an extraordinary manner. History in this case being the demented evil regime of the National Socialists in Germany after January 1933 and in his native Austria after March 1938. But how close to the truth is this seemingly accurate description of the man?

Ordinary in the sense of normal, typical, one of many? Leopold Engleitner was born with a spinal curvature that determined that his physical being would be forever deformed. His paternal grandmother was strongly drawn to Protestantism in a tightly Roman Catholic family and region, which gave rise to social as well as religious tensions. His father's attitude toward his own Catholicism was vaguely liberal, almost indifferent, but his mother believed fervently in the Church and its strictures. This situation evoked in the young man a deep skepticism about religion until his conversion to the faith of Jehovah's Witnesses.

Throughout his childhood he and his family suffered constant hunger because his father could not earn enough to feed them properly. Leopold's deformity cruelly isolated him from his schoolmates. He could not participate in games or other physical exercises and was constantly ragged as being "inferior." As a young teenager, Leopold questioned the moral standards of the Habsburg Monarchy and the gap between its riches and his own family's poverty. At the age of 13, he left school permanently to work intermittently as an unskilled laborer. Nevertheless, he was able to purchase a plot of land, to build his own small house, and to eke out a living while making many things with his own hands, such as a pair of skis.

After being convinced by the teachings of Jehovah's Witnesses that theirs was the way to salvation and a better life, he resigned from the Catholic Church, a formal procedure in Austria, despite great pressure against this from family and friends. Afterward he became an object of contempt in the region, at times spat upon by some villagers. Following his conversion, he made house-to-house visits to explain the Bible to others. He suffered great physical stress and pain when arrested by local police authorities who regularly picked him up for "questioning." He served a short sentence for "peddling without a license" in 1934 and longer stretches in 1936 and 1937 for "libeling" and "offending" the legal religions of the country and for being a "public danger." All of this occurred before Germany and Austria united in March 1938.

An ordinary man?

Leopold Engleitner's history is far from ordinary, and his determination, faith, and strength of will seem far beyond those of an ordinary person. Leopold Engleitner is, in fact, a heroic figure to many, because of the course of his life after the Anschluss.

With the ban on Witness activities in the spring of 1938, Engleitner and his companions went underground but did not cease their activities. They were, however, much more cautious than before. In April 1939 the police arrested a group of Austrian Witnesses that included Engleitner. Authorities moved him from jail to jail, deported him to Buchenwald, then transported him to Wewelsburg (Niederhagen) and Ravensbrück concentration camps, where the guards constantly beat him and unsuccessfully attempted to make him renounce his faith. He worked at hard labor under appalling conditions imposed by the German and Austrian SS barbarians. The story of Leopold Engleitner and other Jehovah's Witnesses in the camps, as recounted in this book, gives details not only about the persecution of the Witnesses but also about the daily life in the camps and the fate of Jews, gypsies, and other victims of the Nazis' persecution and genocide.

Despite his horrendously weakened physical condition, made worse by his deformed spine, he persevered, even refusing release from the camps because this would require him to sign a renunciation of his beliefs. In the summer of 1943, he was released after signing a declaration that he would work in agriculture for the rest of his life.

The final irony of his incredible life occurred when, in the spring of 1946, he applied at the local labor office for a job unconnected with farming. The clerk pointed to that declaration and refused to allow him a nonagricultural position! An appeal to the American military government authorities resolved the matter, and Leopold Engleitner worked as a construction laborer until his retirement in 1969. He never stopped preaching and proclaiming the "good news" of his faith.

An extraordinary life of an extraordinary man.

— Brewster Chamberlin
Key West, June 2002

As a historian, Dr. Chamberlin has focused his research and teaching on European history in the 19th and 20th centuries. A Fulbright-Hays Fellowship and other grants enabled him to conduct research in many European countries, especially in Germany. He has taught for the University of Maryland, the Johns Hopkins University's School for Advanced International Studies, and the Zentrum für Antisemitismusforschung at the Technical

University in Berlin and has been a Research Associate of the Institut für Zeitgeschichte in Munich. The editor and author of numerous articles and books on various aspects of German and European history, archival theory and practice, and the United States Holocaust Memorial Museum, Dr. Chamberlin was the Director of Archives for the Museum from 1986 to 1997, after which he served as the Director and Associate Director of the Museum's International Division from 1998 to 2001. He is currently writing a book about the city of Berlin in the 20th century.

Foreword

Unbroken Will

Peace, liberty, and equality are precious assets that are often taken for granted. But if we are fortunate enough to live in a part of the world where armed conflict has for decades been a thing of the past, we would do well to remember that the elder generation in particular had to undergo the painful experience of discovering just how fragile peace can be and how valuable liberty and democracy are.

During the Nazis' reign of terror in the Third Reich, few people had the courage to stand up for their own religious and political convictions. Many faced imprisonment in a concentration camp and the most inhuman treatment imaginable, which few survived. But for the survivors, their sufferings were by no means over after the war ended. Society often misinterpreted their attitude; unfounded prejudices often resulted in loneliness and isolation for people who had suffered a great deal already.

Much later, in the course of examining the National Socialist era, the courageous stance taken by many civilians in the struggle against the terrifying regime of that time has begun to emerge. This book pays a richly deserved tribute to one of the few surviving Upper Austrian witnesses of that period, Leopold Engleitner. The brutal mistreatment he suffered in the various concentration camps could only bind his hands; it could not break his iron will or his unwavering faith.

His uncompromising stance makes him a pioneer of freedom of speech and worship, and one is wholly justified in describing him as a model for future generations. In my capacity as head of the provincial government of Upper Austria, I would like to express my deep respect and gratitude toward Herr Engleitner for his selfless commitment and wish him many more days of peace and good health.

— Dr. Josef Pühringer
Provincial Governor of Upper Austria

Franz Jägerstätter and Leopold Engleitner

by Andreas Maislinger

There are few books that I have so eagerly awaited as this biography of Leopold Engleitner from the province of Upper Austria. Let's not fool ourselves; not every book that is published is of value. Books often appear that merely reproduce facts already known to us or that are riddled with errors. So it is not always easy for readers to obtain a clear picture. Too often the title of a book promises much when what it contains is in reality nothing more than an artificially padded-out newspaper article.

This book is different. At long last we can read the story of this Austrian, one of Jehovah's Witnesses. In the past two decades, the rising popularity of oral history has led to a wealth of life stories of people from all kinds of backgrounds being recorded for posterity. Historical research discovered ordinary people. In the process the (mostly young) historians covered every conceivable occupational group. But the majority of the biographies recorded and published dealt with people who followed left-wing, socialist, or communist ideals. By way of example, I need only mention the wide range of literature and numerous documentaries on Austrians in the Spanish Civil War.

The persecution of Jehovah's Witnesses has by no means been ignored by Austrian historical research. The comprehensive documentation on resistance and persecution in the individual federal provinces published by the *Dokumentationsarchiv des Österreichischen Widerstandes* (DÖW, the Documentation Centre of Austrian Resistance) deals extensively with Jehovah's Witnesses. But that was all there was until the "amateur historian" Bernhard Rammerstorfer came along and wrote a long overdue book about one of Jehovah's Witnesses who was persecuted by the National Socialists. And he has written a gripping book. This opinion is shared by the historian Detlef Garbe, and he should know, since he is the author of the definitive work on Jehovah's Witnesses in the Third Reich, *"Zwischen Widerstand und Martyrium."*

Not only has Bernhard Rammerstorfer managed to write a gripping story but he has spared no effort in following up every detail, however small. The index forced him to verify the spelling of names and to document other statements made by Leopold Engleitner as well. This meticulousness is (unfortunately) often missing from oral-history books.

Franz Jägerstätter is the real reason why I have looked forward to this book so much. I was born in 1955 in St. Georgen on the border between Salzburg, Upper Austria, and Bavaria. When I was a child, my father told me the story of a farmer from St. Radegund who was executed for refusing to fight for Hitler. I remember that even then there were rumors that he had had close contact with the Bible Students, as Jehovah's Witnesses were then known. In fact, both his aunt (Maria) and his cousin (Johann Huber) were Jehovah's Witnesses. Unfortunately, very little is known about Franz Jägerstätter's relationship to the Jehovah's Witnesses. In her biography of Jägerstätter, Erna Putz writes that he "had numerous theological discussions with them," which "would have been one of the reasons why he took a deeper interest in religious problems."

Leopold Engleitner recalls a conversation he had with Johann Huber. Shortly after World War II, Franz Jägerstätter's cousin told him about the problems he had encountered in St. Radegund following his resignation from the Catholic Church. According to Engleitner's recollection of Huber's statements, the latter was no longer even able to buy milk in the village. The only person who did not spurn him because he had become one of Jehovah's Witnesses was Jägerstätter's mother, and Huber was able to pay the family regular visits. Although Jägerstätter is said to have been rather disparaging at first, he later began to ask serious questions. A study of the Bible in the strictest sense did not take place, however. Engleitner takes care to emphasize this distance and has no intention of claiming Franz Jägerstätter for the Jehovah's Witnesses.

Although the farmer from the Austrian Innviertel became one of the best known opponents of Hitler following the publication in the United States in 1964 of the book *In Solitary Witness: The Life and Death of Franz Jägerstätter* by Gordon Zahn, I would still like to present a short biography of him.

Franz Jägerstätter was born on May 20, 1907, in St. Radegund near the town of Braunau on the river Inn in Upper Austria. His parents were too poor to marry. During the first years of his life, he was brought up by his grandmother. In 1917 his mother married the farmer Heinrich Jägerstätter, who adopted Franz as his son. While living on his adoptive father's farm, he was encouraged to read by a grandfather. Franz had the reputation of being a lively, happy-go-lucky boy. In 1936 he married the deeply religious Franziska Schwaninger. The marriage, which was by all accounts unusually happy, produced three daughters: Rosalia, Maria, and Aloisia. In 1938, Franz Jägerstätter voted against the Anschluss of Austria to the German Reich. In 1940 he was called up. He completed his basic training and swore allegiance to Adolf Hitler. In April 1941 he was exempted from military service at the instigation of the mayor, who maintained that his was a reserved occupation. He made use of the time he had until his second call-up in February 1943 to prepare his decision to declare himself a conscientious objector and to refuse to join the German *Wehrmacht*. On August 9, 1943, Franz Jägerstätter was executed in Berlin.

The film director Axel Corti based his film *Der Fall Jägerstätter* on the above-mentioned book by the American pacifist Gordon Zahn. The leading role was played by Kurt Weinzierl. The film excited such interest that it was repeated on Austrian television after only five months. Franz Jägerstätter's steadfast refusal to serve in the German *Wehrmacht* under Adolf Hitler caused a controversy that still rages today. In the course of the debate, which has often been intense, his attitude has repeatedly been compared to that of Jehovah's Witnesses, although such comparisons were never more than mere allusions. In order to evaluate these comparisons, what has been needed more than anything else is a biography of one of Jehovah's Witnesses whose study of the Bible made it impossible for him to be "a soldier of Christ and at the same time a soldier of the National Socialists," just as Franz Jägerstätter was.

This biography is now available, and we can compare Jägerstätter's actions with those of Leopold Engleitner. Both came from poor backgrounds and were born at almost the same time. Both were raised as Catholics and searched for answers different from those offered in their immediate surroundings. Whereas Leopold Engleitner found his answers with Jehovah's Witnesses, Franz Jägerstätter never left the Catholic Church and was locked in conflict with his parish priest and even with the bishop of Linz.

It is in this conflict that the principal difference between him and Jehovah's Witnesses becomes evident. After all, Jägerstätter had to resist pressure from his church and force himself to make the decision he made, whereas Engleitner and other Jehovah's Witnesses had the approbation of the leaders of their religious community. True though this is, the chapter "Courageous Change of Religion in the 1930s" in this book shows that the resistance Engleitner had to overcome was every bit as strong as it was for Jägerstätter. Despite the support he received from his brothers in the faith, Engleitner had to assert himself in an environment that was at the least disapproving and at worst downright hostile toward his convictions. Jägerstätter and Engleitner held opposing political views. Had they met, they would have found common ground on the subject of serious Bible study but would have disagreed about Dollfuss and Schuschnigg. My personal wish is that supporters of Franz Jägerstätter and Jehovah's Witnesses meet to discuss the similarities and differences between these two opponents of National Socialism, both of whom were motivated by the Bible. We only have fragments of information concerning discussions between Jägerstätter and Jehovah's Witnesses, but this new book offers the interested reader the chance to bring Jägerstätter and Engleitner together for an imaginary dialogue.

Dr. Andreas Maislinger is a political scientist from Innsbruck, Austria, with wide study and work experience. In 1987 he was visiting assistant professor at the University of New Orleans. He has also seen service at the Hebrew University in Jerusalem and was involved in a Holocaust class at Yad Vashem in 1990. From 1992 to 1996, he wrote for the Jüdische Rundschau (Jewish Review), Basel, Switzerland, and has been scholarly director of the Braunau Contemporary History Days (Braunauer Zeitgeschichte-Tage) since 1992. In the same year, he founded the Austrian Holocaust Memorial Service (Gedenkdienst), an alternative to Austria's compulsory military service. Gedenkdienst interns work at major Holocaust institutions. In 2000 he initiated the project House of Responsibility in Braunau, Austria.

Introduction

by Bernhard Rammerstorfer

What prompts a young man to undertake an in-depth study of the experiences of a 98-year-old victim of Nazi atrocities?

I met Leopold Engleitner for the first time in 1994 in Bad Ischl. In the course of the many hours spent together in conversation and various other activities, we developed a special friendship. The longer I listened to him, the more moving I found the life story of this simple man who had had to cope with physical infirmities since birth. The stories he told gave me the unique opportunity to immerse myself in 20th century history, from the monarchy to the First Republic to National Socialism to the Second Republic.

He has encountered many prominent personalities in the course of his life. For example, Emperor Franz Joseph, Katharina Schratt, Hans Moser, and Dr. Heinrich Gleissner. During the Hitler Regime, he had personal experience of the unspeakable cruelty that man is capable of. Despite this, he is today a cheerful man with a thoroughly positive outlook. I have come to appreciate his quick wit, his courage, his enormous faith in God, and his unshakeable belief.

For me, people like Leopold Engleitner who show such great character are a gift and a boon to society, and what they have experienced during their lives should be made available for coming generations. This is why it was so important to me to record his life story for posterity, because we can learn so much from it.

Over the past few years, I have conducted intensive research into the life of Leopold Engleitner. I decided to present his life biographically instead of writing a novel or a fictional diary. I did not want to sacrifice important details or be constrained by a particular style.

The lighthearted anecdotes that have been included are not intended to disguise the barbarity of the conditions that prevailed but are presented to paint as complete a picture of Leopold Engleitner's personality as possible.

This book has not been written to condemn those who did not act as Leopold Engleitner did. The years here discussed were a difficult time for the soldiers too. Many of them felt compelled to serve and were far from convinced of the cause for which they fought. Certainly those who had to fight at the front or at other scenes of battle far from home suffered much.

Leopold Engleitner's choices nevertheless prove that, even in times of violence, terror, and oppression, it is possible to lead a life free of violence and guided by principles. Even a simple, ordinary man can remain unsullied by an unjust regime.

Horrific as it was to be killed in a concentration camp, it was perhaps even more horrific to remain alive and thus be subjected to continuing torment and humiliation. A living death can seem worse than death itself.

What I have found so impressive is the outstanding simplicity and uprightness of Leopold Engleitner's life; he succeeded in maintaining his personal integrity and his faith under the most adverse conditions imaginable. It is phenomenal that a huge, totalitarian system failed to break the will of such an unassuming man.

In a society caught under the spell of National Socialism and that exerted enormous pressure, he showed an alternative to conventional patterns of behavior.

Leopold Engleitner should be a role model particularly for young people, inspiring them to adhere to just principles and to have the backbone to stand up for these values in the face of peer pressure and other forms of coercion. This is especially important in today's society, which is constantly being threatened by radical tendencies. The fact that in the 20th century we actually started numbering world wars should be enough to set us thinking.

It was very important to me to demonstrate by means of Leopold Engleitner's personal history that adherence to principles and the development of conscience are of paramount importance not only to the individual but also to the entire fabric of society. They are, after all, the pillars on which humanity and peace rest and which are essential for resistance against *Gleichschaltung*—forced conformity with authoritarian ideals.

For centuries now, the whole world has longed for lasting peace but has been unable to achieve it. As long as young people the world over are trained for war, we cannot expect this situation to change. It is surely worth considering whether it would make more sense to train them for "peace." I know that I am philosophizing, but the life of Leopold Engleitner leads to that conclusion.

Twentieth-century history would surely have been written differently if more of his contemporaries had acted as courageously as Leopold Engleitner.

Acknowledgments

My thanks go to the following for their expert assistance:

- Dr. Alois Birklbauer, lecturer at the Institute for Criminal Law of the University of Linz
- Dr. Gerson Kern
- Dr. Andreas Maislinger, political scientist, founder and chairman of the Austrian Holocaust Memorial Service, Braunau Contemporary History Days and House of Responsibility, www.maislinger.net
- Julian Rivers, University of Bristol, Department of Law

For their helpful comments on the manuscript I thank:

- Wulff E. Brebeck, curator of the Kreismuseum in Wewelsburg
- Dr. Brewster Chamberlin, historian, lecturer at the University of Maryland, the Johns Hopkins University's School for Advanced International Studies, and the Zentrum für Antisemitismusforschung at the Technical University in Berlin; director of archives at the United States Holocaust Memorial Museum 1986 to 1997, director and associate director of the United States Holocaust Memorial Museum's International Division 1998 to 2001

- Dr. Detlef Garbe, historian, curator of the Neuengamme Concentration Camp Memorial
- Kirsten John-Stucke, assistant curator of the Kreismuseum Wewelsburg
- Dr. Wolfgang Quatember, curator of the Ebensee Concentration Camp Memorial
- Sabine Stein, Buchenwald Concentration Camp Memorial, archives

Proofreading:
- David Wilson

For help with research and access to documentation I thank: Arbeitsmarktservice Oberösterreich, Bezirksgericht Bad Ischl, Bundesarchiv Berlin, Bundespolizeidirektion Linz, Dokumentationsarchiv des Österreichischen Widerstandes, Evang. Pfarramt Ramsau am Dachstein, Filmarchiv Austria, Foto Hofer Bad Ischl, Gedenkstätte Buchenwald, Gemeindeamt Traunkirchen, Informationsdienst der Zeugen Jehovas Österreich, Justizanstalt Linz, Kath. Pfarramt Bad Goisern, Kath. Pfarramt Bad Ischl, Kath. Pfarramt Gmunden, Kath. Pfarramt St. Wolfgang im Salzkammergut, Kath. Pfarramt Straßwalchen, Kath. Pfarramt Strobl, Kreismuseum Wewelsburg, Landesgendarmeriekommando für Oberösterreich, Landesgendarmeriekommando für Salzburg, Landesgericht Leoben, Landesgericht Salzburg, Landesgericht Wels, Landeshauptstadt Magdeburg, Landeshauptstadt München, Landratsamt Stollberg, Lewes Prison, East Sussex, Magistrat der Stadt Wels, Magistrat der Stadt Salzburg, Magistrat der Stadt Wien, Standesamt Wien – Favoriten, Mahn- und Gedenkstätte Ravensbrück, Marktgemeinde St. Wolfgang im Salzkammergut, Nordrhein-Westfälisches Staatsarchiv Detmold, Nordrhein-Westfälisches Hauptstaatsarchiv, Oberlandesgericht Graz, Oberlandesgericht

Linz,   Oberösterreichische   Landtagsdirektion,
Oberösterreichisches Landesarchiv, Oberster Gerichtshof
Wien,   Österreichische   Präsidentschaftskanzlei,
Österreichisches Staatsarchiv, ÖVP Landesparteileitung
Oberösterreich, Salzkammergut-Zeitung Gmunden,
Staatsanwaltschaft Salzburg, Staatsanwaltschaft Wels, Stadt
Augsburg, Stadt Blumberg, Stadt Brandenburg an der Havel,
Stadt Bremerhaven, Stadt Frankfurt am Main, Stadt Hamm,
Stadt Halver, Stadt Konstanz, Stadt Oebisfelde bei Gardelegen,
Stadt Sprockhövel, Stadt Stade, Stadt Treuen, Stadt Ulm,
Stadtamt Bad Ischl, Stadtamt Gmunden, Stadtarchiv der
Landeshauptstadt Saarbrücken, Steiermärkisches Landesarchiv,
Thüringisches   Hauptstaatsarchiv   Weimar,
Verwaltungsgemeinschaft Heideck–Prettin, Wachtturm–
Gesellschaft Selters, Wachtturm Bibel- und Traktatgesellschaft
Wien, Zentralstelle im Lande Nordrhein-Westfalen für die
Bearbeitung von nationalsozialistischen Massenverbrechen in
Konzentrationslagern bei der Staatsanwaltschaft Köln

And for their invaluable help and support my special thanks
go to: Robert Buckley, Reinhard Hannesschläger, and Ingeborg
Wagner Kolodney

Leopold Engleitner: Rehabilitation by the Highest Representatives of the Austrian Republic

Leopold Engleitner presents Dr. Thomas Klestil, President of the Republic of Austria, with a copy of his biography, 2003.

May 5, 2003
Fifty-eight years after Leopold Engleitner's return home following his flight to the mountains of the Salzkammergut from the National Socialist regime, he was received by Austria's President, Dr. Thomas Klestil, in the Hofburg, the presidential palace in Vienna.

This reception by the Austrian head of state was an unexpected gesture of rehabilitation and recognition of Engleitner's courageous stance.

*The Chairman
of the Austrian
National Assembly,
Prof. Dr. Andreas
Khol, with Leopold
Engleitner
in the Austrian
parliament building,
2003*

June 6, 2003

As one of the few remaining survivors of the period, Leopold
Engleitner was invited by the Chairman of the Austrian
National Assembly, Prof. Dr. Andreas Khol, to attend the
symposium in the Austrian parliament on "Austrian Victims
of National Socialist Military Jurisdiction" as guest of honor.
Dr. Khol described National Socialist military jurisdiction as
jurisdiction based on injustice and underlined the great
importance of the two-year research project "Victims of
National Socialist Military Jurisdiction," which was
commissioned by the Austrian Ministry of Education and led
by Prof. Dr. Walter Manoschek. "If the present is unaware of
the past," said Dr. Khol, "it cannot shape the future. And it is
important that this research project places the facts about what
happened on the table. We now see the past beyond the

Left to right: Johannes Peinsteiner, Mayor of St. Wolfgang (Engleitner's home district); Dr. Josef Pühringer, Governor of Upper Austria; Leopold Engleitner with the Silver Order of Merit of the Province of Upper Austria; author Bernhard Rammerstorfer, 2003

constraints of prejudice and have the chance to recognize the wrongs that were committed."

By way of thanks for the invitation and the award of compensation from the state fund of the Republic of Austria for the gramophone that the Nazis had confiscated from him in 1939, Engleitner gave Dr. Khol a copy of his biography containing a dedication, which the Chairman of the National Assembly received with pleasure, saying: "Thank you very much. I will certainly read your book."

June 16, 2003
In recognition of his unwavering adherence to his principles during the period of National Socialism and the countless talks and discussions about his experiences that he has held at universities, schools, and international memorial sites, Leopold

Engleitner was awarded the Silver Order of Merit of the Province of Upper Austria by the Upper Austrian Governor Dr. Josef Pühringer. In his speech Dr. Pühringer said: "As a witness to those times, Leopold Engleitner has patiently answered questions for hours on end, thus affording an enormous number of young people a genuine insight into history. With his courageous stance and his tireless commitment to an objective assessment of our history, he has enhanced our country's reputation both at home and abroad and has thus rendered his homeland a great service.

"Mr. Engleitner, thank you for making this black period of our history known to the next generation. We cannot change what happened in the past; we can only learn from it. And people like you, who lived through it, can make a huge contribution to this learning process. Thank you for your efforts and congratulations on receiving this honor."

May 5, 2004
On the occasion of the "Day of Commemoration Against Violence and Racism in Remembrance of the Victims of National Socialism," and the newly-elected Austrian president Dr. Heinz Fischer gave a cordial welcome to Leopold Engleitner in the presidential chambers of the Hofburg in Vienna. The president showed great interest in Engleitner's life-story and expressed his respect and admiration.

Austrian president Dr. Heinz Fischer with Leopold Engleitner and author Bernhard Rammerstorfer, 2004

1: Map from the time of the monarchy, circa 1915 (adapted), showing Upper Austria, Salzburg and Styria, with the places of significance in Leopold Engleitner's life

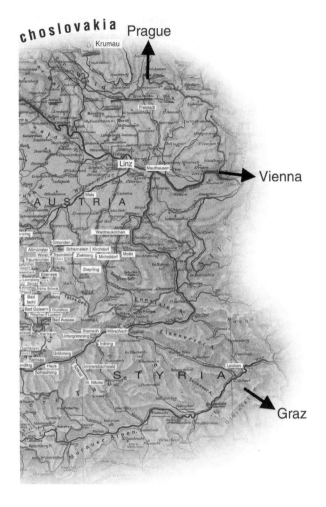

2: German school atlas, 1942 (adapted), published by the Reichsstelle für das Schul- und Unterrichtsschrifttum, *showing Europe with concentration camps*

A Narrow Escape

It is Tuesday, April 17, 1945. World War II rages on, but the people of the Salzkammergut[1] around Bad Ischl[2] sense that this meaningless slaughter is drawing to a close. Almost every family has been affected, either directly or indirectly, by this terrible war and its grim side effects. Despite this, there is work to be done and needs to be met.

It is already late afternoon at the Unterbergerhof, an alpine farmhouse in Windhag in the municipality of St. Wolfgang on the shores of the Wolfgangsee, but people are still working in the fields. The farmer, Johann Unterberger, is not among them; he is in a military hospital, having been badly wounded during the fighting in Normandy. It is left to his wife, Franziska, and former concentration camp internee Leopold Engleitner, a forced laborer, to look after the farm without him.

Franziska and her farmhand Leopold, also known as Poidl, are getting

[1] A region of Austria including parts of Salzburg, Upper Austria, and Styria
[2] Also known as "The Emperor's Village"

3: The Unterbergerhof, 1966

ready to call it a day when they notice the local postman approaching in the distance. Engleitner, feeling troubled, says to Franziska: "I have a sneaking suspicion he's bringing something for me. I'll go ask him what's so important that it can't wait until tomorrow." He hurries towards the postman, who is now waiting at the front door, and asks him: "Who are you looking for?"

"You," comes the terse reply.

"Why—what's the matter?" Engleitner wants to know.

"I've brought your call-up papers!" the postman says.

Engleitner feels himself go weak in the knees. "Surely this is no longer necessary," he thinks despairingly, taking the envelope. Then he hands it straight back to the postman without opening it, saying: "I don't want these papers and will not accept them under any circumstances. You can take them back right now. I'm not going to take part in this crazy war!"

The postman tries to calm him down. "Don't be a fool, Poidl! Another few weeks and the war could be over. If you refuse these orders, you'll be picked up by the military police in no time. Then there'll be no escape. They won't think twice about shooting you like a dog."

"Well, that's a risk I'll have to take," replies Engleitner grimly, "but for me a clear conscience and my faith are more important!"

"Accepting this letter doesn't mean you have to give up your faith," counters the postman. "You're just confirming that it was handed over to you. You're not accepting the orders themselves. What you do with them afterward is your business. Just ignore them if you want to!"

"All right then," says Engleitner and signs the postal receipt.

In the meantime Franziska Unterberger has come over and wants to know what is going on. "I've just received my call-up papers, and I have to report to the military base in Krumau in

Czechoslovakia within six hours. How on earth can I get there in that time?" says Engleitner. "It's impossible!"

The farmer's wife is shattered at this news and bursts into tears. Not content with taking her husband, they now want her farmhand Poidl too, who has been such a great help to her, working as though the farm were his own. "How am I going to manage all this by myself?" she despairs. "Spring sowing is due soon. Those Nazis are nothing but brutes!"

By this time Engleitner has overcome his initial shock and has worked out a plan. He will flee into the nearby alpine forests around the Schwarzensee.

Turning to the distraught woman, he says soothingly: "Don't worry, Franziska, I'm not going to war. I will not support such barbarity. I'll just disappear for a while. I'm sure the war won't last much longer, and as soon as it's over, I'll be back to help you again."

Franziska, guessing his intentions, warns him: "Whatever you do, don't go up to our Meistereben alpine hut. The Nazis know that you're our farmhand, and that's the first place they'd think of looking for you."

After asking her to pack some food for him, he says: "I'll get some rest now, and as soon as it's dark I'll be off. Go to the local council offices in St. Wolfgang tomorrow and tell them I've left. Say that I didn't have time to announce my departure personally because I had only six hours to get to Krumau. And please stop worrying about me. God will protect me as He has done so often in the past. All I need to do is follow His principles and keep my faith in Him!"

Engleitner then goes to say goodbye to the farmer's uncle, Franz Unterberger, who lives in the house next door. Unterberger tells him the way to a secure hiding place and adds a warning: "Never stay too long in one hut!"

These words are a reminder to Engleitner of the fate that befell Joki Steiner (real name Jakob Hillebrand) from nearby Strobl. Failing to return to his unit from leave, Steiner fled to a cave in the Bleckwand area, where his brother, Anton

Hillebrand, secretly supplied him with food. However, because he lingered in one hiding place, a scout patrol found him and executed him as a deserter.[1] His brother Anton was also arrested and sentenced to death, although his sentence was later commuted to seven years' imprisonment.[2]

Engleitner assures the farmer's uncle that he will not stay too long in one place. Unterberger then offers him a rifle to hunt game for food, but Engleitner refuses to take it. "How can I object to military service and then carry a rifle? Chances are I'll be found, and if I'm carrying a gun, that'll be the end of me!" So after saying goodbye to Franz and again reassuring Franziska, he goes off to bed.

Naturally, he sleeps very little and gets up again before midnight. He finds that the Ukrainian girl who helps in the kitchen has prepared bread, meat, and a cake for him to take along. She too tries to talk him out of his plan.

Escape from the Nazi military police now begins in earnest. Outside it is pitch-black. It appears that everyone is asleep; there is no better time to escape without being spotted. The mountains around the Schwarzensee would be the safest refuge, and because he has been hiking in them many times, Engleitner knows the area like the back of his hand. He hastily heads across the fields, northward toward the Wirlinger Wand, climbing a steep path up to the southern slope of the Leonsberg, where he can take shelter in the protection of the forest. He arrives there just in time because the sky is already beginning to lighten. He continues along another mountain, the Zimnitz, which used to be Austrian emperor Franz Joseph's favorite hunting ground for chamois. But this is no time for reminiscing; at this moment Engleitner feels like a chamois himself, fleeing from his hunters. He must avoid leaving any

---

[1] DÖW: Widerstand und Verfolgung in Salzburg 1934-45 (Vienna, 1991) p. 572ff

[2] DÖW file 18175

telltale traces and must stay in one hiding place only as long as is strictly necessary. The army will send out scout patrols to search for him as soon as they realize that he has not responded to his call-up. If he gets caught, he can expect no mercy. As a deserter he will be shot on sight.

So without a weapon of any kind, he moves stealthily through the forest, eventually choosing a secure hiding place in a thicket with a good view of the surroundings. He wants to ensure that any pursuers will not catch him unawares. It is now well after midday, so he fortifies himself with a snack. Of course he eats very little, as he must make his provisions last as long as possible. He has brought his Bible with him to give him spiritual strength. He starts to read, but remains alert and watchful, for as a local Austrian saying goes: "The forest is full of eyes." So still and inconspicuous is he that a deer passing three feet in front of him is unaware of his presence.

His lack of sleep begins to catch up with him. As he thinks about his situation, he is reminded of a saying: *"Und wenn die Welt in Waffen tost, ist Einsamkeit des Weisen Trost"* (When the world echoes to the roar of guns, loneliness is the comfort of the wise). This is part of one of the so-called "Mountain Psalms" by a German poet who spends his summer holidays in St. Wolfgang. Engleitner finds the words most appropriate to his predicament.

Daylight is beginning to wane, so he sets out in search of a lodge, a hut in which farmers collect leaves in the autumn for use in the cowsheds the following spring. Before falling asleep Engleitner prays to God, as he does every night, asking for the strength to endure his trials and keep a clear conscience. Utterly exhausted, he closes his eyes and is soon fast asleep.

He spends the next night in a similar lodge, but on the third day he cautiously moves to higher ground, farther and farther away from Johann Unterberger's farmhouse. He does not want to use up his already dwindling provisions too quickly, so he eats some *waldsalat,* wild dandelions. He used to eat them as a child, when times were especially hard. As darkness begins to fall, he starts searching for a safe resting place for the night. There are no lodges at this altitude. Although it is mid-April and winter has given way to spring, at over 3,000 feet above sea level he needs to be prepared for the return of cold weather. Fortunately, a warm, steady wind blows from the south bringing moderate temperatures, so that it is possible for him to sleep in the open. Engleitner tears off some pine branches, piles them together, and soon has a reasonably comfortable place to rest.

"Actually it's not too bad," he thinks to himself as sleep overtakes him, "and certainly better than it was in the concentration camp."

His sleep is fitful, though, partly because of the great pressure he is under and partly because of the cold night air. Soon he is awakened by a noise. "What was that? They can't have traced me already," he thinks, peering cautiously down the mountainside. Seeing no sign of a scout patrol, he assumes it was an animal and dozes off again, sleeping uneasily until daybreak. He is in constant fear of being caught. He has no companion who can take turns keeping watch. So afraid is he that the sound of a leaf falling to the ground makes him jump.

The days pass slowly. Engleitner divides his time between walking and looking for places to hide that are both comfortable enough to sleep in and able to provide a view of his surroundings. He spends the nights outdoors. Gradually he makes his way down the northern slope of the mountain to the Weissenbachtal.

However, this area is not without its dangers either; a short time ago a poacher fell victim to an overambitious hunter. Who knows what he would do to Engleitner, who, as a fugitive from the law, is now fair game for anyone carrying a gun?

A week passes, and with it goes the warm wind from the south. Heavy rain begins to fall, gradually turning to snow.

Soon the ground is covered by a layer of snow some twenty inches deep.

The constant strain and lack of proper food weaken Engleitner. His provisions run low, and the bad weather takes its toll. He tries to light a small fire for warmth in a hollow under a fallen tree, but the surrounding grass catches fire, and he must hurriedly extinguish it. Soaked to the skin and frozen stiff, he starts making his way back to the Leonsberg, crossing the northern side of the mountain in search of a hut. It is essential that he warm himself and dry his clothes. Unfortunately, the huts he finds are securely locked. He walks on to the Bärenloch, a region once inhabited by bears, in hopes of finding refuge in one of the caves there. However, he soon realizes that none of them is suitable because no fresh water is nearby.

Where can he turn now? There is just one hut left that he could use, because he knows where to find the key: the Meistereben hut belonging to Johann Unterberger. But he also remembers Franziska's warning that it is the one place his pursuers will be sure to look. Now he simply has no alternative.

It is late in the evening. Soaked to the skin, practically frozen to death, and close to total exhaustion, Engleitner slowly climbs to the alpine hut, some 3,500 feet above sea level. Standing at the door at last, he reaches under the doorframe and grasps the key. With a feeling of relief mingled with fear, he unlocks the door and goes in, looking forward to lighting a fire and getting warm again. But before doing so, he takes the time to cover the windows and doors with pieces of cloth so that the fire cannot be seen from outside. He then gathers up the wood stored in the hut and kindles it on the open hearth. The darkness outside should ensure that the smoke will not give him away. He undresses and dries his wet clothes near the fire. Warmth gradually returns to his chilled body, making him drowsy. It has been days since he has had a good night's sleep. Putting his dry clothes back on, he

4: Meistereben alpine hut, circa 1937

clears the embers from the hearth and places a log on the bench in front of it as a barrier between him and the fireplace. Stretched out along it on the warm bench, he falls into a deep sleep.

Suddenly he is jolted awake by a piercing pain in his back. To his horror he sees flames—flames everywhere! The dry log has caught fire, and his clothes have started to burn too! He is literally on fire. Fortunately, he has the presence of mind to roll himself on the floor, which is covered with snow that has blown into the hut. He is also astute enough not to tear open the door, since that might fan the flames all the more. After he manages to extinguish the blaze, a terrible pain makes him aware of the full extent of this horrible accident. His entire back, from neck to buttocks, is covered in burns. His clothes are ruined except for the front part and sleeves of his shirt and jacket. The rear parts of his trousers and undergarments are completely destroyed.

What should he do, half-naked in the middle of the night? He has no choice: he must return to the farm to have his burns tended and to fetch new clothes. He puts his trousers and jacket on backward so that his burns are more or less covered. After looking around the hut to make sure nothing is left that could betray him, he sets off.

Grimacing with indescribable pain, Engleitner passes down the southern mountain slope and heads back toward the Unterbergerhof, well aware that his decision could prove fatal. Shaking with fever and desperately thirsty, he tries to take a few hurried sips of water from every mountain stream he passes, scooping it up with his hands. When he arrives at the farmhouse, on April 30, 1945, it is fortunately still dark. Without losing a second, he awakens the farmer's wife and briefly tells her what has occurred, adding: "I have to stay somewhere here on the farm. I'm in terrible pain, and I need new clothes. There must be a good hiding place somewhere. Please, please don't send me away!"

Although Franziska Unterberger understands his predicament, she replies: "No, you can't stay here. People have been talking about you. They know you've been called up, and no one really believes you've reported for duty. The people who come for their milk every day keep asking me whether we know anything about your disappearance. So you can't possibly stay here. Someone is bound to see you and report you."

"But what else can I do?" asks Engleitner despairingly.

"Go to your parents," suggests Franziska. "It wouldn't occur to anyone to look for you there."

There is little time to think about it. "I suppose she could be right," he thinks. "The military police wouldn't look for me at my parents' house now that I've been on the run for nearly two weeks. Hopefully they won't think me so bold as to hide where they could so easily get hold of me. Anyway," he concludes, "I have very little choice." He heads toward his home in Weinbach, Aigen-Voglhub. He awakens his parents, Leopold and Juliana Engleitner, explains his situation, and begs them to hide him. But they are too afraid to let him in, even though it is his house they are living in. Engleitner is desperate; not only does he need new clothes but his burns are causing him intense pain. Dawn is already breaking. His life is in danger, and no one is willing to help him. Everyone refuses to accept the seriousness of his plight and thinks only of himself. Engleitner, losing patience, says to his parents: "I must stay here whether you

5: Juliana Engleitner, circa 1950

like it or not. It's getting light already, and everybody will see me. Please, have mercy on your son!"

"All right," says his father, yielding to his son's plea, "but you'll have to hide in the barn. The house is far too dangerous. Our neighbor, Anna Gruber, keeps asking us if you've joined up. She has close connections with the Nazis and will report us straight away if she suspects that you're here."

Engleitner's father tells his wife that she must under no circumstances allow herself to be drawn into a discussion with that "Nazi hussy," and should let him do the talking if she crosses their path. Gruber has already managed to get the parish priest of St. Wolfgang, Josef Rohrmoser, sent to the concentration camp. While visiting an ill farmer, Josef Sams in Weinbach, the priest was asked his opinion regarding the probable outcome of the war. He answered: "Has England ever lost a war?" The housekeeper overheard him and told Anna Gruber, who immediately reported the incident to an SS man she knew. When he failed to take an interest, she contacted another SS man, who instigated Rohrmoser's arrest on October 20, 1939. Because of his "anti-Nazi statements" he was charged with violating the

Heimtückegesetz (the law against so-called insidious behavior).[1]
He was arrested and sent to Dachau concentration camp.[2]

Engleitner fetches fresh clothes and settles down in the
hay. His mother makes him some soup and brings it to the
barn in a milk can. Using a pitchfork, she lifts the soup up to
her son, who is resting in the loft. Grateful for the warm food,
he wolfs it down and asks her for wet towels to cool his burns.

In the excitement of the last few moments, he had
completely forgotten his injuries, but now that he has calmed
down a little and hopes to get some sleep, the pain returns
with a vengeance and the full extent of his accident back at the
hut becomes apparent to him. However, he has no choice but
to live with it and try to regain enough strength to face any
ordeals that may still be in store. Stretching out on his stomach
in the hay and feeling happy just to be alive, he falls asleep.

The next morning his father tells him of the reports that Hitler
committed suicide the day before. The news of the death of
this great enemy, the man responsible for the unspeakable
suffering of the past few years, is good news for Engleitner. It
gives him hope that the war will soon be over. His father, on
the other hand, thinks it will last another two weeks. He
informs his son that a requiem mass[3] will be celebrated for the
Führer in St. Wolfgang parish church the next day. "Can you
believe it?" Engleitner thinks to himself. "Even in death, this
mass-murderer who spread fear and horror throughout the
world is still honored by the church."

Despite signs that the end of the war may be only days
away, his parents are afraid of the punishment they might have

---

[1] dRGBl. (deutsches Reichsgesetzblatt, Law Gazette of the German Reich)
1934 I, p. 1269
[2] DÖW: Widerstand und Verfolgung in Oberösterreich 1934-45 (Vienna,
1982), Vol. 2, p. 21
[3] When Cardinal Bertram received the news of Hitler's death, he ordered
"a solemn requiem to be held in memory of the Führer...." Rolf
Steininger (ed.), *Vergessene Opfer des Nationalsozialismus*, (Innsbruck
2000), pp. 68-9.

to face for hiding a deserter. Unable to bear their constant moaning any longer, Engleitner decides to leave the very next night. Taking with him some kitchen utensils, a portion of polenta (a kind of porridge made of maize meal), other food supplies, and a woolen blanket, he crosses Russbach and disappears into the mountains once again.

Where to now? It is dark as he warily makes his way through the trees. He remembers Franz Unterberger, the farmer's uncle, telling him once about a cave on the northern mountain slope, close to the Meistereben hut, and decides to look for it. In Haleswies, he uses a trick often employed by poachers: he covers much of the distance walking backwards so that his steps appear to lead in the opposite direction. In this way any pursuers might be thrown off the scent, if only for a time.

It is dawn when he finds the cave. Situated in the middle of a steep wall of rock, it is an ideal hideaway. In an emergency he can escape either upward or downward. He climbs up the steep slope and inspects the interior of the cave, which is only about a cubic yard. "This won't be very comfortable," he thinks. "A man can't even stand upright." The chamois droppings on the cave floor make it even less appealing. Engleitner climbs down the slope to gather twigs and branches to make himself a place to sleep in the cave. He is still in agony from his burns. He collects moss to use as bedding and cover part of the cave opening as a protection against the cold and to reduce the chance of his being seen, without obstructing his view from the cave.

That is vital, because unknown to him a scout patrol is searching the area around the Schwarzensee for him and any other fugitives. He feels quite safe in his hiding place, though. He decides to make a fire for warmth, and climbs up the mountainside to the nearby forest. Glancing all about him, he cautiously collects firewood.

Suddenly he stops, horror-struck. A hunter is standing near the Meistereben hut and looking in his direction through binoculars. The hunter is a few hundred yards away and separated from the cave only by a deep gully. "He must have seen me," Engleitner thinks. "He's sure to come over here." He drops the firewood, clambers back down into the cave, and hastily gathers up his belongings. Breathlessly he waits, wondering from which side the hunter will appear, getting ready to flee in the opposite direction. He begins to panic because he knows that the hunter could easily shoot him without warning. But Engleitner is fortunate. The hunter never appears, so he is able to stay in the cave—until that is, a change in the weather thwarts his plans.

It is early May, and the snow is starting to thaw. Water drips from the limestone of the cave and soaks him to the skin. But worse is to come—he develops bad diarrhea, and since it is of course impossible for him to answer the call of nature in the cave, he has to do so clinging to the cliff, relieving himself over the edge. Soon the melting snow forms a stream that flows through the cave and forces him to move out.

The painful burns and severe diarrhea take their toll on Engleitner. Completely soaked and utterly exhausted, he reaches a point where he no longer cares whether he is caught. He decides to go back to the Meistereben hut after dark. When he gets there, freezing, shivering, and exhausted, it is well into the night.

As he did the week before, he dries his wet clothes in front of the fire, warms himself, and eats some soup and polenta. This time, however, having learned from his previous experience, he makes a comfortable resting place on a heap of hay in the loft and is soon fast asleep.

The next morning he eats more polenta and decides to stay in the hut. He spends most of his time in the loft so that if anyone knocks on the front door he can escape through the back door and along a ditch. The back door affords a good view of the Attersee, allowing him to watch for signs that the war has ended.

But the danger is not over yet.

A scout patrol searches for him relentlessly. The three Nazis have forced a local man who knows the area, Franz Kain from the village of Windhag, to guide them through the mountains. Kain is a former workmate of Engleitner's and is familiar with his objection to military service.

6: Franz Kain, circa 1950

The scout patrol searches several huts and lodges in the neighborhood of the Schwarzensee. Guessing that Engleitner has gone into hiding in the Meistereben hut, Franz Kain tries to keep the Nazis away from it. Thick fog moves in as the group reaches Breitenberg mountain, dangerously close to where Engleitner is hiding.

On a hill only a few yards away from the hut, the leader stops. He examines his map and says: "There must be another hut down there!" Franz Kain, fearing that his friend Poidl could indeed be hiding there, tries to dissuade him, but the Nazi says decisively, "Let's pay it a visit," and starts to make his way down to the hut.

The noose is around Engleitner's neck. Have all his efforts been in vain? After the adventures of his flight from the military authorities and the nightmare of the last few years, is he destined to be caught and executed after all?

EARLY YEARS

Leopold Engleitner was born on July, 23, 1905, in Aigen-Voglhub, in the municipality of Strobl, on the shores of the Abersee (as the upper part of the Wolfgangsee was called) in the Austrian province of Salzburg. His father, Leopold Engleitner, Sr., worked in a sawmill. His mother, Juliana, née Haas, was the daughter of the owner of a large estate who was a member of a proud clan of farmers. She had been brought up a strict Catholic. Her father, Matthias Haas, was mayor of

7: Matthias Haas, grandfather, circa 1890

Strobl am Abersee from 1889 to 1893. Because of his political and social standing, he was invited every year to take part in Emperor Franz Joseph's annual hunt, a privilege granted only to the most prominent citizens. Leopold's paternal grandfather, also called Leopold, made a living digging pits for ice. The ice produced during wintertime was cut into blocks and sold to local innkeepers to keep their meat and drink cool. Both

grandfathers died soon after
Leopold was born, so he had
no personal recollection of
either of them. His maternal
grandmother, Juliana Haas,
died young, his mother
being only twenty-one at the
time. Elisabeth Engleitner,
his paternal grandmother,
was the grandchild of the
well-known maker of clocks
and violins, Ignaz Kefer of
the famous Kefer family of
violin makers from Bad
Goisern.

8: Ferdinand Haas (Photo by Hofer of Bad Ischl, circa 1914)

Leopold grew up with his brother Heinrich, who was a
year younger. The family was very poor. Five other brothers
and sisters died in infancy. He had a half-brother, Ferdinand
Haas, who was eight years older than Leopold and was the
result of a brief affair his mother had with a hunter when she
worked as a dairymaid one summer. Ferdinand was killed
while felling trees at the age of 21. Leopold himself was born
with curvature of the spine, making it virtually impossible
for him to stand up straight without severe pain. His parents
refused to accept his physical infirmity and chided him
continually because of it.

When Leopold was three years old, his family moved
into his grandmother Elisabeth's house in Pfandl in Bad Ischl.
Although his grandmother was a Catholic, she felt drawn to
Protestantism, causing great religious tension within the
family, especially because his mother was a fervent Catholic.
Leopold's father took a noticeably less pious stance.

It was in the midst of these differing religious views that
Leopold grew up, influenced both by his liberal father and his
conservative mother.

Leopold had a very close relationship with his grandmother, closer in fact than with his mother. His grandmother was caring and understanding and did not hold so closely to tradition. This loving attachment to each other was particularly important during those days of need and deprivation. Food was scarce; on most days dinner was only cabbage and potatoes, and there was never enough to end the constant hunger. Of course, there was never money for toys, so the two brothers carved little wooden boats for themselves from the bark of pine trees and floated them in puddles and nearby streams. They spent many happy hours together despite their poverty.

The sawmill where their father worked was in Aigen-Voglhub. During the summer months the two boys had to wash themselves in the canal that ran from the river Ischl to the Zahlermühle sawmill. One day Leopold dived into the water headfirst but failed to resurface. A passerby pulled the motionless boy out of the water, saving his life.

The time approached for Leopold to start school, and he was looking forward to it, although in his neighborhood people did not attach much importance to reading and writing. The standard of education was extremely low, as

illustrated by one of the anecdotes his mother told him about her own childhood:

One day when a farmer's son came home from school, his father urged him to lend a hand with the farm work. The boy said: "I have to finish my homework first."

9: Engleitner's grandmother's house in Pfandl, 1998

His father then asked: "What's so important that you have to do it now?"

"I have to write an essay about Europe," the boy answered.

"You silly boy!" the father exclaimed. "You don't need to write about that! You're never going to be able to go to Europe as long as you live!"

The population really only appreciated physical labor, which inevitably led to a certain ignorance.

Even the teachers were not always abreast of the latest developments, as illustrated by a favorite local story:

A wealthy summer guest presented the school in Strobl with a globe. This was something very special at that time, so the teacher told his students they ought to appreciate this scientific teaching aid. He placed it on top of a cupboard where everyone could see it. Some days later the school inspector paid them a visit. When he entered the classroom, his glance immediately fell on the globe. He told the students that he had rarely seen one himself and that it was very special. He then said to one young boy: "I wonder if you can tell me why the globe is slanting?" Before the young lad was able to reply, the teacher interrupted: "Sir, it's not the boy's fault. The globe was already slanting when we got it."

The story soon spread round the district, to the teacher's great embarrassment. Leopold found it very amusing, as did his mother, who could not help laughing every time she told it.

In 1911 the time finally came for young Leopold to start classes at the primary school in Pfandl. Living in a region that had been home to many notable historical figures, he was naturally most interested in history. His teacher had been an officer in the army, and his teaching method reflected his military background. Since Leopold had great difficulty standing up straight because of his back problems, he was regarded as inferior, and the teacher did not allow him to take part in any physical education. This was very depressing for the boy and made him feel like an outcast. He shed many tears when he had to sit and watch the other children play games. His schoolmates picked up on the discrimination shown by their teacher, and they began to tease and taunt Leopold. On one occasion seven girls held him down and rubbed snow in his face. That incident led to further mockery from his peers. He was shocked by the shameless behavior of many of the boys and girls at school, though most cases were hushed up.

In those days it was fashionable to display a liking for soldiery, so many children were given war toys. Not Leopold, though. His father hated war. Generally, serving as a soldier was regarded as a great honor, and many men aspired to join the army, no matter how low the rank. Soldiers strutted about in their uniforms, even when off duty, basking in the admiration they received. The high social standing that soldiers enjoyed especially among older women in those days is shown in the saying:

She wanted no soldiers when she was young
But now that she's old, she wishes for one.

It was regarded a great ignominy to be declared unfit for military service, and those who were had to pay a "cripple tax." However, Leopold's father could not have cared less about that social stigma and did everything he could to avoid being accepted into the army. In the weeks leading up to his medical examination in the mid-1880s, he began to drink several cups of very strong coffee every day and tied his stockings up so tightly that the veins in his feet were badly swollen. The medical board, noticing his unusually rapid heartbeat (from the coffee), concluded that he must have a serious heart condition, and after taking a close look at his legs they were sure that he suffered from varicose veins as well. They declared him unfit for military service. Naturally, Leopold Engleitner, Sr., who was in reality as fit as a fiddle, was delighted to have hoodwinked the medical board and paid his "cripple tax" with great relish.

Impressions of the Monarchy

One of the things that puzzled young Leopold was the Church's exaggerated veneration of the Austrian Emperor (Kaiser). The Church claimed that it was an honor and a duty to serve the Emperor, and that his subjects should be willing to finance his luxurious lifestyle. After all, he reigned by divine right. Leopold's parents related stories about Emperor Franz Joseph, many of which illustrated his knowledge and love of hunting.

For instance, it was said that a count invited the Emperor to hunt for chamois in the Tennen mountains one day. The head forester of that area was told to be at the Emperor's disposal. While the count and the Emperor were looking for a target, the forester spotted a chamois and whispered: "Look, Your Majesty! A magnificent buck!"

The Emperor raised his binoculars and immediately replied: "That's no buck. That's a doe!" The forester, who was considered an expert on the subject, vehemently defended his opinion, pointing out the animal's protruding horns. The Emperor, however, explained that some very mature females have horns that bear a striking resemblance to those of a buck, and he was sure that the animal before them was a doe. The Emperor proposed that they shoot the animal, although it was normally against his principles to kill female game. "We shall see who is mistaken," he said. Raising his gun, he took aim and brought the animal down. When they reached the dead chamois and inspected it, they found that the Emperor had been right after all, much to the embarrassment of the forester.

This incident was one example of the Emperor's great knowledge of hunting and confirmed the local opinion that "Franzl," as he was called in Bad Ischl, was indeed an excellent hunter.

Apart from hunting, however, he was considered by some to be a bad monarch, one who had little compassion for his poverty-stricken subjects. Some resented the pomp, the pride, and the showy display of the high nobility during the summer

10: *Emperor Franz Joseph (right), hunting for chamois in Bad Ischl, 1909 (reproduction)*

months, which contrasted sharply with the poverty the population had to endure. Young Leopold found the situation repugnant, since he did not even have enough bread to satisfy his hunger.

He also did not understand why the local people were not allowed to use the spa gardens during the summer season unless they wore their Sunday best. The aristocratic guests apparently had to be spared the sight of poor people. To make sure no one turned up in his everyday clothes, a policeman patrolled the park all day.

Peter Grabner, a local farmer, did not think much of such rules. One day in the park he needed to relieve himself, and did so near the Wirer Monument. A policeman caught him and ordered him to pay a fine of one krone. Grabner gave the policeman a two-krone piece, then said dryly: "Keep the change. I passed wind as well."

Another situation that Leopold found shocking was the unseemly relationship between the Emperor and the imperial court actress Katharina Schratt. Her husband was sent to South Tyrol on a long assignment at the instigation of the Emperor. Leopold was well aware of the Emperor's regular visits to the lady's residence, sometimes seeing him leave the imperial villa after morning service to stroll through the court gardens to the wood alongside the river Ischl on the way to his lover.

Although neither the clergy nor the general public seemed to take offense at the Emperor's affair with a married woman, young Leopold found it quite disturbing. He asked himself: "Is there one set of morals for the Emperor and another for us?"

These observations meant that Leopold held the Emperor in anything but admiration and awe. A close encounter with the Emperor in May 1914 did little to change Leopold's opinions. The Emperor wished to see all the schoolchildren in Bad Ischl. They lined up along the road from the railway station to the imperial villa as the Emperor went by in his carriage surrounded by his pompous generals. Since Leopold had been told to throw flowers into the carriage as it passed, he was close enough to see the Emperor's chest decorated with numerous medals. "I wonder where he got those?" he said to himself as he went home completely unimpressed.

Leopold considered the Emperor to be a man like any other, but one who could do more to alleviate the poverty of the country. Because he did not do this, Leopold began to develop a strong dislike of the monarchy, just as many of his contemporaries had done. He was sure that if he had that kind of power, he would do everything he could to put a stop to all the suffering of the poor. But this sincere and laudable desire was not something he could put into practice.

The First World War

In the autumn of 1914, World War I broke out. Leopold, nine years old at the time, had to endure the terrible consequences of that appalling destruction of life and property. The economic situation worsened, and Leopold felt constant pangs of hunger. He heard the war propaganda urging everyone to defend the fatherland and the faith, but did not think much of it. Nor could he agree with the clergy's support of the war.

He was particularly mystified that church bells had been taken down to make bullets. This was once the topic of a heated discussion between him and his aunt at his parents' house, which revealed his capacity for logical thought. When his aunt, Katharina Haas, visited his family, she mentioned that the priest in Bad Ischl had said in a sermon that every soldier killed by such a "holy" bullet would go straight to heaven. Leopold could not help laughing at such nonsense, much to the annoyance of his aunt. "What are you laughing about, you cheeky little brat?" she scolded.

Leopold replied: "The Austrian soldiers will be firing those bullets at their enemies the Russians. Why would they want their enemies to go straight to heaven? Some people will believe anything!" Using common sense he was able to draw logical conclusions even at that tender age.

Leopold closely observed the details concerning how men were drafted into the army. Call-up papers were not sent by post; instead an employee from the local council offices went to each address to inform those concerned. This was done to save the conscript the trouble of going to the council offices to give notice of his absence.

However, not everyone obeyed the call-up. Georg Steiner from Ramsau near Schladming, a mountain guide in the Dachstein region, disappeared into the mountains after receiving his call-up orders. Although he was constantly searched for, he was never caught, and he remained in hiding throughout the war.

In 1916, Emperor Franz Joseph died at the age of 86. Leopold was not especially sad about this; it was a subject of no great interest to him. The Emperor's death had a drastic effect on the social standing of his mistress, Katharina Schratt. People began to treat her with contempt. To increase her popularity, she started giving sweets to the children she happened to meet, including Leopold. His father once had a long discussion with her about her changed situation, during which she complained bitterly about the treatment she was receiving. Although grieving over the death of her "Franzl," she made no secret of her aversion to the Habsburgs, who felt the same way about her.

Although Leopold's father was approaching 50, he was still afraid of being called up for military service. So in January 1917 the family moved from Pfandl to Russbachsaag in Abtenau, in the province of Salzburg, where the senior Engleitner found work in a sawmill. In this way the local council lost track of his whereabouts, and he was able to avoid conscription. The move to a new area was not too unpleasant for young Leopold, since a temperate wind blew that winter and no snow had fallen, so the children were able to go barefoot even in January. Leopold attended the local primary school until the summer of 1918, which was to be the last of his seven years of schooling.

Young Leopold Engleitner worked hard that summer. As a lowly sawyer, Leopold's father only earned about one krone a day. To boost his income, he began collecting roots of the gentian plant, used for making medicine. One kilogram (a little over two pounds) of gentian root brought one krone. So every day he and his son went into the mountains of the Dachstein region to dig up these roots. He managed to collect as much as 25 kilograms (55 pounds) a day and demanded the same effort from his son. Although weakened by the rigors of war, young Leopold toiled with him from sunrise to sunset, digging with a pick and his bare hands. Much to the delight of his father, he was able to collect some eight to ten kilograms a day all on his own.

Shortly before the end of the war, the Engleitners moved back into his grandmother's house in Pfandl. There Leopold was able to attend school briefly until it was closed in October 1918 because of the Spanish flu. The virulent disease spread rapidly among the population already weakened by war. The flu eventually affected some 500 million people and claimed 22 million[1] lives in a relatively short period of time—more fatalities than were caused by the war.

The Salzkammergut, with its "Emperor's Village" of Bad Ischl, was also affected. Leopold suffered from a high fever and profuse perspiration for many weeks, losing a lot of weight. The *Salzkammergut-Zeitung* of November 3, 1918, reported that 19 people in Bad Ischl between one and 87 years of age (eight under 19) died from October 8 to October 31, 1918[2] because of the "sinister epidemic," as it was called in the article.

Fending for Himself

In mid-February 1919, Leopold, then 13½, decided it was time to stand on his own two feet and end his days of constant hunger once and for all. Going around to all the farms in the neighborhood, he offered his services as a domestic laborer in exchange for food and accommodations. Again and again he heard the same answer: "What are we supposed to do with a weakling like you? You'd be more of a hindrance than a help!" This was very discouraging for poor Leopold.

Finally, a hill farmer on the Buchberg in St. Wolfgang, Johann Appesbacher, took pity on him and told the dejected boy: "All right, you can stay here. I don't suppose we'll starve

---

[1] Brockhaus Encyclopedia (Mannheim, 1992, 19th edition), Vol. 9, p. 154

[2] *Salzkammergut-Zeitung,* Gmunden, November 10, 1918, p. 4, Ischl news section, Deaths, Flu Victims

on your account!" But it was over a year before the farmer noticed any signs of recovery in his young employee. Having left home Leopold was now on his own; he chopped wood in the forest and helped on the farm. The farmer's 18-year-old son, Johann junior, teased Leopold mercilessly about his physical limitations. Johann would chase him across the meadows and force him to work ever faster. No matter how hard Leopold tried, the farmer's son was never satisfied and always found something to complain about.

Leopold mucked out the cowshed once a week and collected leaves from the nearby beech trees to cover the floor. Beech wood, in German "Buchenwald"—little did Leopold know at the time what terrible connotations this word would one day have.

He spent his evenings reading any instructive books he could lay his hands on. The farmer ridiculed him for this because he considered it to be a waste of time.

But Leopold's thirst for knowledge proved useful. Since he was only 13, he was really still too young to work and should have been in school. One day the headmaster of the school in St. Wolfgang saw him working on his own in a field. He began to ask the lad questions to find out what this "permanent truant" knew. Because Leopold had read so many educational books, he was able to answer the headmaster's questions.

"I really ought to report you for not going to school," said the headmaster. "But times are hard, so we'll say no more about it." The war and the collapse of the monarchy meant that rules were not applied as strictly as they might have been. But Leopold would much rather have gone to school than have had to work so hard to earn his daily bread.

He left that farm in February 1921 to work for another farmer, Moabauer[1] in St. Wolfgang, where he stayed until July 1, 1923.

---

[1] Moabauer was the name given to the farmer who owned this particular farm. Engleitner worked for two different owners; the family name of the first was Hörak, the second, Eisl.

After that he worked for Josef Leitner, the innkeeper of the "Branntweinhäusl" in Russbach, and for Johann Baier, an innkeeper in Radau, looking after their small farms. Then on November 5, 1923, an opportunity arose for him to work regulating the beds of mountain streams. He also worked intermittently as an unskilled laborer for Brandl Building Contractors, the district works management in Gmunden, and the council offices in St. Wolfgang. In the winters he worked as an ice cutter. All these jobs in the 1920s were interspersed with periods of unemployment. When his job at the paper and cardboard factory in Weinbach came to an end on May 14, 1932, he was given no more work.

During the 1920s Leopold spent some time working with woodsmen on the Rettenbachalm. From spring to autumn he worked in a tree nursery. Leopold and the other woodsmen slept from Monday to Saturday in a wooden hut where discipline was very strict. The head foreman had been a corporal in the army, and he saw to it that anyone who broke a rule was given extra chores. For example, if anyone left his spoon on the table after he finished eating, he would have to clear stinging nettles or chop wood. Once, though, the head foreman broke one of his own rules by leaving a pan on the table. It was the pan he always made his dumplings in. The men grabbed the pan and hung it from the roof in front of the hut. Now unable to find his pan, he made pancakes instead, although dumplings were his favorite food. Days passed. The workers feigned innocence and asked why he had stopped making his favorite dumplings. The foreman, not having noticed the pan hanging outside the hut, said that it was because he no longer liked them. The men waited a week before finally telling him where his pan was. The foreman, however, did no extra chores as a punishment— and after that, neither did anyone else.

During those difficult years following the war, both Leopold's mother and his brother worked on various farms. His father moved to Radau in St. Wolfgang, since financial difficulties had made it necessary to sell his parents' house in Pfandl. When the four family members were eventually reunited, they moved into a two-room apartment in Weinbach, St. Wolfgang.

In 1926, Leopold's grandmother, Elisabeth Engleitner, with whom Leopold had remained very close, died.

The suffering that World War I had caused left deep scars on young Leopold and created in him a deep desire for peace for all mankind. He therefore found the following saying, which was popular at the time, particularly apt:

> *When kingdoms crashed, came tumbling down*
> *The tyrants were cursed by all peoples.*
> *O that war nevermore plow the earth*
> *May war ensure from which all suffering stems*
> *For eternal peace to reign on Earth*
> *No more war, no more war.*

This became his favorite quotation and he often recited it to his friends, who were not especially impressed by them, however. But that did not bother him. He had begun to cherish the dream of a government that would finally bring enduring peace to the world.

In the summer of 1930, St. Wolfgang was chosen as the location for several scenes of the film *Liebling der Götter* (Favorite of the Gods), featuring the famous actors Hans Moser and Emil Jannings. The employment office in Bad Ischl arranged for Leopold Engleitner to appear as an extra in various crowd scenes, including scenes of people cheering near the starring actors. His pay was to be the continuation of his unemployment benefits, which would have been stopped had he refused the job. The bustle of the three-day shoot under the hot lights during the summer heat convinced him that working in films could be more difficult than it seemed.

In the spring of 1931, Engleitner began thinking about a home of his own. His family lived in extremely cramped conditions, and ever since his father had sold the house in Pfandl, he had set his heart on building his own home one day. He took on any odd job that came his way and saved all he could, but still had far too little to buy land on which to build a house. One day a golden opportunity arose. Bad Ischl council was selling more than a third of an acre of industrial land in Weinbach in St. Wolfgang, some six miles from Bad Ischl. This was the site of the former paper and cardboard factory in Weinbach, and the asking price was low because of the poor quality of the land. Engleitner jumped at the opportunity. His house would stand where the river Ischl had once run, now a dry, stony riverbed. In order to fill the former riverbed with earth, he offered to drain the marshy parts of the meadows of the neighboring farmers, taking as payment only the soil he would remove. His neighbors were more than happy to have this arduous task taken off their hands, and Engleitner was equally happy to have the earth with which to cultivate his own land. But with the vehicles of the time, it was going to be very difficult to move all this earth to his plot. He waited for winter to come so that when the meadows were covered with snow he could load the earth onto a sled to transport it with reasonable ease to his site.

Where would he get the building material for the house? One day his father, who had worked in the paper factory's boiler house, received an offer. If he tore down the walls of the boiler house, his son could keep the bricks. If any of the firebricks from the factory furnace were found to be damaged, he could keep them too. Thus Leopold had a unique chance to obtain his building material free of charge.

Leopold and his father began dismantling the boiler house. They carefully removed the mortar from the bricks, laying any undamaged firebricks to one side as agreed. When they had finished, Engleitner junior had some fourteen thousand bricks. He later sold the broken firebricks for a good price.

He had already erected a wooden hut on his land with the intention of building his brick house beside it. But financial difficulties put an end to that plan. Instead he decided to line the inside walls of the hut with the bricks that he and his father had labored so hard for. Then he built a chimney for the little two-roomed house.

Some time later he added a shed with a hayloft where he could house a goat, whose milk became one of the main sources of nutrition during those hard times. For the roof of his new house, he purchased the old factory's porch for a bargain price. The wood was high-quality red larch that has survived intact in the roof of his house into the 21st century. Soon after the building was completed, Engleitner allowed his parents and brother to move in with him, since they could no longer afford the rent for their small apartment in St. Wolfgang. The two brothers shared the attic, while his parents occupied the ground floor. As the family could not afford a bathroom, Engleitner would wash himself in the nearby river Ischl during the summer months. The remaining bricks were sold to make ends meet.

In the 1920s any leisure time that Engleitner had was spent where he most loved to be—in the open air. For hours on end, he would go hiking through the mountains of the

11: Leopold Engleitner's house, Weinbach 27, circa 1934-36

12: Hiking tour in the Zimnitz mountain region: Leopold Engleitner standing in the background, with his friend Leopold Mair and girlfriend, 1928/29

13: Johann Unterberger, circa 1925

Salzkammergut, even reaching the Königssee in Bavaria, Germany. He would take a book with him and stop at tranquil, scenic spots to read. His favorite writers were the country novelist and poet Peter Rosegger and Ludwig Ganghofer. Sometimes one of his friends would accompany him— Wolfgang Bachauer, Johann Unterberger from St. Wolfgang, or Leopold Mair from Bad Ischl. Even the cold of winter could not keep him indoors. He took planks of ash wood, cut them to size, and boiled them in water to make himself skis. Thus he was able to explore further the mountain region of his homeland.

Hunting, or rather "poaching," had always played a large part in the life of the people of the Salzkammergut. Like most young men at that time, Leopold Engleitner found the idea of poaching appealing, partly because of his constant hunger but also because of the sense of adventure it awoke in him. Whereas these escapades had to be kept secret from his father, he knew that his mother's heart was filled with pride, since she came from a family with a long tradition of hunting and poaching.

It was not so much the shooting that Engleitner liked—he never actually bagged an animal—it was more the excitement and camaraderie.

One night he went looking for game with his friend Leopold Mair in the Zimnitz mountains. Engleitner sat in Emperor Franz Joseph's former look-out while his friend tried to drive a herd of chamois in front of the damask barrel of his gun, a Lefaucheux breechloader inherited from his grandfather Matthias Haas. However, two lovers looking for a secluded spot scared the animals off. Engleitner was forced to return home without having fired a shot. To cap it all, he tripped over a tree root in the darkness and bent the barrel of his treasured Lefaucheux.

On another occasion it seemed he had been given a golden opportunity. Franz Unterberger told him of a place on the Radau mountain where success was virtually guaranteed. The bark of a particular tree had been scraped in such a way as is only found where a large roebuck often frays its antlers. On a pitch-dark night, Engleitner took up his position a few yards away from the tree, squatting beside a six-foot-high wall of rock. He waited patiently for the buck to appear. Eventually the animal came into view and began rubbing its antlers against the tree. It was indeed a magnificent specimen! Engleitner quickly raised his gun, took aim, and was just about to pull the trigger when several leaves fell from the rock above him. The leaves disturbed the buck, which took fright and ran off. Foiled again! His dream of a delicious meal of venison remained just that.

However, it was not until some days later that he discovered that he had in fact been very fortunate. Franz Unterberger had spoken to a local gamekeeper who told him that he had been lying in wait for the selfsame buck in the same place and on the same night as Engleitner. The gamekeeper waited at the top of a rock, when, much to his annoyance, he accidentally pushed some dry leaves off the high rocky ridge just as his finger was poised on the trigger of his gun. The roebuck had immediately sensed the danger and disappeared. When Engleitner heard this, he was glad that he had not had the opportunity to shoot. He certainly would have been punished. It was shortly after this that he decided to end his unsuccessful "career" as a poacher.

COURAGEOUS CHANGE OF RELIGION IN THE 1930s

Leopold Engleitner's father often told his family that many of their ancestors had been forced to flee from Bad Ischl to Transylvania—then an autonomous principality, now a part of Romania in Eastern Europe—in the 17th century because they were Protestants. They had been rich landowners whose estates were named after them, and they had enjoyed certain tax privileges. The region along the river Traun between Bad Ischl and Lauffen still carries the name Engleiten today.

Even as a young boy, Leopold could not understand how one could be persecuted for reading the Bible. Little did he realize then that he himself would one day be a victim of religious intolerance.

His mother was a strict Catholic. But since his father did not require it, Leopold rarely went to church. He found the worship of images, common in that area, particularly incomprehensible. It was considered a crime and a serious insult to the saint in question if one passed a religious image without tipping one's hat or making the sign of the cross. He could not understand why anyone should have to bow down in front of a statue, which was, after all, made only of wood or china. Leopold largely inherited his father's skepticism, but his mother insisted that Leopold and Heinrich kneel down every evening before a picture of the Virgin Mary to say their prayers.

One day at school during religious instruction, the class discussed one of the Ten Commandments, which read:

> **Exodus 20:4, 5a[1]**
> Thou shalt not make unto thee a graven image, nor the likeness of any form that is in heaven above, or that is in the earth beneath, or that is in the water under the earth; thou shalt not bow down thyself unto them, nor serve them: for I the LORD thy God am a jealous God.

Leopold wanted to apply what he had learned right away. That evening he refused to kneel down in front of the picture of the Virgin Mary, telling his mother what he had learned at school that day. After she cuffed him around the ears a few times, he was forced to give in, at least outwardly. But deep down he was determined not to let the matter rest and began searching diligently for further confirmation of his views on image-worship. And it was not long before he found it.

Inquisitive, as small boys tend to be, he was poking around his grandmother's attic one day and found buried under a heap of junk an old book of sermons. The book had once belonged to his paternal great-grandfather, a zealous Lutheran. Every day Leopold stole upstairs and began to quench his thirst for spiritual knowledge with this old book, until one day he could no longer find it. His mother had found out what he had been doing so secretly in the attic, and had burned it.

Experiences of this kind, together with the things he learned at school about the meddling of religions in war and the blessing of weapons by the clergy, raised many questions in his innocent mind. He wondered about the way God was portrayed by these religions. Not even his religion instructor,

---

[1] Unless otherwise stated, all Bible quotations are taken from the Revised Version of the Holy Bible, published by the Cambridge University Press, London, 1903.

a priest, was interested in answering his genuine questions about the catechism. He even rebuked Leopold on several occasions when he thought the boy was becoming too inquisitive, stopping his questions with a harsh "Silence!"

Leopold's doubts grew as he watched the soldiers return home from World War I in 1918. Many of them had anything but a favorable view of the Church because of the terrible things they had seen. After he had started work as a farmhand at the age of 13½, he was shocked to see how reverently the clergy were treated. He found it amazing that other people could so naïvely follow traditions while remaining blind to the iniquities perpetrated by the Church. Leopold's contemporaries seemed to him to be spiritual prisoners, spellbound by rituals and permitting themselves to be exploited financially.

Despite his mother's extraordinary zeal for the Catholic Church, young Leopold's personal experiences and unanswered questions left him unsatisfied with the doctrines he had learned. But this did not mean that he had no interest in religion. Nature, with its multitude of wonderful living things and which he loved so much, was proof to him that God must exist. The infinite intelligence, variety, and love manifest in creation convinced Leopold that Almighty God deserved to be worshipped and praised.

But just "how" was one of the countless questions the clergy could not answer satisfactorily. His desire for spiritual freedom grew. Yet how difficult to defy the conservative ideas that held the rural population in their thrall! He encountered the views of atheists and devout Protestants, but none could satisfy his craving for answers.

To his great surprise, his thirst for spiritual knowledge was finally quenched in October 1931, when he found what seemed to him to be exactly the answers he was looking for.

One Wednesday evening Leopold Engleitner's friend and hiking companion Wolfgang Bachauer introduced him to a way that, despite many adversities, he was never to abandon.

Bachauer made an unusual request of Engleitner. He invited Leopold to accompany him to a meeting of Bible Students,[1] as Jehovah's Witnesses were then called, which was being held in an apartment in Bad Ischl. The public generally avoided the Bible Students and treated them with suspicion, so Bachauer felt uncomfortable about going there alone. Still disappointed with religion as a whole, Engleitner thought: "If it makes him happy, I'll go along with him." So off they went, feeling very proud of themselves for having the courage to visit these people.

The Bible Students' discussion turned out to be too intense for Bachauer. Engleitner, on the other hand, found the meeting captivating. At long last he began to receive answers to the questions that had troubled him for so long, such as, "Does God approve of image-worship? Does a fiery hell really exist? Will the dead be resurrected? Does the papacy represent Jesus Christ here on earth? Is God part of a Trinity?" What inspired him more than anything else, however, was the realization that God does not approve of man's wars, even if fought in His name. He learned that God is love and that He has a name that is exalted. In Hebrew this name is represented by the four consonants YHWH, which in English is rendered as "Jehovah." Furthermore, he discovered that anyone can establish a personal relationship with God.

Psalm 83:18
That they may know that thou alone, whose name is JEHOVAH, Art the Most High over all the earth.

Engleitner had already come across the name "Jehovah" before, having read it once in a book by the German poet Heinrich Heine. His father had borrowed it from the public library in Strobl, of which he was a founding member. In the ballad

---

[1] In 1931 the Bible Students adopted the name Jehovah's Witnesses. The original name, Earnest Bible Students, remained in use for many years.

Belsazar,"[1] the utensils of Jehovah's temple are mentioned, but at the time it had not meant anything to the young Engleitner. Empress Elisabeth of Austria (known affectionately as Sisi) also mentioned the name Jehovah quite often in her poems and in her diary.[2]

According to Jehovah's Witnesses, Jehovah God would bring peace and happiness to all mankind in a worldwide paradise on earth. This would be accomplished through God's Kingdom, a heavenly government, which has at its head God's son, Jesus Christ. So this was the Kingdom that millions of people prayed for in the Lord's Prayer and was the "good news" that Jesus had talked about in his famous Sermon on the Mount. No human emperor, king, or president would ever be able to achieve this.

Engleitner immediately bought a Catholic Bible translated by Leander van Ess and found corroborating evidence for all he had learned. At long last he had found what he had been looking for—a promise of world peace, guaranteed by the highest Sovereign of the universe.

A New Way

Over time, Leopold Engleitner became firmly convinced that he needed to live in harmony with what he had learned. It would prove to be a difficult and dangerous way involving hardship and suffering but one that would bring him great satisfaction and joy. His recently found faith and the strength he drew from his relationship with his God Jehovah left him in no doubt that this was the only way that would give his life real meaning, and he was prepared to pay any price to stay on that path.

It was not long before that faith was subjected to its first test. Engleitner realized that he would have to break with his

---

[1] Heinrich Heine, *Gesammelte Gedichte und Verse* (Lechnerverlag, Switzerland, 1994) pp. 79–80

[2] Brigitte Hamann, *Elisabeth - The Reluctant Empress* (New York, 1986), p. 286

former religion. The first hurdle was therefore his resignation from the Catholic Church. In Austria during the 1930s, the church held remarkable power and exerted enormous social pressure. After thorough study of the Word of God, Engleitner informed his parents of his decision to leave the Roman Catholic Church. His father was very upset at the news; evidently he was not as self-confident as he had always claimed to be. Fear of his fellow man was manifest in his motto: "You don't have to take part in everything, but only fools swim against the tide." On hearing his decision, his mother fell to her knees in front of him, wrung her hands, and pleaded: "Poidl, you can't possibly bring this disgrace upon me. Please, please don't do it!" Though her fervent plea deeply touched him, she could not persuade him to go back on his decision. He told her that although he knew it would be hard on his mother, he had to follow his convictions. If she would only study her own Bible, she would see that he was doing the right thing. She refused to do so, however, because like her husband she did not really have anything against her son's newfound faith; what she feared was the damage it would do to the family's reputation.

In order to leave the church officially, Engleitner needed his certificate of baptism (see following page). To get it he went to Franz Seitz, the parish priest of Strobl am Abersee. This required courage, since the priest was reputed to be an ill-mannered lout. It was said that he regularly boxed the ears of the sexton and the altar boys in a fit of rage.

Nevertheless, Engleitner went to ask him for his certificate of baptism from the parish registry. Looking through the register of births and baptisms, the priest asked him: "Are you applying for a government post?"

"No," came the reply.

"Do you want to get married?"

Again the answer was: "No."

"Then what do you need it for?" snapped the impatient priest.

nr. 66.

Land Salzburg
Erzdiözese Salzburg

Geburts= und Taufschein

Aus dem hiesigen Tauf-Register tom. _V._, fol. 122 wird hiemit ämtlich bezeugt, daß am 23 Juli des Jahres 1905

Eintausend neunhundert fünf

zu Aigen 24, um ½11ʰ mittags

geboren und am 23. Juli 1905 von hochw. Herrn

Pfarrer Johann Draxel nach katholischem Ritus getauft wurde:

Name des Täuflings	Vater deſſen Tauf- und Zuname, Charakter und Religion	Mutter deren Taufname, ihres Vaters und ihrer Mutter Tauf- und Zuname	Paten mit Tauf- und Zuname und Charakter
Leopold Engleitner,	Leopold Engleitner, ... Aigen 24, zu Hans, ... in Bad Ischl, geboren 28.8.1867, gestorben 4.7.1904.	Juliana Haas, ... Haus, ... gein, ... Juliana, geb. Schmidt, geb. 2.6.1871.	Katharina Stehrer, ... Gattin fam.

Urkund deſſen ist des Unterzeichneten eigenhändige Unterschrift und das beigedrückte Amtsiegel.

F. e. Pfarramt Draxel a/Aigen

am 18. Februar 1932.

Franz Seitz, Pfarrer.

14: Leopold Engleitner's birth certificate and certificate of baptism
(issued on February 18, 1932)

"For my resignation from the church," said Engleitner courageously.

Franz Seitz angrily threw the book back onto the shelf and began to laugh scornfully. "You'll never get it from me!" he said with an air of finality. Then he wanted to know the reason for this decision. Engleitner readily told him about his newfound faith, quoting from 2 Corinthians 6:17:

> Wherefore come ye out from among them, and be ye
> separate, saith the Lord, and touch no unclean thing;
> And I will receive you.

This did not go down well with the priests and was perhaps not the most tactful thing to say. This layman not only quoted the Bible to a theologian but had the audacity to tell him what it meant. "That's what comes of your free interpretation of the Bible," the priest retorted, marching him to the door.

But before the priest closed it, Engleitner made another attempt: "I'll give you one last chance," he said. "Either you give me my certificate now, or I'll report the matter to the local authorities."

"You do what you like! You're not getting it!" shouted the priest and threw him out.

Engleitner was not the least bit intimidated by the priest's display. He reported the matter to the local government office in Gmunden, asking for its support. The office contacted Seitz and ordered him to hand over the certificate of baptism at once. Engleitner's resignation from the Roman Catholic Church was officially registered on February 27, 1932 (see following page), with the proviso that he explain in person the reasons for his entry into a new church or religious community to its leader or minister.[1] So it was that on the following Sunday the parish priest of Strobl announced Engleitner's departure from the church from the pulpit with the words: "That upstart from Weinbach has left the Church!" From that day on,

---

[1] Article 6 of the Law on Interconfessional Relations RGBl. No. 49/1868, Resignation from the Church RGBl. No. 13/1869

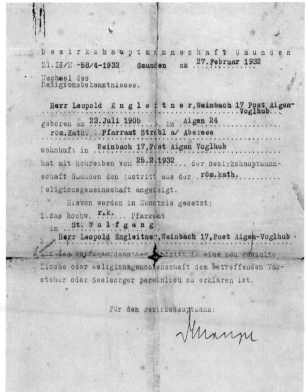

15: Resignation of membership from the Catholic Church (issued on February 27, 1932)

Leopold Engleitner became the object of general contempt, some people even spitting at his feet as they passed by.

With the first major obstacle out of the way, there was nothing to prevent him from announcing his newfound faith to others. So in May 1932, he was baptized as one of Jehovah's Witnesses in a washtub decorated with daffodils in a house in Bad Ischl. By so doing he declared that from that time on he would endeavor to live his life in accordance with the requirements of his God Jehovah. He was now determined to follow the example of Jesus Christ and proclaim the good news contained in the Word of God to as many people as possible.

He began this task in the immediate vicinity of his hometown. But in 1932, Austria's economic situation worsened, and in June of that year, Engleitner found himself out of work again. This gave him the chance to preach further afield, spending whole days going from house to house in distant areas. At the same time, he had the opportunity to work on his house and take on any odd jobs that came his way.

Approaching complete strangers and talking to them about the Bible was of course not easy, particularly as very few of these conservative people owned a Bible in those days. Besides, he had had no training for this sort of work and had only been to school for seven years. Because of his upbringing and the way he had been treated by certain teachers, classmates, and the farmers he had worked for, he saw himself as inferior. He was just a simple man with little self-confidence. But that did not stop him from talking to people wherever he could about the things he had learned, for he was convinced that he had found the true religion.

In the autumn of 1933, he embarked on one of his many preaching tours. He went to Lupitsch in Bad Aussee, some 22 miles from his home, to speak to the people there. It was there that another obstacle threatened to dampen his enthusiasm.

While Engleitner was going from door to door, a policeman who had something against him stopped him and asked for his identification papers. Engleitner showed him his unemployment card. The officer wrote down the information and informed the labor exchange in Bad Ischl of his activities. The next day Engleitner received a visit from a member of the labor exchange staff, Josef Nöstlinger, who informed him that his unemployment benefit payments had been stopped, effective immediately. This meant that he would have no income whatsoever and had no hope of a job in the foreseeable future.

Nöstlinger justified this measure by explaining to Engleitner that sects were not tolerated in Austria and that only Catholics and Protestants had the right to preach. But this was in direct violation of the Treaty of Saint Germain, signed in 1919, which stipulated in Section V, Articles 62 and 63, that Austria was obligated to recognize these laws:

Section V
Protection of Minorities
Article 62 (Fundamental Law)
Austria undertakes that the stipulations contained in this section shall be recognized as fundamental laws, and that no law, regulation, or official action shall conflict or interfere with these stipulations, nor shall any law, regulation, or official action prevail over them.

Article 63 (No Discrimination, Religion)
(1) Austria undertakes to assure full and complete protection of life and liberty to all inhabitants of Austria without distinction of birth, nationality, language, race, or religion.
(2) All inhabitants of Austria shall be entitled to the free exercise, whether public or private, of any creed, religion, or belief, whose practices are not inconsistent with public order or public morals.

In the knowledge that he had the law on his side, Engleitner bicycled to Gmunden the very next day to visit the labor office there. The staff refused to listen to him and held that the action taken was quite legitimate. He had only one option left, to write to the labor exchanges in Linz and Vienna, asking that this unlawful decision be revoked. A friend helped him to write a letter of complaint, which may have overstepped the mark somewhat. A short time later the officer in charge of Bad Ischl police station stopped by to inform him of a report received from the labor exchange that Engleitner had "libeled an official authority," and had to pay a fine.

When Engleitner explained to the policeman how the letter had come about, the friendly officer said: "I see. You may have written the letter, but the actual wording is someone else's. Don't worry about it. I'll take care of this, and you won't have to pay the fine." The man duly kept his word, and Engleitner heard no more about it. This problem may have been solved, but soon afterward Engleitner received letters from both the labor exchange in Linz and the one in Vienna confirming the stoppage of his unemployment benefits.

They too refused to correct this arbitrary act that violated the constitutional right to freedom of religion in Austria. This was only the first of a series of attacks by administrative bodies against Engleitner, which increased in ferocity under Chancellor Schuschnigg. They aimed to force him to abandon his newfound convictions.

What should he do now? He had no job and would receive no benefit payments. Although he had the Austrian constitution on his side, no one would assist him in fighting for his rights. Not only that, at home he had to contend with a furious father who ranted and raved, bitterly reproaching his son with the words: "That's what you get for all your clever ideas! What are you going to do now?" The easiest thing would have been to give up his faith and return to the fold, accepting the traditional views of society. This would have been the path of least resistance, but it was a path he could not and would not take. He made it plain that his religious convictions were of much greater importance than any social or material convenience. Confident that he had the Almighty on his side, he decided to devote his entire time to proclaiming the good news and soon received a letter from the branch office of the

Jehovah's Witnesses in Bern, Switzerland. This office supervised the work of their Austrian counterparts at the time, and it invited Engleitner to move to a territory where no member of this religious organization had ever worked before.

So it was that on Monday, January 1, 1934, this unassuming young man, with physical limitations but also enormous vitality and sense of purpose, left his home in Weinbach. Carrying a few schillings, a rucksack full of Bible literature, a little food, and an old coat, he boarded a train from Bad Ischl to the village of Untergrimming in the Ennstal. On arrival at his destination, he looked over the territory he had been assigned. It included the entire Styrian Ennstal from Mandling in the west following the river Enns eastward to Schladming up as far as Stainach and Wörschach and all the neighboring valleys, including the Donnersbachwald and Sölktal valleys to the south. It was literally a mountainous task that faced him. He was to carry the Bible's message into the homes and hearts of everyone living there without letting himself be discouraged by the adversities that surely awaited him.

He was a long way from home, and therefore needed a place to spend the night. With his savings almost gone, he was forced to rely on the hospitality of the people he met. Often he slept in haylofts or cow barns and sometimes in the manger of a sheep pen, where he was once woken by several sheep busily nibbling at his coat. Occasionally, an especially friendly farmer would offer him a bed in the house, adding a hot meal for good measure. But when his message met with little enthusiasm, he would go several days without food.

The weather was not kind to him, either. He spent one day trudging through the Ramsau region around Schladming in icy cold weather and deep snow for hours, and when he eventually reached his lodgings that evening, he was unable to take his shoes off, as they had frozen to his feet. It was only with the help of the farmer's son that he managed to pry them off, only to find that the bottom of his socks had remained stuck in his shoes. He came down with a high fever during the night and felt terrible the next morning. Fortunately, in the course of that day, he met a man who offered him a warm bed to sleep in.

He never spent more than one night anywhere. An innkeeper advised him that if he stayed too long in one place, he would soon be arrested by the police, as had already happened to an Adventist preacher.

As it turned out, though, even this constant moving around could not prevent his arrest. Even prior to the Nazi annexation of Austria in 1938 (the so-called Anschluss), National Socialism had gained a strong foothold in Upper Styria, so much so that a state of emergency had been declared in many regions. For example, a kind of civilian militia patrolled the town of Schladming, where the population was predominantly Protestant, following a series of riots that had been instigated by the National Socialists. Some had even gone so far as to blow up a number of bridges. In view of this precarious situation, Engleitner had to proceed with great caution.

One day at a laundry, he struck up a conversation with the owner. He tried to find out the man's opinion on various topics, asking him among other things about his political views. In this way, he hoped to find out whether it would be safe to mention Biblical matters. The man seemed trustworthy, advising him to be very careful because there were a lot of informers about, so Engleitner asked him if he could leave his rucksack of Biblical pamphlets with him for safekeeping. That way, if he was arrested, he would not lose them all. He only took his Bible and a few leaflets with him in his coat pocket. Before going to the next house, Engleitner always took a long detour through the village to shake off anyone who might be trailing him. But despite all his efforts, he was arrested and taken to the local police station where a large group of policemen waited for him. As soon as the duty officer saw him, he cried out: "Now we've got him!" and Engleitner realized that the police must have known what he was doing in spite of all the precautions he had taken. After his pamphlets had been taken away from him, the sergeant asked him: "Are you carrying any kind of weapon?"

"Yes, of course!" replied Engleitner promptly.

"Then hand it over!" demanded the policeman. Engleitner drew his Bible out of his coat pocket and, grinning broadly, tossed it onto the table. The policemen burst out laughing, taken off guard by the quick-witted response. Engleitner then picked up his Bible and walked out of the police station, relieved that he had avoided further interrogation.

Returning to the laundry, he picked up his rucksack and set out for Haus, a village in the Ennstal where it was a little safer, and continued his work there.

In Stainach, Styria, Engleitner's quick thinking saved him from another brush with the authorities. He had been having a discussion with a woman on her doorstep and had left her some Bible pamphlets. Her irate husband, a local policeman, came running after him and stopped him, shouting: "Are you allowed to preach here at all? Do you have a permit?" Engleitner always carried a document with him signed by the provincial governor of Upper Austria, Dr. Heinrich Gleissner, entitling him to distribute religious publications and leaflets. Although the permit had already expired and had only been valid in Upper Austria, Engleitner handed it to the policeman, who after examining it briefly, cried out: "It's already expired!"

Engleitner quickly snatched the document away from him. "Why ask me to show you my permit when you can't even read properly?" he said. Without waiting for a reply, he turned and quickly walked off. The policeman wondered if he had read it correctly or not. Embarrassed to ask for the document again, he let Engleitner go.

Although most people were not willing to listen to what he had to say about the "good news," he managed to have brief conversations with at least some of them. In the spring of 1934, he happened to meet a farmhand in St. Nikolai im Sölktal who was passing by with a wooden cart. This man was David Meissnitzer, although Engleitner did not know his name at the time. Engleitner explained what he was doing and gave him a brochure to read before moving on to the next farmhouse. As there was no one at home, he stuck a leaflet into the door. On his way back, he met the farmhand again, who told him that he had already finished reading the brochure. Although he was rather indignant about the revelations it made about the Church's shortcomings, he had to admit that the subsequent explanations were quite plausible. Engleitner was delighted that the young man had made the effort to read the information so quickly, and encouraged him to study the Bible. Little did he realize what consequences this chance encounter would later have.

His activities, however, rarely went unnoticed by the authorities. The local government offices in Gröbming sentenced him to 48 hours' detention in Bad Ischl prison for alleged "peddling." Kajetan Achleitner, with whom Engleitner had worked regulating riverbeds of mountain streams, was now his jailer. "I've brought my Bible along," said Engleitner, "in case I get bored."

"That's all right," replied Achleitner.

Thus he was able to spend his enforced "holiday" studying his favorite book.

Engleitner left Upper Styria in July 1934 and moved to a new territory in Upper Austria. The area covered the Krems and Steyr valleys in the Lower Traunviertel from the village of Scharnstein eastward over Kirchdorf, Micheldorf, and Krems Ursprung, where the river Krems rises, continuing on to Ramsau and Molln, and then northward up the Steyrtal to Waldneukirchen. This was a vast area for one man to cover. Engleitner continued his work as before, going from house to house from early morning to late at night, then sleeping in a hayloft. But brushes with the authorities could not be avoided in this region either.

At the beginning of August, when he was staying in Molln with a couple called Franz and Franziska Unterbrunner, it was pure chance that saved him from one such encounter. It was evening and he had just returned to his lodgings from a preaching tour. There he found a letter waiting for him from St. Wolfgang, his local authority, requesting him to call at the office there immediately. Because he still wanted to attend a Bible study group that evening, he planned to start the 60-mile journey to St. Wolfgang early next morning. However, after the meeting had ended, he changed his mind and cycled home right away, even though it was already ten o'clock and pitch-dark. He went by way of Micheldorf, Ziehberg, Scharnstein, Gmunden, and Ebensee, arriving in Weinbach early next morning having covered 60 miles of rough, potholed roads. Although very tired, he proceeded directly to the council offices in St. Wolfgang. There he was told that the local government office in Kirchdorf had sentenced him to 48 hours' detention in Bad Ischl prison. The police in Waldneukirchen had charged him with unlawful peddling. Engleitner explained that he had not broken this law and refused to allow himself to be detained. "I haven't got time to serve this sentence now," he said. "I'll come back another time." What really annoyed him was the behavior of the policemen in Waldneukirchen. During the questioning at the police station there, one of them had asked him for a Bible, so he would never have expected such a charge from that source.

Returning to the Unterbrunners' house the next day, he learned of the turbulent events of the previous night. Franziska Unterbrunner told him that their house had been surrounded at four o'clock in the morning by some 20 policemen wanting to arrest him. But because he was not there, they had taken her husband and their two sons into custody instead. However, the Unterbrunners were not Jehovah's Witnesses, and on top of that, the father, Franz, was master of the chimney sweeps' guild and as such responsible for all the chimney sweeps in the area. His arrest would cause serious problems. He was taken to Garsten prison, furious about his detention, and demanded to be allowed to phone his guild's lawyer, who did not manage to secure his release until three weeks later.

(As a result of these events, Franz Unterbrunner started to study the Bible seriously and was eventually baptized as one of Jehovah's Witnesses in 1937. Two years later, in April 1939, the Gestapo arrested him at his house, confiscated Bible publications, and charged him with high treason. He scarcely had time to say goodbye to his family. In September 1939 he was interned in Mauthausen concentration camp in Upper Austria, where he died on January 19, 1940. The official cause of death given was "apoplexy," but according to the testimony of a fellow prisoner, Valentin Eder, he was in fact starved to death.)

Engleitner was naturally happy to have escaped arrest once again, as otherwise he would have been put out of action for quite some time.

However, since he was still regularly picked up for questioning at various police stations, in August 1934 the branch office of the Jehovah's Witnesses in Bern asked him to return home and continue working in his home congregation in Bad Ischl.

So after eight months on the road, he returned home. His clothes were by now so shabby and worn that his parents barely recognized their son; he looked more like a tramp.

Engleitner hoped to attend the convention of Jehovah's Witnesses in Basel, Switzerland. The purpose of the convention was to provide spiritual encouragement and strength by means of Bible-based discourses, to help them withstand the tests they would soon have to face. Leopold Engleitner felt the need for such encouragement very badly and was determined to attend. But he faced a seemingly insoluble problem: Where would he find the money for the train ticket? Sitting in his room one day racking his brains over this problem, his eyes fell on a silver watch chain lying on the table. He had inherited it from his half-brother Ferdinand. It was very old and was inlaid with a number of heavy silver coins. Although this memento meant a great deal to him, he decided to sell it. He went to Gmunden, found a goldsmith shop, and showed the watch chain to the owner's wife. She said she would have to show it to her husband, who would be in a little later on. Engleitner left the silver chain with her while he went to the local government office to apply for a passport. The man at the desk wanted to know why he needed one, so Engleitner explained that he was one of Jehovah's Witnesses and wanted to attend the convention in Switzerland. The clerk found this very interesting and issued the document. During this exchange Engleitner noticed that there was a man in the room whose clothing made it clear that he was a Nazi. When the man heard Engleitner say he was one of Jehovah's Witnesses, his lips curled into a contemptuous sneer. Engleitner, his passport safely in his pocket, then headed back to the goldsmith's.

Entering the shop, he caught sight of the owner, and gasped. "Oh no! It can't be!" he thought. "That's the Nazi I just saw in the passport office. Well, I might as well take my chain and leave." Sure enough, the goldsmith threw him the chain, saying: "This is just old rubbish. Nobody buys stuff like this anymore. Take it and go!"

Engleitner was naturally disappointed, but he refused to lose heart and went to look for an antiques shop. When he found one, the owner bit the chain to make sure it was real silver but said he did not want to purchase it, since he knew of no prospective buyer. Engleitner left the shop dejectedly and was about to set off for home when the shopkeeper came running after him, shouting: "Come back! I've found a buyer, but I'll fix the price!"

Reentering the shop, Engleitner saw an aristocratic-looking man. He was interested in purchasing the chain. The shopkeeper named a price that Engleitner would never have dared to ask for, but the gentleman took out his wallet without hesitation and paid immediately. The shopkeeper then turned to Engleitner and gave him the entire amount without keeping anything for himself.

Now he could afford a train ticket to Basel and was able to attend the international convention of Jehovah's Witnesses. The gathering lasted for several days and had a profound effect on Engleitner. When it was time to leave, he felt as if he were leaving home. A fine article about the convention appeared in one of the Basel papers, so Engleitner took a copy home as a present for his father, an avid reader. His father was so excited about reading a genuine Swiss newspaper that he practically snatched it out of his son's hands, but when he came across the article about the convention, he moaned: "I might have known you wouldn't bring me anything good!"

Next winter Engleitner voluntarily reported to the courthouse in Bad Ischl[1] to serve the 48-hour prison sentence he had received from the local government office in Kirchdorf. He could have paid a fine instead, but he was short of money and decided to make himself comfortable in a heated cell. This enabled him to regain much needed strength while enjoying free board and lodging.

In the spring of 1935, his economic situation worsened considerably. He was still disqualified from receiving unemployment benefits and had no income whatsoever. He searched the newspaper advertisements every day but could find nothing until he spotted a notice that a snail farm near Mattighofen was in need of edible snails. The moist meadows of the Ischl valley were just the place to look for such snails,

---

[1] *Bezirksgericht* ("district court") Bad Ischl, court of first instance.

so Engleitner started collecting large quantities of them, keeping them in a wooden box made just for this purpose. When he had enough, he sent them on to the snail farm. This and other odd jobs working for Alois Unterberger and other neighboring farmers allowed him to keep his head above water during this difficult time.

An Unprejudiced Police Officer

In the autumn of that year, he began to devote more time to proclaiming the "good news" again, despite the increasing danger of making himself known as one of Jehovah's Witnesses; the population, stirred up by the clergy, was becoming more and more aggressive. Engleitner had a taste of this growing animosity one day in Traunkirchen when he escaped the clutches of a mob by the skin of his teeth.

He was cycling home from Winkl when he noticed a large crowd at the narrow end of Traunkirchen town square. At first he thought that there must have been an accident and so continued unsuspectingly on his way. Not until he was in the middle of the crowd did he realize that they had come for him, to beat him up and teach him a lesson he would not forget.

Just as the mob closed in for the attack, the officer in charge of Traunkirchen police station, Inspector Franz Bachmair, happened to pass by. He asked the angry crowd what was going on and was told that they had just caught one of the Bible Students. After commending them on their initiative, he told them to go home. Seizing Engleitner in front of the mob, he led him off to the police station. At this the crowd calmed down a bit, and for the first time in his life, Engleitner was glad to be arrested. Who knows what would have happened to him otherwise?

When they arrived at the station, the policeman said: "You were lucky there, my friend. If I hadn't turned up, you'd have been in trouble, make no mistake!"

"I know I owe you a great deal, officer," replied Engleitner, who then proceeded to start a lively conversation with him.

After a while the inspector glanced out of the window, which afforded a good view of the town square, and turning to Engleitner said: "The coast is clear now. The crowd has dispersed, and there's nothing more to worry about. Fetch your bike, and be on your way!"

Engleitner was all too happy to comply, and jumping onto his bicycle, he quickly rode home.

On another occasion the same policeman had to arrest him after he had been reported for peddling. Engleitner asserted his innocence, maintaining that he was wrongly accused. But how could Franz Bachmair find out whether he was telling the truth or not? Engleitner therefore made the following suggestion: "If you really want to know if I ask for money when I hand out Bible leaflets, you'll have to come with me. It's the only way for you to see that I'm not peddling."

At first the policeman was indignant and replied: "I can't possibly do that! What would people think?" But he soon realized there was no other way to form a fair judgment on the matter and agreed.

So the two of them set off. Engleitner smiled to himself on account of his unlikely preaching companion and was amused to see how uncomfortable the policeman felt at having to explain to everyone what he was doing. After they had visited several houses and Bachmair had made inquiries about Engleitner's activities, he concluded: "Herr Engleitner, you're right! You're not violating the law. You don't ask for money for the leaflets you hand out, and no one has said anything to the contrary. Whatever money you receive is given voluntarily as a donation, which you are perfectly entitled to accept. I can therefore drop the charge against you. You're free to go!" Bachmair then headed back to the police station, visibly relieved that this embarrassing task was finished.

The police in Altmünster, however, were less well disposed toward him, and he found himself having to appear in court in Wels[1] together with another Witness, the optician Josef Hahn, charged with violating the peddling law.

> Imperial Patent, issued on September 4, 1852,
> as amended BGBL[2]
> No. 324/1934 § 1
> *Peddling is to be understood as trading in commodities*
> *while moving from place to place and from house to house,*
> *and without a fixed sales outlet.*

In court the two men explained to the judge that they distributed their material free of charge and that their activities served purely religious ends and involved no commercial gain. They pointed out that they both had a permit for the distribution of religious pamphlets and publications, issued by the governor of Upper Austria, Dr. Heinrich Gleissner. These sound arguments helped the judge reach the conclusion that neither of them had broken the peddling law, and they were both acquitted.

The same year, in spite of his financial straits, Engleitner bought a gramophone so that he could convey the Word of God using recordings of lectures on Bible subjects. If a householder showed interest, Engleitner would set up the machine and play one of the records. Using the latest technology available, he spared no trouble or expense to convince his fellowman of the importance of the message.

During a round of questioning at the police station in Traunkirchen, Engleitner found out how much of an irritation his activities were to the Church. He also learned that it was often the Church itself that incited the authorities to hound

---

[1] *Kreisgericht Wels*
[2] *Bundesgesetzblatt:* Federal Law Gazette

Jehovah's Witnesses. One day as Inspector Franz Bachmair prepared to read a charge against Engleitner, a small boy burst into the room. "Officer!" he shouted breathlessly. "Reverend says to tell you that the Bible Students are going round again and you should see to them!"

The policeman thanked the boy and sent him back to the parish priest with his regards. He then turned to Engleitner and said: "Did you hear that? Now you know who it is behind the persecution of your group. We keep getting tip-offs like that. But don't worry, you have nothing to fear from me."

Now he had definite proof that the clergy were abusing their power to stop his activities. This simple man was not going to be intimidated, however; on the contrary, the harassment only served to strengthen his conviction that spreading the "good news" contained in the Bible was necessary, even if it was becoming more and more dangerous to do so. But from that time on, brushes with the authorities were not so harmless.

In the Clutches of the Authorities

On Sunday, January 5, 1936, Leopold Engleitner was arrested in St. Gilgen on the Wolfgangsee while preaching. He was taken to the local police station where the authorities confiscated his entire stock of Bible literature on the grounds that the distribution of Bible Student publications was prohibited in Austria.[1]

"We'll soon put an end to all your running around!" threatened the officer on duty.

"The message we bear is not our own," explained Engleitner fearlessly. "It comes from the Bible and originates from above. You can't prohibit that."

"We don't interfere with what he does up there," said the policeman, "but down here we're in charge!"

---

[1] File number: 351927-G.D. 2, decree of the Federal Chancellery (Office for Public Security) of November 25, 1935

"Yes, Officer, I've noticed that already," replied Engleitner with a grin.

"What are you insinuating?" snapped the policeman.

"Merely that I've been disqualified from unemployment benefits for several years now, and although you say you're in charge, you can't even give me work!" The policeman, taken aback, did not say another word.

At 12.30 p.m., Engleitner and Roman Franzmeier, another Witness, were transferred to the prison in St. Gilgen. Both were held "under suspicion of having caused a breach of the peace and under strong suspicion of collusion."[1] That same day, St. Gilgen police searched Engleitner's house and seized fifty more books and other literature.

After Otto Haahs, the judge, had examined the literature on January 6, 1936, at St. Gilgen court, he told Engleitner and Franzmeier that they were being taken into custody under §§ 175 no. 4, 179 StPO (*Strafprozessordnung,* code of criminal procedure relating to the danger of recidivism) on suspicion of offenses in connection with § 303 of the Penal Law (StG) of 1852, amended 1919 (libel on a legally recognized church or religious community).[2]

Of course Engleitner was absolutely convinced that he had not broken that law, but his arguments fell on deaf ears. He believed that this ruling blatantly violated the Peace Treaty of Saint Germain, Section V, Articles 62 and 63. It seemed further evidence of the enormous influence that the legally recognized churches in Austria exercised. For instance, a ruling of the Supreme Court illustrated just how sensitive they were to challenges to established doctrine:

"The claim that several other children issued from the marriage between the Blessed Virgin Mary and Joseph, the adoptive father of Christ, conflicts with the Catholic teaching

---

[1] File number: Z 2/36, charge filed by the police in St. Gilgen on January 5, 1936, at St. Gilgen court

[2] Examination of the accused at St. Gilgen court, January 6, 1936

of the virginity of the Mother of God and constitutes an offense under § 303 StG." [1]

On January 24, 1936, Leopold Engleitner and Roman Franzmeier, manacled like dangerous criminals, were put on the local Salzkammergut train[2] and taken to Salzburg court[3] where, after several rounds of questioning, they were taken into custody pending trial.

Although indignant about this further act of vindictiveness, Engleitner felt honored to suffer for God and Jesus Christ as the first Christians had done. Imprisonment gave him the opportunity to prove his steadfastness under adverse circumstances, and he drew strength from the promise Jesus gave in the Sermon on the Mount:

Matthew 5:11, 12
Blessed are ye when men shall reproach you, and persecute you, and say all manner of evil against you falsely, for my sake.
Rejoice, and be exceeding glad: for great is your reward in heaven: for so persecuted they the prophets which were before you.

In prison, Engleitner had to share a prison cell with very rough characters who harassed him because of his religion. So he had to keep his wits about him and asked the warden to give him a Bible. The warden thought that he probably wanted to use it to convert the other inmates, so he put him in solitary confinement and gave him books by Goethe instead of a Bible. Solitary was what Engleitner had secretly hoped for, and he

[1] Supreme Court ruling, September 11, 1897, collection 2110
[2] Known locally as the *Kleinbahn* (Small Train) or *der feurige Elias* (The Fiery Elias)
[3] Landesgericht Salzburg: as the court with jurisdiction over the province of Salzburg, also court of second instance.

gladly accepted his "punishment," pleased that he would have some peace. Unfortunately though, this also marked the end of the English lessons he had been taking from a teacher who was serving a prison sentence because of his National Socialist activities, and who had been among his jeering cell-mates. He had had a very attentive student in Engleitner, who picked up things very quickly and also learned to pronounce words such as "Washington" and "New York" correctly, words that only well-educated people would have known how to pronounce in Austria at that time.

On February 7, 1936,[1] the decision to dissolve the Watchtower Bible and Tract Society in Austria—a decision issued on June 17, 1935,[2] by the federal director of security in Vienna—was declared legally binding with immediate effect by the Supreme Court. This had no direct effect on Leopold Engleitner and Roman Franzmeier, though, since they were on remand for alleged violation of the Penal Law, § 303.

On March 30, 1936, the main hearing was held before a court of lay assessors at Salzburg court. The public prosecutors in Salzburg arraigned the two on charges in connection with § 303 and § 122 of the Penal Law (*Religionsstörung*),[3] whereby § 123 section 1 was also cited as applicable, as it was assumed that "this activity involved a danger to the public."

§ 303, Penal Law 1852, amended 1919
Libel on a legally recognized church or religious community
Whosoever publicly, or before a group of people, either in print or by distributing a pictorial representation, or in writing, either mocks, ridicules, or seeks to degrade

---

[1] File number: A108/36.1
[2] File number: MAbt. 2/5363/35, ruling of June 17, 1935
[3] Literally "Disturbance of religion": activities likely to cause offense to practitioners of legally recognized religions.

the doctrines, practices, or institutions of a legally recognized church or religious community, or offends a religious minister of such a church or community during the practice of services of worship, or behaves indecently or in such a way as is likely to cause offense to others during the public exercise of their religion, is committing an offense, in so far as this does not constitute the crime of "Religionsstörung" (§ 122), punishable with close arrest of one to six months.

§ 122, Penal Law 1852, amended 1919

The crime of "Religionsstörung" is committed by

a) whosoever, either through speech or actions, in publications or distributed writings, blasphemes against God;

b) whosoever disturbs the exercise of an existing religion recognized by the State, or publicly displays contempt for it, either by defiling through misuse the utensils used during religious services, or by actions, speeches, publications, or distributed writings;

§ 123, Penal Law 1852, amended 1919

If the act of "Religionsstörung" leads to any public offense, or any seduction, or any public danger, the crime is to be punished with imprisonment of one year to five years; in cases of extreme maliciousness and danger, this sentence is to be increased to up to ten years.

In Engleitner's opinion the charge that their religious activity represented a public danger conflicted with the constitutional right to the free exercise of religion in Austria. He would have understood such unjust treatment in the days of the monarchy, when even the slightest protest against the existing religious order was severely punished. But now that Austria was bound by the Peace Treaty of Saint Germain, it should have been impossible for anyone to consider constructive criticism a danger to the public. How could freedom of religion exist if it was considered a crime to point out discrepancies between the Bible and the teachings and behavior of those claiming to believe in it?

After the indictment was read, the two defendants pleaded not guilty and were given the opportunity to defend themselves. They stated: "We have not disturbed any religious service, committed the crime of *Religionsstörung,* or shown contempt for any religion whatsoever. Rather we have merely proclaimed the truth as it is written in the Holy Scriptures. The books and publications that were confiscated from us and which we distributed contain the whole truth of the Bible. While the clergy of the recognized denominations preach the laws found in the Bible, they do not obey them. We, the defendants, know what the Bible says because we possess a copy of it. The clergy teach 'Thou shalt not kill,' and yet they bless weapons, in disobedience to God's laws. The established religions preach parts of the Holy Scriptures, but other parts they ignore. Therefore, they do not reveal the whole truth. The Holy Scriptures contain divine prophecies. We always respect state laws that conform to God's laws, but at the same time, we tell people that only God's Kingdom offers genuine help. We tell them not to meddle in politics and warn them not to get involved in any revolutionary movement. We Bible Students have enemies not only in Austria but also in Germany and Russia. We do not ridicule any religion or church. What matters is whether a thing is approved by *God*, not whether it is approved by a government. If a government claims to be Christian, then it has to permit interpretation of the Bible."[1]

The judge, Dr. Langer, noted this statement and asked the two Witnesses to answer the following question: "Is the president of the Watchtower Society, Rutherford, inspired by God?"

Franzmeier said yes, he was. The judge then turned to Engleitner and asked for his opinion.

"By no means!" replied Engleitner without a second's hesitation.

"Why not?" the judge wanted to know.

The explanation Engleitner then gave proved his thorough knowledge of the Bible and ability to draw logical conclusions. He said: "According to the Holy Scriptures, the inspired writings end with the book of Revelation. For that reason, Rutherford cannot be inspired by God. But God most certainly gave him a measure of his holy spirit to help him understand and interpret his Word by means of thorough study!" The judge was obviously impressed by such a thoughtful answer from this uneducated man. He realized that he was not just repeating something mechanically that he had heard, but had a firm personal conviction based on the Bible.

The court passed the following judgment:

"The defendants have committed the crime of libel on a legally recognized church under § 303 of the Penal Law and are hereby sentenced as follows:

1. Roman Franzmeier, sentenced to 3 (three) months' close arrest

2. Leopold Engleitner sentenced to 2 (two) months' close arrest each sentence to be augmented by 1 day of fasting per month."[1]

---

[1] File number: 5 Vr 99/36.28

In the court's opinion, some passages from the confiscated publications were deemed to mock Christian churches. In particular the pages 13, 21, and 22 of the booklet *Liberty* were cited:

"There are numerous churches or congregations throughout the land, and their worship is mere formalism, bowing down to images and repeating certain rituals.... [They] address their prayers to stones or statues made of wood or to other inanimate objects. Some turn wheels and count that as a prayer; while others count beads while they repeat some words, and believe this is prayer."

After reading this, the court made the comment: "It is claimed here that the church practices idolatry by worshipping inanimate objects, and that its veneration of God is choked by forms and formulas. This is obviously a distortion of the facts, since the wording as well as the meaning of this statement are not aimed at the thoughtless use or even misuse of objects such as images or the rosary, but at the objects themselves. It is therefore indisputable that a degradation of the paraphernalia of the Christian churches has taken place."

On the other hand the court stated: "The defendants cannot be numbered among those who have completely lost their faith in God. On the contrary, they are seeking knowledge of God and His relationship to mankind by means of the Holy Scriptures. Therefore they do not show any contempt for religion itself, rather for those theological teachings, church institutions, and practices which, in their opinion, do not originate from the Holy Scriptures, or are, at least, not interpreted correctly. In the light of this, the court subjectively finds that the offenses with which the defendants are charged merely constitute an offense under § 303 of the Penal Law, since the evidence produced shows that it was not the defendants' intention to hold religion in contempt, but to mock and degrade the previously mentioned doctrines, practices, and paraphernalia of legally recognized religious communities. The court cannot share the view expressed by the prosecution that

16: Certificate of arrest,
March 30, 1936,
Salzburg prison
administration

the defendants have also committed the crime of *Religionsstörung* as defined in § 122 of the Penal Law, despite the fact that there are undoubtedly grounds for suspicion that such an offense was committed."

Finally, the impounded publications were declared forfeited under § 41 of the Press Law, because of their punishable content.

Turning to Engleitner, the judge, Dr. Langer, said: "In fixing the sentence, we have shown particular consideration for you by deciding on the minimum penalty." Despite this, Engleitner made it quite clear to the judge that in his view even this was too much, since he held himself to be innocent. He therefore filed a nullity appeal. Franzmeier, on the other hand, accepted the verdict.

Engleitner was allowed to return home the same day, since he had already served three months' imprisonment (see next page), longer than the sentence he had just received. The judge, however, ordered him to leave the city of Salzburg immediately.

Convinced of his innocence, Engleitner was in no hurry to obey this order. He went to visit Johann Pichler, a brother in the faith who lived in Salzburg, and accompanied him to a meeting of Jehovah's Witnesses in the evening to gain spiritual strength after his long imprisonment. He spent the night in Pichler's home, and the next morning he leisurely made his way to St. Gilgen to pick up his bicycle, which he had left there following his arrest.

He returned home to the scathing remarks of his parents, who had always told him that his new faith would bring him nothing but trouble. He considered this parental opposition further proof of the fulfillment of Bible prophecy.

Matthew 10:36, 37
A man's foes shall be they of his own household. He that loveth father or mother more than me is not

worthy of me; and he that loveth son or daughter more than me is not worthy of me.

Engleitner was sure that he was on the "right way," and that it would be narrow and stony, just as Jesus had said it would be:

Matthew 7:14
Narrow is the gate, and straitened the way, that leadeth unto life, and few be they that find it.

He continued resolutely on his chosen path; nothing and nobody could make him abandon it. When the case against him was finally dismissed on July 22, 1936, by order of the Austrian president Wilhelm Miklas (see page 69), even his parents saw that their son had been the victim of injustice.

The international convention of Jehovah's Witnesses took place in Lucerne, Switzerland, in the late summer of 1936. The timing could not have been better for Leopold Engleitner. Spiritual strength and encouragement would be needed to withstand the tests awaiting his faith. He only wondered how to finance his trip to the convention. Around the Feast of Corpus Christi in June, the works management of the hydroelectric power station in Weinbach wanted to clear the channel of moss. Since this was a Catholic holiday, it was difficult to find laborers who were willing to do the job. Engleitner was asked to take on the task together with a few local farmhands. He was happy to do so, and the double time he received for working on a holiday meant he had enough money for the journey to Switzerland.

On October 4, 1936, while going door to door in Altmünster, Engleitner spoke to a man who turned out to be a member of the *Heimwehr*, a kind of voluntary civilian guard.

The man locked Engleitner up in a room and went to fetch
the police. However, the man's mother, who had been watching,
unlocked the door after her son left and urged him: "Come
out quickly! Go before he comes back!" Engleitner heaved a
sigh of relief, thanked the woman, and hurried off without
delay.

Unfortunately it was not long before the authorities picked
him up again. The police in Altmünster charged him with
"endangering public safety." His "crime"? He had distributed
leaflets published by the Bible Students. Four days after his
arrest, police from Strobl searched his house and confiscated
more printed material. At Strobl police station, Engleitner gave
a statement to the duty officer, Johann Stassny: "On October
4, 1936, at seven o'clock in the morning, I left Weinbach on
my bicycle and rode to Altmünster. I arrived there alone at
about half past eleven. In Altmünster I distributed some leaflets
before leaving at three o'clock in the afternoon of the same
day to return home. I did not ask for any money for the material
I distributed, but I did accept voluntary donations."[1]

Although President Wilhelm Miklas had ordered the
proceedings against Engleitner be stopped only three months
before, Engleitner now faced another charge. In November
1936 he received the indictment from the public prosecutors
in Wels. Once again he was charged in connection with § 303
of the Penal Law with having committed libel against a legally
recognized church, and an application was filed with the court
in Wels for a trial before a court of lay assessors.[2]

The prospect of another trial did not worry him much.
He soon returned to Altmünster to share his message as before.

---

[1] File number: Z 326/36 Charge filed by the police in Altmünster on
October 19, 1936, at the local court in Gmunden
[2] File number: 1 St 3305/36

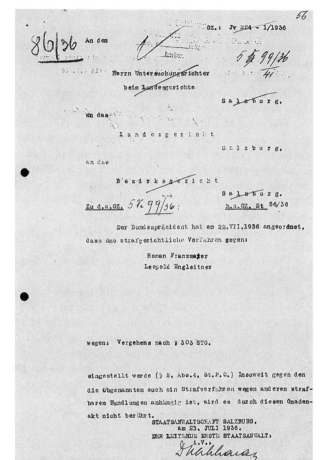

17: Letter from the public prosecutors in Salzburg to Salzburg court, dated July 23, 1936, concerning the dismissal of the case against Roman Franzmeier and Leopold Engleitner by order of Austria's president, Wilhelm Miklas

Once again he was arrested and taken to the local police station. His entire stock of Bible literature was confiscated on the pretext that his activity violated the law. Engleitner told the policeman on duty: "I'll be back for my publications because we have freedom of religion in Austria."

The policeman replied: "You'll never see them again. What you're doing is against the law."

Engleitner bicycled to friends of his in Altmünster and considered what to do next. He decided to go on the offensive, and the very next day he went to the local government office in Gmunden to state his case and lodge a complaint. So early next morning, he stood before the official in charge, Dr. Eduard Pesendorfer, who asked him: "What's so important that you get up at the crack of dawn to come and see me?"

"I wish to make a complaint against the police in Altmünster," Engleitner answered.

"Well now, what have they been up to?" Pesendorfer asked him calmly.

Engleitner told him what happened the day before, adding: "Herr Doktor, you have the statute book lying on your desk in front of you. Please be so kind as to read the Peace Treaty of Saint Germain, Section V, Articles 62 and 63!"

Pesendorfer, surprised to hear Engleitner's specific reference to the law, opened the book and read the two articles out loud. When he had finished, he closed the book and said: "That sounds like freedom of religion, doesn't it?"

"Precisely!" replied Engleitner. "And that's why I'm here, to ask for your support."

"All right, I'll see to it that your material is returned to you," promised Pesendorfer and dismissed him.

The official responded exactly as Engleitner had hoped. At long last a representative of a public authority expressed willingness to speak up on behalf of his right to practice his religion and to do so even during that time of religious intolerance. With a light heart, he cycled home, full of hope that the friendly Dr. Pesendorfer would keep his promise. Two weeks later he received a small parcel through the mail containing some Bible leaflets and an accompanying letter. Engleitner was pleased to receive the parcel, but saw that the publications were not his. Furthermore, the parcel contained only six booklets—the police had confiscated 60 from him. What could be done about that? Should he forget the whole matter and consider it a victory that he had at least received something?

Not satisfied with the outcome, Engleitner worked out a plan to secure the return of the rest of his booklets. Since it was midwinter, he could not use his bicycle, and he had no money for the train fare. So he decided to cross the Alps on foot. Although 15 inches of freshly fallen snow covered the ground, the sun was shining and there was not a cloud in the sky. He trudged through the snow along the banks of the Schwarzensee and crossed two mountain passes, the Moosalm and the Grossalm. He spent the night in Neukirchen with some acquaintances, continuing on his way the following morning. By the time he arrived at Altmünster police station, he had covered some 30 miles. An elderly policeman asked him what he wanted. Reaching into his pocket for the letter from the local government office in Gmunden that had accompanied the returned booklets, Engleitner held it up in such a way that the policeman could read the official stamp. "I've come to collect the printed matter that was confiscated from me and that has been promised to me by the local government office in Gmunden."

The policeman barely glanced at the letter, and merely remarked: "We've already deposited it at the council offices. Go and get it from there."

Engleitner thanked him, relieved that the policeman had not asked to read the letter, since it said that he had already received the literature.

At the council offices in Altmünster, he used the same tactic. Again the man at the desk did not bother to read the letter and said: "We've got your papers in the next room. You can take them with you. We'll be happy to be rid of the rubbish!"

Engleitner had cleared the last hurdle. He stowed the publications into his rucksack and headed home, satisfied that he had, against the odds, been successful.

Despite his extreme caution, Engleitner was arrested again on December 22, 1936, in Bad Ischl. He was at Friedrich Zwerger's optician office. A man named Benedikt Pichler was there too and seemed to take an interest in what Engleitner had to say. Then Pichler revealed his identity as a plainclothes policeman, arrested Engleitner, and confiscated his literature. A charge was filed against Engleitner[1] with the local court in Bad Ischl, passed on to the court in Wels, and added to the legal proceedings already pending.

Engleitner was set free until he was due to appear on trial at Wels court. The local newspaper, the *Salzkammergut-Zeitung*, carried the following highly inaccurate report under the headline "An Agent as a Bible Student":

> The unemployed Ferdinand Engleithner of Bad Ischl, Weinbach 27, was caught red-handed distributing publications of the Bible Students and was arrested by the local police. Pamphlets found in his possession were confiscated, and he was taken into custody at Bad Ischl court, charged with violating the peddling law. [See the original report on the facing page.]

Engleitner, who was in fact still enjoying his freedom, could only shake his head in disbelief on reading this report. Even his parents and acquaintances could only laugh at this sort of journalism.

---

[1] File number: Z 497/36, report by the police in Bad Ischl

> **Ein Agent als Bibelforscher.**
> Der arbeitslose Ferdinand Eng-
> leithner aus Bad Ischl, Wein-
> bach Nr. 27, kolportierte Schriften
> der Bibelforscher und wurde dabei
> von der Gendarmerie betreten.
> Diese beschlagnahmte seine Schrif-
> ten und lieferte ihn wegen Ueber-
> tretung des Kolportagegesetzes
> dem Bezirksgerichte Bad Ischl ein.

*18: "Salzkammergut-Zeitung," Gmunden, issue
dated December 31, 1936, page 7*

The court hearing in Wels on Wednesday, January 20,
1937, was adjourned at the request of the prosecuting counsel.
The judge, Josef Höffinger, told Engleitner that his presence
would not be required and that he could therefore save himself
the long journey.

On Wednesday, March 3, 1937, the adjourned hearing
resumed at Wels court before a court of lay assessors. The public
was not admitted. Determined to defend himself, Engleitner
rode all the way to Wels on his bicycle.

*19: Josef Höffinger, judge
at Wels court, circa 1935*

When judge Josef Höffinger
saw him, he asked in surprise:
"What's this? So you came after
all?"

"Of course I came. You can't
start without me, can you?"
Engleitner replied with a twinkle
in his eye. After the indictment
had been read out, he pleaded not
guilty, adding: "I admit to
distributing the publications in
question, but I never asked for
money. I only accepted voluntary

donations. Our literature explicitly says that our teachings are in no way intended to offend any religious organization or private individual. Our aim is merely to offer instructive criticism of the doctrines of the Christian churches and to point out how these conflict with the Holy Scriptures. Our supreme lawmaker is God. The purpose of the publications I distribute is not to ridicule or denigrate the institutions or practices of churches recognized by the state, but rather to warn their religious leaders not to ignore what's written in the Bible. I know that every citizen must obey the law. But I'm standing here as one of Jehovah's Witnesses, and as such it is primarily God's law that I have to obey. It is impossible to convey the message in more palatable words than those contained in our booklets. I receive nothing for the distribution of these publications. The voluntary donations that people give to me are used to buy more literature.

"I was once convicted of the same offense, but I was pardoned on July 22, 1936."[1]

Engleitner waited tensely for the verdict. The judge, Dr. Höffinger, unintentionally provided some comic relief for the courtroom. After returning with the lay assessors from their deliberations, he attempted to sit down but missed his chair, landing on the floor. Engleitner had great difficulty stifling his laughter. At least the judge was human.

Then the verdict was pronounced. Dr. Höffinger was known to be a relatively lenient judge, who had on occasions bought convicted defendants a snack after the trial. Turning to Engleitner, he said: "We have been very accommodating and have, in consideration of your good reputation and clean record, allowed for extenuating circumstances. You will therefore be sent to prison for one week only."

"All the same," replied Engleitner, "I do not accept this verdict."

"Why not?" asked the judge sharply.

---

[1] File number: 6 Vr 1577/36.18.

"Because I haven't libeled anyone and am not guilty!"
Engleitner filed a nullity appeal and requested that legal aid
be appointed and entrusted with asserting his rights of appeal.

The nullity appeal was rejected on July 2, 1937. So was
the appeal against the court ruling which Dr. Franz Pühringer,
his court-appointed counsel, had filed with the Supreme Court.
The court ruled that the appeals had not been executed
correctly. Although they had been lodged within the required
time, the substance of the appeals had been submitted too
late, and so the ruling of Wels court, the court of first instance,
became final.[1]

For the time being, however, Engleitner did not have to
serve the week's imprisonment he had been sentenced to on
March 3, 1937.[2]

In the summer of 1937, Jehovah's Witnesses held a convention
in Prague, Czechoslovakia. Because money was scarce once
again, Engleitner and five other Witnesses from Bad Ischl and
the surrounding area decided to cover the 220 miles to Prague
by bicycle. After riding two days, they reached their destination
and were able to join with about 3,000 fellow believers in
receiving encouragement and being strengthened for the trials
and tribulations ahead. Reports were already coming in from
Germany that Hitler was ruthlessly persecuting the Witnesses
there. Engleitner and his colleagues shuddered at this news.
Carefully chosen words were addressed particularly to the
Witnesses from Austria, urging them to remain true to the
faith and to trust in God completely, come what may. The
end of the week brought tears of joy, and Engleitner feared
this might be the last large gathering he would be able to attend

---

[1] File number: 4 Os 435/37.2, Supreme Court of Vienna, Department 4,
dated July 2, 1937

[2] Set aside by order of Leoben district court of December 12, 1955, file
number: 10 Ns 1029/55

as a free man. Although he and his friends still had some time left, it was not long before their worst fears were realized.

Once home, Engleitner soon resumed his house-to-house visits with great zeal in Bad Aussee. At noon on September 19, 1937, a young man in Praunfalk in the municipality of Grundlsee answered Engleitner's knock. Engleitner explained the reason for his visit, enthusiastically telling the man about the Bible's message of the Kingdom of God and offering him some pamphlets. Then his eyes fell on a policeman's hat hanging on a peg in the hall. "Oh, no! Not another policeman!" he thought. Sure enough, a few moments later the young man said: "You are carrying out an unlawful activity and are in possession of illegal printed matter. You're under arrest! Come with me to the police station at once!" On their way to the station, Engleitner tried to convince the eager policeman that he was wasting his time, since his activity was permitted by the constitution, as stipulated in the Peace Treaty of Saint Germain. He also showed him the amnesty decree signed by President Wilhelm Miklas, which had been issued to quash his previous year's conviction in Salzburg. He always carried this document with him so that he would be able to vindicate himself if necessary.

Arriving at the police station, Engleitner repeated his arguments, whereupon the officer on duty, who was standing in for his superior who was away on holiday, tried to placate his young colleague. "Jehovah's Witnesses are good people," he said. "I know them well. We can let Herr Engleitner go."

Engleitner was naturally very relieved to hear this, and was already on his way out when he heard the angry retort of the young policeman: "He must stay here! I will not allow you to let him go. Either you keep him under arrest, or I'll report you to the chief."

In the face of this threat, the other police officer was afraid to release Engleitner and began with the official proceedings. Engleitner was questioned, and his publications were confiscated yet again. Since the eager policeman thought the prisoner might try to contact whoever had published the pamphlets and warn him, Engleitner was arrested and put into custody at the local council offices.[1] The young police officer felt quite pleased with himself.

Later that evening, a man in dirty, bloodstained clothes was brought into Engleitner's cell. Engleitner asked what had happened to him. The man answered: "I was poaching with a friend of mine when a young policeman saw my friend and shot him. If I'd run away, I could have escaped, but I stayed with my friend and tried to help him. Unfortunately, he died and I got caught." Engleitner later learned that the policeman who had fired the fatal shot was the same ambitious young man who had insisted on his arrest. People in the area were so incensed by the shooting incident that they sent vast numbers of angry letters to the police, who were forced to transfer their young colleague as soon as possible.

The day after his arrest, Engleitner demanded of the council secretary that his case be brought before a court of law. This request was granted, and he appeared in court in Bad Aussee before the judge Dr. Emil Pregler-Grundeler.

"You have no right to keep me under arrest," said Engleitner to the judge.

"Why not?" replied the latter.

"Read what it says in the Peace Treaty of Saint Germain, Section V, Articles 62 and 63," answered Engleitner handing him the letter signed by the Austrian president.

The judge opened the statute book and examined the letter. Naturally, he could find no reason to keep him under arrest. But instead of letting Engleitner go, he remarked: "Well, we'll just have to find another reason, won't we?" Whereupon he had Engleitner taken to Bad Aussee jail where he stayed in custody awaiting trial until October 7, 1937. In the meantime, the police in St. Wolfgang searched his house in Weinbach for

---

[1] File number: Z 135/37, charge brought by the police in Bad Aussee on September 20, 1937, filed with Bad Aussee district court

The following appears in the *St. Lucia Catholic Magazine* of October, 1933: "The Catholic Church alone has the right to teach Christ's doctrine to the world. She alone has the right to explain the Bible." If that statement were true, then let Protestants take notice that they have no right either to teach or to exist. The claim, however, is entirely false and in keeping with many other false claims that deceive the people.

Falsely and fraudulently the Catholic hierarchy claims that the pope is a successor of the apostle Peter, whereas the Scriptures show there are no successors to the apostles. It has caused the people to believe that their beloved dead are in "purgatory", and the priests of this hierarchy have collected enormous sums of money from the people upon the false and fraudulent claim that they can by their prayers shorten the duration of punishment in "purgatory".

20: Publication "World Recovery," p. 8, Watchtower Bible and Tract Society, Brooklyn, NY, USA 1934, facsimile

publications of the Bible Students. They found none because Engleitner had hidden them carefully. Following the three weeks in custody pending trial, he had to serve the week's imprisonment he had been sentenced to on March 3, 1937, by the court in Wels. He spent an entire month in Bad Aussee jail.

Fortunately, a coincidence made his time in prison less unpleasant than it might have been. He shared the cell with the poacher and a hotel owner who had been involved in a brawl. Both men had their meals sent to them—the poacher by his family and the hotelier from his own hotel. They were kind enough to share the generous portions with Engleitner, who, used to meager fare at home, left prison four weeks later looking better than he had going in. When he arrived home, his parents thought he had been away on holiday!

An indictment arrived, once more charging him in connection with § 303 of the Penal Law. Among the charges the public prosecutors in Leoben brought against him were: "In the publication *World Recovery*, on page 8, the doctrine of the Catholic Church which states that the Pope is the successor of the apostle Peter, and at the same time Christ's representative on earth, is degraded. Similarly, the publication *His Vengeance* contains propaganda of Jehovah's Witnesses and accuses the Christian Church in particular of following selfish and untrue paths."[1]

Engleitner lodged an appeal on December 19, 1937, with the wording:

> Having received and understood the charges brought against me, I hereby lodge an appeal against them on the grounds that the publications distributed on August 19, 1937, in Bad Aussee are intended neither to ridicule nor to degrade. Representatives of religious, political, and financial interests have, as history proves, used religion to suit their own selfish ends on many occasions and have, as a result, not only dishonored God's name but also destroyed the faith people had in God's Word (see The Great War, Abyssinia, Spain). The ministry as an occupation is not attacked by these publications—on the contrary, it is defended. An ordained man, a leader of people, or a custodian of goods or monies who acts in accordance with the Holy Scriptures, is to be respected. But when disloyal, hypocritical, and selfish elements or representatives of one of these professions act wickedly and turn against the commandments of God, then it is not ridicule or degradation to draw attention to that. On the

---

[1] File number: 5 St 5220/37

contrary, by doing so we honor all those who carry out their duties with responsibility before God and man. This is not disparaging religion, but putting God's Word in its rightful place. Every fair and attentive mind realizes immediately that these publications do not speak against the true religion of Jesus Christ but against the perversion of it to diabolical ends, such as warfare, murder, and crime. Whoever abuses God's name and his Word in this manner is disloyal to him. Such deeds have severely shaken the faith of millions of Christians in the Almighty; when they distribute their literature, Jehovah's Witnesses have no intention of deriding Christianity—no, the faithless clergy have done this already. Rather, Jehovah's Witnesses regard it as their foremost duty to defend Christianity by exposing errors, and this cannot be done without pointing out the mistakes made by those who publicly claim to be Christian while at the same time serve the interests of world politics and world finance. The prophet Ezekiel repeatedly stressed how terrible the approaching Day of Judgment will be and therefore how necessary it is to warn mankind. (Ezekiel chapter 33) It is the duty of dedicated and pious Christians to carry these Bible truths to their fellowman.

Anyone who studies the content of the literature objectively must come to the conclusion that no disparagement of Christianity is intended. Therefore, as a true Christian, I consider myself not guilty.

Awaiting your kind acknowledgment

I remain most respectfully

Leopold Engleitner[1]

---

[1] Leopold Engleitner's appeal against the charges brought against him, lodged with the council chamber at the district court in Leoben, December 19, 1937

However, the court of appeal in Graz rejected Engleitner's appeal and upheld the charges against him.[1]

The trial was to be held at Leoben court.[2] This posed quite a problem for Engleitner, since the Pötschen mountain pass he had planned to bicycle through was closed for the winter. Nevertheless, determined to defend himself and prove his innocence, he called at the courthouse in Bad Ischl and asked the staff for assistance. They explained to him that if a warrant for his arrest had been issued, it would have been their responsibility to see that he was present at the trial. But since this was not the case, he would have to finance the journey himself if he wished to attend his trial. Engleitner just did not have the money. On January 19, 1938, he was sentenced *in absentia* to one month for offenses in connection with §303 of the Penal Law.[3]

He never had to serve that sentence, though. On March 8, 1938, the sentence was conditionally remitted by Leoben court on the application of the public prosecutors in Leoben following a pardon issued by the Austrian president on February 16, 1938. Engleitner was placed on probation until December 31, 1941.[4,5]

Was Leopold Engleitner a pioneer and champion of freedom of religion, free speech, and freedom of the press?[6]

---

[1] File number: 4 Bs 1240/37.17, Oberlandesgericht Graz, December 28, 1937

[2] Kreisgericht Leoben

[3] File number: 20 Vr 1932/37.19

[4] File number: 20 Vr 1932/37.23, ruling of Leoben district court, March 8, 1938

[5] Set aside by Leoben district court on December 1, 1955, file number: 10 Ns 1029/55

[6] See Appendix I

HITLER OCCUPIES AUSTRIA

March 12, 1938, was a Saturday. Engleitner was cycling home from a meeting of Jehovah's Witnesses in Bad Ischl at about ten o'clock at night when he heard heavy footfalls marching in step. "That surely can't be Hitler's troops already, can it?" he thought to himself. But his worst fears were realized as he watched a seemingly endless column of German soldiers march past him in the direction of Bad Ischl.

That day German troops advanced across the border and began the occupation of Austria, the Anschluss. Hundreds of thousands of Austrians lined the streets, cheering Hitler and his troops, but for many the annexation of Austria by the German Reich had catastrophic consequences. Within days the Gestapo had arrested 90,000 people (two percent of the adult population).[1] Communists, Social Democrats, Christian Socialists, and Jews were either thrown into prison or deported to concentration camps. Under the wave of repression, the entire leadership of the anti-National Socialist opposition was removed. In the civil service, thousands of so-called "unreliable" officials lost their jobs.

---

[1] *Geheime Staatspolizei*—Secret State Police

Dr. Heinrich Gleissner, governor of the province of Upper Austria, and Dr. Eduard Pesendorfer from the local government offices in Gmunden were among those relieved of their duties and deported to Dachau concentration camp. [1]

The chairman of the senate, Josef Höffinger, who had presided over Engleitner's hearing at Wels court on March 3, 1937, was removed from office on March 12, 1938, and ordered to "leave the court building immediately" (see illustration 21). He was subsequently threatened with prosecution under § 28 of the transitional constitutional code, since his remaining in office "would clearly be detrimental to the reputation of the judicial office."[2] However, he avoided these legal proceedings by applying for early retirement, although he had to accept a 25-percent reduction in his pension.

Engleitner followed the events surrounding Hitler's seizure of power very closely. The Führer instituted a new greeting that established a personality cult, which was tantamount to worship. Engleitner could not understand how millions of people were ready to follow Hitler, blind to his true intentions. For his part, Engleitner prepared for the worst.

The convention in Prague had discussed the brutal treatment meted out to Jehovah's Witnesses in Germany. Engleitner was realistic enough to imagine what might be in store for him. Consequently, he intensified his study of the Bible to deepen his faith and devoted more time to prayer to strengthen his close relationship with God. He felt more determined than ever not to compromise and to adhere to the principles of the Bible, no matter what atrocities Hitler might bring on him.

The first problem he faced was how to handle the impending referendum on Austria's Anschluss to Germany,

---

[1] They were removed under § 4, Section 1, Decree for the Reorganization of the Austrian Permanent Civil Service of May 31, 1938, Reichsgesetzblatt (RGB1.[2]) I p. 607.

[2] File number: Jv 942-4pers/38, letter dated April 23, 1938

Jv 580–4p/38

V e r f ü g u n g :

Über Auftrag der Kreisleitung Wels der
NSDAP. enthebe ich mit sofortiger Wirkung ihres Dienstes
beim Kreisgerichte und Bezirksgerichte Wels :

1.) den OLGR. und Senatsvorsitzenden Josef Höffinger,

2.) den HiRi.Dr. Wilhelm Grösswang,

3.) den JOA. Otto Drnowitz,

4.) den w.A.R. Alois Hirsch,

5.) den JAss. Roman Dickinger,

6.) den Amtsgeh. Franz Holub.

Die enthobenen Richter und Beamten haben
des Kreisgerichtsgebäude sofort zu verlassen.

Über ihr zukünftiges Schicksal wird später
entschieden werden.

Der Präsident des Kreisgerichtes
Wels, am 12. März 1938.

21: Decree of the presiding judge at Wels court, March 12, 1938

Volksabstimmung und Großdeutscher Reichstag

Stimmzettel

Bist Du mit der am 13. März 1938 vollzogenen

Wiedervereinigung Österreichs mit dem Deutschen Reich

einverstanden und stimmst Du für die Liste unseres Führers

Adolf Hitler?

Ja

Nein

22: Original ballot-paper

Referendum and German Reichstag

Ballot Paper

Do you agree with the reunification of Austria with
the German Reich that took place on March 13, 1938,
and do you vote for the programs of our Führer,

Adolf Hitler?

Yes

No

Translation of the ballot-paper

Zur Führerrede in Stuttgart:

„Ich werde vom 10. April ab der reichste Mensch der Welt sein!"

Stuttgart, 2. April. Gestern traf der Führer unter dem Jubel von Zehntausenden in der Hauptstadt des Schwabenlandes ein. Am Abend sprach er in der überfüllten Schwabenhalle. Im Laufe seiner großen Rede erklärte er: „Ich werde vom 10. April ab der reichste Mensch der Welt sein, ich werde das höchste besitzen, was es gibt, — ein ganzes Volk".

Die evangelische Kirche Oesterreichs zur Volksabstimmung

Der Evangelische Oberkirchenrat hat anläßlich der Volksabstimmung am 10. April folgende Erklärung beschlossen, die am Sonntag den 3. d. in allen evangelischen Kirchen verlesen werden wird:

„Für den 10. April ist das deutsche Volk Oesterreichs aufgerufen, um in einer ehrlichen und freien Abstimmung vor aller Welt zu bekunden, daß die Rückkehr ins Reich und damit die politische Neugestaltung unserer Heimat dem tiefsten Verlangen und Wünschen des Volkes entspricht. Mit diesem Herzenswunsch hat sich unsere evangelische Kirche in Oesterreichs stets, ohne Rücksicht auf Gunst oder Mißgunst früherer Machthaber, einig gewußt. Wenn daher der Evangelische Oberkirchenrat sich heute an das evangelische Kirchenvolk wendet, so geschieht dies nicht aus der Sorge heraus, daß einer von uns nicht wüßte, was er an diesem entscheidenden Tag zu tun habe. Die evangelische Kirche in Oesterreich hat schon am 12. März und seither wiederholt ihrer ungeheuchelten Freude über die geschichtliche Wende Ausdruck gegeben. Als Trösterin und Helferin, die unsere Kirche in den letzten Jahren vielen kämpfenden Deutschen in Oesterreich war — weit über den Kreis unserer Glaubensgenossen hinaus —, empfindet sie die ganze große Freude dieser Tage mit und nimmt sie dankbar aus Gottes Händen als sein Geschenk.

Wir stehen zur rettenden Tat des Führers. Das vorbehaltlose „Ja" der Evangelischen Oesterreichs als die dem Führer schuldige Antwort des Volkes ist für uns nicht nur selbstverständliche völkische Pflicht, an die wir niemand zu erinnern brauchen. Dieses „Ja" ist aufrichtiger Dank an den gnädigen Gott für Rettung und Befreiung unserer Heimat.

Evangelischer Oberkirchenrat A. u. H. B.
gez. Dr. Kauer."

Hiezu erklärt der Präsident des Evangelischen Oberkirchenrates:

„Unsere evangelische Kirche ist ihrem Wesen nach die christliche Tat, getragen von aufrichtiger Ueberzeugung, stets maßgebender als bloß lehrhafte Worte. Im Führer und in seiner Bewegung, in den Leistungen des deutschen Volkes erkennen wir solches Christentum, denn der Führer hat dem durch Materialismus zerrissenen deutschen Volk vorgelebt und daher auf die wirksamste Art gelehrt, wie Liebe zum Nächsten durch die Tat verwirklicht wird. Dadurch hat er es aus tiefstem Abgrund emporgeführt zu stolzer Höhe. Auch eine christliche Kirche, die unverrückt auf ihren geistlichen Grundlagen verharrt, wie die des deutschen Volkes Reformatoren wieder aufgedeckt haben, muß dies anerkennen. Wir stehen vorbehaltlos zum Werk des Führers und danken Gott dafür, daß er dem deutschen Volk in schwerster Stunde Rettung brachte."

24: "Salzkammergut-Beobachter", Gmunden, issue dated
April 2, 1938, front page (facsimile)

5

The Austrian Protestant Church on the Referendum

On the occasion of the referendum on the 10th of April, the Protestant Church Assembly has agreed to the following declaration, which will be read out in every Protestant church on Sunday, 3rd inst.

"German nationals in Austria are called upon to declare to the whole world in a fair and open referendum on April 10 that the return to the Reich and the political reorganization of our homeland it entails are in accordance with the greatest wishes of the people. Our Protestant church in Austria has always shared this heartfelt desire. . . . If the Protestant Church Assembly chooses to speak to the Protestant faithful today, it is not because we fear that any one of us may not know what he has to do on this decisive day. The Protestant church expressed its sincere joy at this historical watershed on March 12 and has done so repeatedly since then. . . .

"We fully endorse what the Führer has done to save the nation. The Protestant church's unconditional 'Yes' is the answer that the whole nation owes him and is not only our undeniable nationalist duty, of which we need remind no one; it is also a sincere "Thank you" to merciful God for the salvation and liberation of our homeland."

Protestant Church Assembly

(signed)
Dr. Rauer

Translation of the highlighted text

Salzkammergut Beobachter

Einzelnummer 30 Groschen   **Wochenausgabe**   Einzelnummer 20 Pfennig

Erscheint jeden Donnerstag vormittags / Schriftleitung u. Verwaltung: Gmunden, Adolf-Hitler-Platz 2. Tel. 513.

Nummer 3   Gmunden, 31. März 1938   **1. Jahrgang**

Feierliche Erklärung der österreichischen Bischöfe zur Volksabstimmung in Österreich am 10. April

Wien, 27. März. Die österreichischen Bischöfe haben eine feierliche Erklärung erlassen, in der sie aus innerster Überzeugung und mit freiem Willen anläßlich der großen geschichtlichen Ereignisse in Deutsch-Österreich erklären, daß sie die Leistungen der nationalsozialistischen Bewegung freudig anerkennen und ihr Wirken mit den besten Segenswünschen begleiten. Die Bischöfe bekennen sich ausdrücklich als Deutsche zum Deutschen Reich und fordern auch die Gläubigen dazu auf.

Ein Schreiben an Gauleiter Bürckel

Die feierliche Erklärung der österreichischen Bischöfe wurde dem Beauftragten des Führers für die Volksabstimmung in Österreich, Gauleiter Bürckel, mit folgendem Schreiben überbracht:

Der Erzbischof von Wien.

Wien, 18. März 1938.

Die feierliche Erklärung der österreichischen Bischöfe lege ich hiemit bei. [...]

Heil Hitler!
Th. Kard. Innitzer e. h.

Die feierliche Erklärung hat folgenden Wortlaut:

Feierliche Erklärung!

Aus innerster Überzeugung und mit freiem Willen erklären wir unterzeichneten Bischöfe der österreichischen Kirchenprovinz anläßlich der großen geschichtlichen Geschehnisse in Deutsch-Österreich:

Wir erkennen freudig an, daß die nationalsozialistische Bewegung auf dem Gebiet des völkischen und wirtschaftlichen Aufbaues sowie der Sozialpolitik für das Deutsche Reich und Volk und namentlich für die ärmsten Schichten des Volkes Hervorragendes geleistet hat und leistet. Wir sind auch der Überzeugung, daß durch das Wirken der nationalsozialistischen Bewegung die Gefahr des alles zerstörenden gottlosen Bolschewismus abgewehrt wurde.

Die Bischöfe begleiten dieses Wirken für die Zukunft mit ihren besten Segenswünschen und werden auch die Gläubigen in diesem Sinne ermahnen.

Am Tage der Volksabstimmung ist es für uns Bischöfe selbstverständliche nationale Pflicht, uns als Deutsche zum Deutschen Reich zu bekennen, und wir erwarten auch von allen gläubigen Christen, daß sie wissen, was sie ihrem Volke schuldig sind.

Wien, am 18. März 1938.

Th. Kard. Innitzer   A. Hefter   S. Waitz

Pawlikowski   Johannes Maria Gföllner

Michael Memelauer

23: Salzkammergut-Beobachter," Gmunden, issue dated March 31, 1938, front page (facsimile)

Solemn Declaration of the Austrian Bishops on the Occasion of the Referendum on the 10th of April

The declaration is worded as follows:

Solemn Declaration

With the deepest conviction and of our own free will, we, the undersigned bishops of the Austrian ecclesiastical province, hereby make the following declaration in the light of the great and historical events in German Austria:

It is with pleasure that we acknowledge the marvelous achievements of the National Socialist Movement in the realm of national and economic development and social welfare for the German Reich and people, in particular for the poorest classes. Furthermore, we are also convinced that the threat of utter destruction posed by godless Bolshevism has been averted by the work of the National Socialist Movement.

The bishops bestow their blessings on this work and will also exhort the faithful to support it.

On the occasion of the referendum, we bishops have as Germans the clear duty to the nation to recognize the German Reich, and we therefore expect all Christians to be aware of what they owe to their nation.

Vienna, the 18th of March, 1938.

Th. Cardinal Innitzer   A. Hester   S. Waitz

Pawlikowski   Johannes Maria Gföllner

Michael Memelauer

Translation of the Solemn Declaration

which was held on April 10, 1938. In the days prior to the
referendum, the leading church dignitaries in Austria declared
their support of the Anschluss in most of the country's
newspapers and left their flocks in no doubt as to how they
expected them to vote. The issues of the *Salzkammergut-
Beobachter* of March 31 and April 2 ,1938 (see preceding
pages), clearly proclaimed the church's views. Engleitner had
absolutely no doubt that he would not vote for Hitler; he
had already decided to follow a different "Führer,"[1] the King
in Heaven, Jesus Christ. How was he going to deal with this
difficult situation? But a few days before the referendum, he
received an unexpected solution to his problem. A policeman
from St. Wolfgang came and told him: "Because of your
previous convictions, you have lost the right to vote."
Engleitner heaved a sigh of relief. His unjustified prison
sentences had turned out to have a positive side after all.

The result of the referendum, 99.6 percent in favor of the
Anschluss, led to an immediate ban on the activities of Jehovah's
Witnesses. From that point on, they had to be even more careful
than before, changing their meeting places as often as possible.
In addition, it became increasingly difficult to obtain biblical
material. Although the Swiss branch in Bern managed to smuggle
some literature into Austria, it was not enough to meet demand.
It became necessary to print material secretly in Vienna. It was
virtually impossible to send such publications by mail.

The head of their Vienna branch, August Kraft, arranged
meeting places with fellow Witnesses where the material could
be secretly handed over at an appointed time. In Wels, for
instance, the apartment belonging to Egmund and Anna
Stadtegger served as one such "hand-over point." Whenever
he went there, Engleitner bicycled under the cover of night. It
would have been far too dangerous to take the train. Everything
went well for a time, until one day Anna Stadtegger had to

---

[1] German for leader.

Decree of the Federal Government regarding the Referendum to be held on April 10, 1938, RGBl. No. 2/1938

Article 1. Right to vote.

§ 2 Section 1

Excluded from the right to vote are Jews and all those who count as Jews.

Section 2

A Jew is an individual who is descended from at least three grandparents who were, racially, full Jews. Full-blooded Jewish grandparents are those who belonged to the Jewish religious community.

Section 3

A Jew is an individual of mixed Jewish blood who is descended from two grandparents who, racially, were full Jews if

he was a member of the Jewish religious community on September 16, 1935, or joined the community later;

on September 16, 1935, he was married to a person who was a Jew, or was subsequently married to a Jew.

Section 4

Excluded from the exercise of the right to vote is

any person who is completely or partially legally incapacitated;

any person whose right to exercise paternal authority over his children has been revoked by a court ruling, for as long as the children are in the care of legal guardians, but at least for three years following the court ruling;

any person who has been finally convicted of any offense during the last five years;

any person who is currently serving a prison term, is on remand, or is in the workhouse.

send him and his companion Franz Rothauer away empty-handed because the Gestapo were on their trail.

Some days after this unsuccessful trip, Engleitner received a postcard from August Kraft asking him to go to Steyrling, a small, out-of-the-way railway station on the Pyhrn line, to pick up several issues of *The Watchtower*. Risky as it may seem to put such a message on a postcard that anyone could read, it was in fact safer than a letter in a sealed envelope, which would certainly have been opened and read.

Early in the morning of the appointed day, Engleitner rode off to Steyrling, more than 50 miles east of Weinbach, and waited at the little station for the train from Vienna. When it pulled in, some passengers disembarked, others got on. Then August Kraft suddenly opened the window of his compartment and tossed out a roll of *Watchtowers*. Quick as a flash, Engleitner pounced on the roll, jumped on his bicycle, and rode off as fast as he could go. When he reached a spot that he judged to be safe from prying eyes, he opened the roll and began distributing the magazines to the addresses written on them. This meant his having to go as far as Oberwang, nearly 30 miles northwest of his home in Weinbach. This underground activity occupied most of his Sundays during the years 1938 and 1939.

Shortly after Hitler's troops occupied Austria, Engleitner received a letter from the labor exchange in Bad Ischl requiring him to appear there in person without delay. By this time he had been disqualified from unemployment benefits for five years and was therefore surprised at this summons. He set off immediately and was received at the labor exchange in Bad Ischl by the National Socialist Karl Beichl.

Beichl asked him why he had been disqualified from unemployment benefits. After listening to Engleitner's explanation of the authorities' unlawful measures, he said sympathetically: "Herr Engleitner, we are well aware of the fact that you have been treated very unjustly. But we, the National Socialists, will do all we can to make amends."

He then sent him to Franz Zimmermann, a policeman from St. Wolfgang who was responsible for assigning jobs to all those seeking work. As soon as he saw Engleitner, he exclaimed in front of all the others who had come for a job: "We must give Engleitner a job right away! He suffered under the Schuschnigg government more than anyone else and is the only one who was disqualified from unemployment benefits!"

Never in his wildest dreams would Engleitner have dared hope for such a development. He had feared that the National Socialists would subject him to even worse treatment than the previous government. But it was clear to Engleitner that the Nazi party intended to use such measures to curry favor with the Austrian population, similar to their deferment of payment of farmers' debts.

From May to August 1938, the St. Wolfgang council hired Engleitner to widen the Seestrasse, the road that ran along the shores of the lake, and for sewer construction. Although he worked side by side with zealous Nazis, they respected his religious attitude and his refusal to perform the Hitler salute.[1] He overheard his workmates say that high-ranking Nazis always carried a capsule of poison with them so that they could take their own lives should their party's policies fail.[2] From this Engleitner concluded that on the one hand the Nazis were far from convinced of their own success but that on the other hand they were determined to pursue their political ends at all costs. It became clear to him that he would face fierce resistance, since the Nazis' attitude was "all or nothing."

---

[1] *Heil Hitler!* (Salvation through Hitler). Jehovah's Witnesses refused to perform this salute because, according to Acts 4:12, salvation is only possible through Jesus Christ, not through man. *"In none other is there salvation: for neither is there any other name under heaven, that is given among men, wherein we must be saved."*

[2] Guido Knopp, *Hitler's Helfer* (Munich, 1998), p. 204

After this job Engleitner was taken on by the firm Siemens & Schuckertwerke until December 1938. This company laid electric power cables from Kaprun im Pinzgau across the area around the Schwarzensee up to Lenzing in Upper Austria. While engaged in this work, Engleitner and his workmates lived in an alpine hut on the Ackeralm and helped lay the paths that were needed to transport parts of iron pylons. Later on he worked on erecting barriers to protect the pylons from avalanches. This was dangerous work, since he had to climb up and down the rock face secured only by a rope.

When this job came to an end, the construction firm Mayreder, Keil, List & Co., which was based in Graz, hired Engleitner. This company needed about 100 people for excavation work in preparation for the laying of telephone lines from Bad Aussee to Salzburg. This job proved very convenient for Engleitner because the pay was very good[1] and because he could reach his place of work from home. That meant that he could make full use of his weekends to carry out his underground work, secretly delivering magazines.

On April 4, 1939, Engleitner's life took a dramatic turn for the worse. His boss had given him the day off, and he made use of the opportunity to prepare for a celebration which was to take place that evening.

The time had come for the National Socialist regime to show its true colors.

---

[1] The salary was 0.65 Reichsmarks per hour, 27 Reichsmarks per week

PERSECUTED BY THE NAZIS

Arrest

At eight o'clock in the evening, Tuesday, April 4, 1939, five Witnesses—Leopold Engleitner, Rosalia Hahn, Pauline Schlägl, Franz Rothauer, and his wife, Emilie—gathered at the Rothauers' house at Kreutern 58, Bad Ischl, to commemorate the Last Supper. They did this every year after sundown on Nisan 14, according to the Jewish calendar. On this evening, Leopold Engleitner had prepared a short talk highlighting the significance of Jesus' death. Because the National Socialists had stepped up their persecution of Jehovah's Witnesses, the atmosphere among the group was understandably tense. Some thought it would be wise to return home and commemorate Jesus' sacrifice alone. Engleitner thought otherwise, saying: "If the Gestapo are lying in wait for us, leaving now would mean running straight into their

25: The house of the Rothauer family, Kreutern 58, 1945

arms. Wouldn't it be better just to carry on?" Then he started his discourse.

Moments later he was interrupted by a loud knock at the window. "That must be the Gestapo!" they all thought, and started trembling with fright. Engleitner, trying to remain calm, volunteered to see who it was, since he had some experience dealing with the authorities—in fact, more than he would have liked. Opening the door, he said amiably: "Good evening, gentlemen! To whom do I have the pleasure of speaking?"

"To the Gestapo!" answered one of the five men harshly, opening his jacket to show his insignia. Two of the other four were SS[1] men, one was a member of the SA,[2] and one was another Gestapo man.

"What brings the Gestapo here?" Engleitner asked in feigned surprise.

"We'll show you!" one of the men bellowed. Pushing Engleitner aside, they forced their way into the house.

How did the Secret Police know about this meeting? It had long been rumored that Jehovah's Witnesses met at Franz Rothauer's house, and a few days previously the Rothauers' five-year-old son, Friedrich, had been asked by the daughter of a neighbor whether Bible meetings were held at his house. The boy, not knowing any better, gave her all the details, which the girl immediately reported to her father, a Nazi.

The intruders started turning everything upside down in the hope of finding some of the prohibited *Watchtower* magazines. Failing to find any, they grew angry and shouted: "Where have you hidden *The Watchtowers*?"

Engleitner placated them by saying: "We haven't got any! You've banned them! We wish we still had some." The Nazis were persuaded that it was pointless to search any further. *The Watchtowers* remained safely hidden.

---

[1] *SS – Schutzstaffel*, the Elite Guard that originally served as Hitler's personal body guard.

[2] *SA – Sturmabteilung*, Storm Troopers

One of the SS men was Robert Krainz from Bad Ischl. He and Engleitner knew each other quite well, since Krainz's mother had some contact with the Witnesses. Krainz asked Engleitner what time he had arrived at the Rothauers' house.

"At six o'clock this evening," was the reply.

"That's a lie!" shouted Krainz. "I saw you arrive before that!"

"Don't you have anything better to do than to spy on me?" asked Engleitner. "If you already knew the answer, why did you ask?"

Surprised by Engleitner's tone, the SS man nervously asked: "You won't hold it against me, will you?" Engleitner saw that the man was not so sure that the Hitler regime would last and was worried how he would be viewed if a different government came to power. Engleitner reassured the SS man that he would bear no grudges.

One of the men asked why the five Witnesses had come together that evening. Engleitner replied: "We are commemorating the death of Christ, who died over 1,900 years ago to deliver us from our sins. We are reading the account of it in the Bible. Is there something wrong with what we're doing?"

The five men, surprised by this direct answer, responded: "No, no. The Bible is not prohibited." The Nazis debated among themselves what to do next, then placed a document in front of the group. It was a declaration that the undersigned were members of a splinter group that was separate from Jehovah's Witnesses and were willing to submit to Hitler's orders and support him. "If you sign this paper," they were told, "you can go home. If not, you're under arrest, and then you know what'll happen to you!"

Leopold Engleitner knew that signing that declaration was tantamount to renouncing his faith and giving up his neutral position. He answered: "I can't agree to that, and I will not sign this document under any circumstances. As to the others, you must ask them yourselves."

Everyone refused to compromise and resisted this attempt to force them to accept Hitler's ideologies. As a result, Leopold Engleitner, Franz Rothauer, Rosalia Hahn, and Pauline Schlägl were arrested. Only Emilie Rothauer was allowed to stay, since she had a baby to look after. She would have been taken into custody too had it not been for one of the Gestapo men, who refused to comply with the demand of the SA man Peter Hödlmoser to arrest Emilie Rothauer and take away custody of her children.

As they were led away, they wondered: "Will we ever be free again?" Only one of the four would see his homeland again.

At Bad Ischl police station, the particulars of the four were taken down and the reason for their arrest officially documented. In the process one young policeman remarked: "It's not our fault you've been arrested!"

Hearing this, one of the Gestapo men said sharply: "Do not apologize to these criminals! They're enemies of the state and are getting no more than they deserve."

Engleitner could not help but wonder at that remark and thought to himself: "So we're enemies of the state now, are we? Funny that you're an enemy of the state if you commemorate the death of Jesus, read the Bible, and refuse to point a weapon at your fellowman. Either there's something wrong with this state or I'm just not intelligent enough to understand it." But he did not voice his thoughts; he knew perfectly well that it would not change anything if he did. The official reason for their arrest? Holding a Bible discourse and being followers of the Bible Students, activities deemed hostile to the state.

At half past ten that evening, the four detainees were taken to the courthouse in Bad Ischl,[1] where they were held in custody

---

[1] Amtsgericht Bad Ischl. During the Nazi era, courts of first instance in Austria (otherwise known as *Bezirksgerichte*, "district courts") were known as *Amtsgerichte*.

as political prisoners (see following page). Their freedom was now a thing of the past. This most basic of civil rights was to be subjected to prolonged and brutal suppression.

At noon the next day, a group of men from the Gestapo in Linz took them in two cars to the Gestapo headquarters in that town at Langgasse 13. Under normal circumstances Engleitner would have enjoyed the journey a lot more, since it was the first time in his life that he had traveled any distance by car. Franz Rothauer was put in the front seat, while Engleitner sat in the back next to one of the Gestapo men. The two prisoners asked the officers whether a universal kingdom under which there was no war, no crime, no misfortune, and even no death would appeal to them. "Of course that would be nice," they replied, "but it's only a utopian dream, nothing but Jewish propaganda."

Engleitner and Rothauer replied: "Is it reasonable to think God is incapable of fulfilling what he promises in the Bible but to believe that the Führer, a mere human being, will be able to fulfill his promises?" The Nazis said nothing in reply.

Interrogation by the Gestapo in Linz

On their arrival in Linz, they were taken into a large room with other Witnesses who had been arrested the previous night in raids throughout Upper Austria. Here Engleitner saw Alois

Moser again, the head of the post office in Braunau whom he had met for the first time at the convention in Basel, and Franz Wimmer from Manning. During the coming years of hardship and suffering, their paths would cross several more times.

As Engleitner waited in this large room, a Gestapo man

27: Franz Wimmer, 1930

GENDARMERIE STATION Bad Ischl
Bezirk Gmunden, Oberösterreich

E.Nr.923.

Hahn Rosalia,Schlägl Pauline,
Engleitner Leopold u.Rothauer Franz,
Festnehmung wegen staatsfeindlicher
Betätigung.

                          An das

                  A m t s g e r i c h t

                          in

Bad Jschl,am 5.April 1939.   Bad Jschl.

                     Nationale:
        Rosalia Hahn,am 1.11.1901 in Flitsch,Italien geboren,
Wien zuständig,Optikersgattin,Bad Jschl,Grazerstraße 52
wohnhaft.
        Pauline Schlägl,am 3.1.1895 in Wien geboren,nach Bad-
Jschl zuständig,verheiratet,Bad Jschl,Siedlungsgasse 15
wohnhaft.
        Leopold Engleitner,am 24.7.1905 in Strobl geboren,Bad-
Jschl zuständig,ledig,Hilfsarbeiter,Weinbach Nr.27,Gemeinde
St.Wolfgang wohnhaft.
        Franz Rothauer,am 14.7.1906 in Bad Jschl geboren und
zuständig,verheiratet,Forstarbeiter,Bad Jschl,Kreutern Nr.55
wohnhaft.

                     Tatbestand:
        Die Obgenannten sind Anhänger der Bibelforscher
und haben am 4.April 1939 in den Abendstunden in der Wohnung
des Franz Rothauer einen Bibelvortrag abgehalten.Sie wurden
hiebei von Beamten der Geheimen Staatspolizei betreten und
festgenommen.Die Einlieferung erfolgte am 4.April 1939 um
22 Uhr 30 Minuten in das Amtsgericht Bad Jschl.

        Die Festgenommenen befinden sich vorderhand in
politischer Verwahrungshaft und werden voraussichtlich am
5.April 1939 von der Geheimen Staatspolizei,Staatspolizei-
stelle Linz,nach Linz abtransportiert.

                              Der Gend.Sationsführer:
                                    I.V.

26: Statement of the particulars of the four detainees and the facts of
the case, April 5, 1939, filed by Bad Ischl police station at Bad Ischl
court

approached him and accused him of having double standards: Engleitner was perfectly happy to accept work that the Nazis found for him but refused to support Hitler. Engleitner answered: "I'm grateful for all that governmental institutions do for citizens. In fact, I don't smoke or drink and am therefore not a burden on the national health service."

"Well, that's very commendable," said the man, "but you must also defend the Fatherland!"

"There's no fatherland for me to defend," Engleitner replied, "because all men are brothers. I take God as my guide, and he knows no borders. If *you* want to make war, I'm not going to stop you, but I won't join in!"

That ended the conversation. Engleitner was then fingerprinted and photographed.

It was on the basis of these photographs that his mother Juliana would later have to identify her son. Engleitner then had to wait outside an interrogation room. Alois Moser had been taken into the room immediately before him. Engleitner heard a loud noise, as if someone had been struck. On being taken into the room, he saw Moser pick up his glasses and

28: Leopold Engleitner, April 5, 1939, photos by the Gestapo in Linz

hurriedly leave; he realized that he had not been mistaken and braced himself for what was to come.

Because he came from the area around Strobl, the two interrogators asked him if there was still enough snow on the Postalm to go skiing. "More than enough!" replied Engleitner pleasantly. This answer seemed to clear the air somewhat. The interrogators' superior happened to look in, and they got permission for time off for the next day. One of the interrogators stopped work immediately; the other, detective Rudolf Stangl, took down Engleitner's information.

When it came to the question of what to put down as his religion, however, there was a difference of opinion. Engleitner wanted his religion listed as "Jehovah's Witnesses," but Stangl said: "I can't write that! Jehovah's Witnesses aren't recognized in this country. I'll put non-denominational or independent liberal Christian."

Engleitner would not accept that. "I insist that you write 'Jehovah's Witnesses,'" he declared. "That's why I'm here, after all. If you must arrest me because of my religion, it should at least be listed correctly."

"No," said Stangl. "It's just not possible. Officially, that religion doesn't exist!"

Engleitner replied: "Well, in that case, I should be able to go home. The religion for which I was arrested doesn't exist."

Stangl now had no choice but to comply with Engleitner's request. Then the interrogation began. Engleitner explained his position, stating:

"I am one of Jehovah's Witnesses. I regularly attended their meetings and conventions. I distributed literature I received from Switzerland to people in order to attract new members. After the National Socialists came to power, my visits to Rothauer's house became sporadic. At these meetings we discussed the Bible. It is true that I have spoken to my workmates about the Bible since the annexation, in order to win them over to the truth. Whenever I talk to someone about the current situation, I naturally refer to the Bible, since it is my duty to do so.

"I have never been a member of any unions or political organizations, nor have I ever been actively involved in politics of any kind. As far as my attitude toward the state, I can only say that I abide by all laws that do not conflict with the teachings of the Bible. I do not give the Hitler salute, and I have not joined the DAF.[1]

"I have told the truth and can give no further information."[2]

Rudolf Stangl placed a piece of paper on the table and told Engleitner to sign it. Engleitner replied politely: "I have to read it before I sign it. I can't possibly sign something I haven't read beforehand." Stangl started reading the document out loud, but Engleitner interrupted him: "Excuse me, please! It's very difficult for me to concentrate. I can't follow the text when you read it out to me. May I read it myself, please?"

Stangl agreed, and Engleitner saw that it was in fact an indictment. He was accused of pursuing underground activities and distributing publications. But the indictment also contained accusations against other Witnesses. Engleitner asked for a pen and crossed out several sentences, especially those concerning his fellow believers. By the time he had finished, there was not much left. He then signed the document and handed it back to Stangl, who remarked: "You didn't leave much, did you?"

Engleitner replied: "Well, I can't confirm something that I haven't done, can I?"

By this time it was already eight o'clock in the evening, and Stangl, visibly in a hurry, left it at that.

---

[1] *Deutsche Arbeitsfront* - German Labor Front
[2] Translation of an extract from the original statement as recorded by the Gestapo in Linz, April 5, 1939

He told Engleitner that he had to leave because his girlfriend was waiting for him outside. "Could you walk several steps in front of me to the police station so that I can follow you with my girlfriend?" asked Stangl.

"No, I'm afraid I don't know the way to the station," answered Engleitner.

"But how can I take you there?" said the policeman impatiently.

"If I may make a suggestion," said Engleitner, "you go to the police station with your girlfriend, and I'll follow at some distance behind. That way, she won't notice that you're taking me there. Don't worry, I won't run away."

Stangl had not expected that. "How do I know I can trust you? Then again, what else can I do?"

They set out for the police station in Mozartstrasse. Rudolf Stangl greeted his girlfriend and went on ahead. Engleitner followed behind them, chuckling to himself. They had to go down Landstrasse, the provincial capital's main shopping street, which was still very busy. Stangl, appearing to be extremely nervous, kept glancing behind. Engleitner gave him an encouraging smile and a nod to show that he had no intention of running away. It would have been easy for him to disappear into the crowd, though, especially since it was dark. As they approached the police headquarters, Stangl pointed to the entrance, indicating to Engleitner that he was to go in there, and then continued his walk with his girlfriend, who had evidently noticed nothing unusual.

Engleitner obeyed this wordless command and reported to the doorman. He was then led to the jail, where all his belongings were taken from him. After changing out of his civilian clothes into the uniform of a prisoner, he was registered as number 149 and locked up along with his brothers in the faith.

The inmates chose Engleitner to act as a "mailman," carrying secret messages to and from his fellow Witnesses and from other prisoners to their wives, who were interned on the floor above.

His cell was directly next to the gate that closed off the section. Every morning the prison guards unlocked the cells and made the prisoners line up in front of them. Engleitner was the first one to leave his cell and stood longest in the corridor, next to the gate. Pauline Schlägl had been given the task of sweeping the stairs every day. Whenever the guards went out of sight into a cell, the prisoners lined up along the corridor with their hands behind their backs were able to pass messages and letters for their wives to the next in line. When Engleitner had all the messages, he would quickly step across to the other side of the corridor, behind an open washroom door that was deliberately left at an angle that would hide him. He would then stand against the bars, back to back with Pauline Schlägl, to pass on the messages. Pauline would immediately conceal the letters in her blouse or her trouser pocket.

The men would use prearranged signals to indicate the precise moment for passing on letters undetected. In this way the imprisoned men and women were still able to communicate and encourage one another.

The guards had no idea what was going on. One day Engleitner was seen by some of his sisters in the faith as he was being escorted by a guard. As soon as the ladies saw him, they waved enthusiastically. The guard had no idea that they were thanking him for his services as a "mailman" and said: "That's peculiar. These women have strange taste if they find an ugly creature like you attractive." Engleitner ignored the derogatory remark, happy that the guard knew nothing of the secret correspondence.

Some time later, Franz Wimmer, assigned to clean the windows of an office, saw Engleitner's indictment lying on a desk. One point in particular caught his eye. As soon as he

could, he told his friend about it. "You are accused of being
work-shy!" he informed him.

Engleitner was surprised that they could evidently find
so little against him that they had to resort to such blatant
untruth on his record. He asked a guard to find out from the
official responsible what grounds there were for this accusation.
The answer was that on April 4, 1939, the day of his arrest,
Gestapo men observed that he had spent the whole day at
home instead of going to work. Engleitner insisted that this
accusation be removed from the indictment, explaining that
his boss had given him that day off. After the official checked
the information, the accusation was removed.

From April 20, 1939, onward, most of the male Witnesses,
including Alois Moser and Franz Rothauer,[1] were deported to
Dachau concentration camp. The female Witnesses were sent
to Ravensbrück[2] concentration camp.

The Trial

On May 20, 1939, the Gestapo filed a charge against Engleitner
with the public prosecutor at the court in Linz,[3] accusing him
of illegal activities for the sect of the IBV[4]:

"Taking into account that Engleitner freely admits his
fanatical adherence to this heresy, that this sect was banned
because of its seditious attitude, and that it is feared that he
will misuse his liberty to commit further criminal acts, a writ
for a warrant for his arrest seems to be essential." (see following
page)

---

[1] Franz Rothauer arrived at Dachau concentration camp on May 27, 1939
[2] Rosalia Hahn and Pauline Schlägl arrived at Ravensbrück concentration
camp on June 2, 1939
[3] Landgericht Linz: During the Nazi era, the Austrian courts of first instance
and of appeal (*Landesgerichte*) were known as *Landgerichte*
[4] *Internationale Bibelforschervereinigung*: International Bible Students
Association

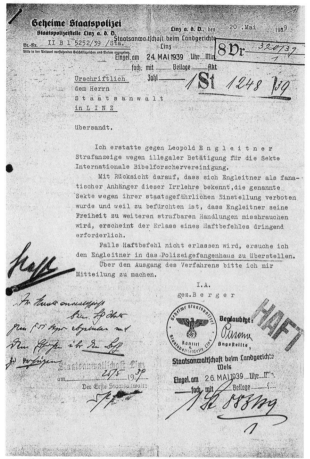

30: *Charge brought against Leopold Engleitner on May 20, 1939, by the Gestapo in Linz, filed with the public prosecutor's office in Linz*

With this report the Gestapo instigated legal proceedings against Engleitner, accusing him of being the ringleader of the small group that had assembled on April 4, 1939, in Bad Ischl, in an attempt to give the affair a veneer of validity.

On May 23, 1939, at a quarter past four in the afternoon, Engleitner was taken to the prison in the courthouse in Linz, where he underwent a thorough physical examination. The arch of his forehead, the shape of his nose, the condition of his teeth, and the color of his mustache were examined and recorded. His four handkerchiefs, one belt, 13 Reichsmarks and 36 pfennigs cash were taken from him. He was then registered as prisoner number 376 and locked in cell number 59 (see below). Franz Wimmer, Wolfgang Mattischek from Attnang-Puchheim, and Georg Pointner from Braunau were interned in the same prison.

At eleven o'clock on the morning of May 24, 1939, the accused were brought before the court in Linz for the first hearing. Also present was a member of the German Nazi monitoring body from Berlin, whose task it was to keep an eye on the Austrian court officials, police, and Gestapo. Observing Engleitner and Wimmer, the official decided that Wimmer's posture was too casual. "Pull yourself together, and stand up straight!" he shouted. At the sound of his distinctive Berlin dialect, the two defendants grinned at each other.

29: Prison register of Linz court, dated May 23, 1939

Engleitner stood before the judge, Dr. Rudolf Löbel and stated:

"I was put in prison on suspicion of being a member of the prohibited sect, the Bible Students. I plead not guilty. I accept that I have to stay in prison for the time being."[1]

Since he had led the group in their commemoration of Christ's death, Engleitner was regarded as a ringleader, as were Wimmer, Mattischek, and Pointner, who had led their respective groups. He hoped to be able to defend himself with the same arguments he had used following his arrest at the beginning of April: "The Bible is not a prohibited book, and commemorating Christ's death can hardly be called a criminal act. So I don't know what you can possibly hold against me!"

The judge, completely ignoring Engleitner's comments, urged him to give up his faith. He handed Engleitner a piece of paper, saying: "Here is a list of twenty-two religions recognized by Hitler and that have deferred to him. The choice is large. If you must be religious, all you have to do is choose one of these and you can go home."

Signing the paper would have sent him down a much easier road, but he was unwilling to compromise. Without a second's hesitation, he said firmly: "I choose none of them."

"Why not?" Dr. Löbel wanted to know.

"Because they don't meet the requirements of the Bible," Engleitner replied. "And I'd like to find happiness my way."

The judge, realizing he could not change the prisoner's mind, remarked: "Well, if you're prepared to go to prison for your faith, so be it!"

"Still," added Engleitner, "I have a clean conscience and have stayed faithful to my convictions."

Engleitner's fellow believers also refused to abandon their faith, and all four remained imprisoned in the courthouse in Linz.

---

[1] Translation of the original transcript of the hearing recorded on May 24, 1939, at the court in Linz

On May 25, 1939, the public prosecutor's office in Linz sent
Engleitner's file to Wels court, under whose jurisdiction the
case fell.

On May 27, 1939, the public prosecutor's office in Wels
opened proceedings against Engleitner. An application was filed
with section 8 of the local court for the institution of
preliminary investigations regarding a violation of § 304 of
the Penal Law (StG) of 1852 with a view to taking him into
custody pending trial under § 175 nos. 2-4, and § 180 (StPO).
Legal proceedings and further investigations were also
instigated with regard to all the others who had taken part in
the meetings at Franz Rothauer's house.[1]

§ 304, Penal Law 1852, as amended 1919
Supporting a religious sect which has been declared
unlawful by the state:
Further, it is a criminal act punishable with a prison
sentence of one month to three months to organize
meetings, hold or publish discourses, proselytize, or
undertake any other activity with a view to establishing
or propagating a religious society (sect), the recognition
of which has been declared unlawful by the state
authorities.

On May 30, 1939, Wels court instructed the court in
Linz to question Leopold Engleitner, to inform him of the
court's decision to initiate preliminary investigations against
him, and to take him into custody pending trial. The court in
Wels then contacted the St. Wolfgang local council, asking for
the accused's character reference. The reply from St. Wolfgang
stated: "Leopold Engleitner has a good reputation, and we

[1] File number: 1 St 883/39, application and order of the Department of
Public Prosecutions in Wels, dated May 27, 1939

know of no complaints against him."¹ The office of criminal
records in Vienna also had "no record of any previous
convictions."² They clearly did not regard Engleitner as a
dangerous citizen, but despite this he was still regarded as a
threat to state security.

On June 2, 1939, the judge, Dr. Egon Orosel, informed
Engleitner of the decision of the prosecutor's office at Wels
court on May 27, 1939, whereupon Engleitner stated: "I hereby
take note of the order to institute preliminary investigations
against me on the grounds that I am suspected of having
committed a criminal act in connection with § 304 of the
Penal Law (StG), and the order to remand me in custody
pending trial because of the risk of escape, collusion, and
recidivism under § 175 nos. 2-4 and § 180 (StPO), and I
abstain from lodging any complaint. I plead not guilty.

"I am not able to swear an oath on military service, nor
can I carry any weapons, since this conflicts with my faith, to
which I unconditionally adhere. I recognize the Führer and
this government, and I submit to the authorities, as long as
their orders do not contradict Bible principles."³

Following this uncompromising statement, Engleitner was
led back to his cell and did not have to undergo further
questioning until the beginning of September 1939. But
unknown to him, further preliminary investigations were
pending. In June, for instance, investigations had been started
into the activities of all those who had been at that
fateful meeting of April 4, 1939. They were suspected of having
committed an offense under § 304 of the Penal Law (StG).
This occurred even though, with the exception of Emilie
Rothauer, they were already interned in concentration camps.

¹ Character reference, dated June 1, 1939, sent from St. Wolfgang council to
Wels court
² Information supplied by the office of criminal records in Vienna to Wels
court, June 1, 1939
³ Translation of an extract from the original transcript recorded on June 2,
1939, at Linz court

On September 13, 1939, the examining magistrate at Wels court requested the transfer of the prisoner Leopold Engleitner from Linz to the Wels court cells.[1]

At that point Engleitner had already spent more than three and a half months in prison awaiting trial, whereas the maximum penalty for his offense would only have been three months. This was further evidence of the arbitrariness of the authorities.

On September 16, 1939, two prison guards entered Engleitner's cell carrying his civilian clothes and barked: "Put these on immediately! You're being taken to court in Wels. You're really in for it now. They're cracking down on conscientious objectors." In an attempt to intimidate him, they then told him about Hitler's new decree.

The *Kriegssonderstrafrechtsverordnung*[2] (KSSVO) had come into force on August 26, 1939. This decree on the special criminal code for wartime and military operations introduced the offense of *"Wehrkraftzersetzung"* (undermining the military). Any attempt to avoid military service was now punishable by death.[3]

Fearing the worst, Engleitner was taken by taxi to the courthouse in Wels, where he was handed over to the prison administration. The atmosphere in the interrogation room made it clear to him what sort of treatment conscientious objectors would now have to face. A crowd of prison guards and policemen soon surrounded him, bombarding him from all sides with questions about his objection to military service. Engleitner explained that Jehovah's Witnesses are completely neutral and do not interfere in any political or national affairs. He added that such an insignificant man as he could never

---

[1] File number: Hs 548/39, official entry of Linz court of September 13, 1939
[2] dRGBl. 1939 I page 1455
[3] Under this decree, Josef Wegscheider and Johann Pichler, with whom Engleitner had stayed on March 30, 1936 (see p. 44), were shot at the military range in Glanegg, near Salzburg.

constitute a danger to such a large country, and that this was not his intention anyway. Besides, all he wanted to do was obey the Biblical commandment "Thou shalt not kill" and live in peace with all men. These arguments mollified the officials surrounding him to such an extent that some were even moved to comment: "Actually, he's right, isn't he?"

Despite this, the examining magistrate, Dr. Edgar Tintara, before whom Engleitner appeared on September 19, 1939, continually tried to persuade him to join up. "Engleitner, Engleitner," he intoned, sounding very serious. "I'm warning you for the last time! If you continue to object to military service, then you already have both feet in the grave. Change your ways!"

But Engleitner just said: "If I've already got both feet in the grave just standing here, what on earth will it be like on the front lines? Or do they shoot with candy out there?"

It was clear that the judge had understood what he was getting at, and he looked at the defendant very sternly. "It's nothing to joke about, Engleitner!" But when he realized that he had made no impression, his face slowly changed, even turning to a gentle smile. Tintara adopted a new tactic and tried to appeal to his feelings, reading him a letter from his mother which contained the entreaty: "Dear Poidl, give up this silly religion, do what Hitler wants you to do and go to war."

Engleitner knew that his mother meant well, but he had already made his mind up. He wanted to stay neutral at all costs, obeying the Christian law of brotherly love and adhering to the Biblical principle of never harming his fellowman. He felt more accountable to God than to his mother, and said: "Sir, my mother is an old woman, and traditions and customs govern her life. I myself choose to be guided by the Bible, a document which has remained valid for thousands of years, and not by an aging woman who fears her fellowman."

When the judge found that nothing would change Engleitner, he remarked: "My word, you're a tough nut to crack."

Engleitner then made a statement, recorded in the minutes, in which he insisted that even after more than five months' imprisonment he was still determined not to turn aside from his chosen way and would resolutely maintain his principles. He stated that he was perfectly willing to do any kind of work for the public good as long as it did not relate to military activities, and would on no account approve of the National Socialist Party's racial laws. Then he added: "The gramophone confiscated at our meeting place is my property. I bought it in 1935. I received the records from a brother in the faith, whose name I will not disclose. If I were set free today and could start a conversation with someone, I would try to bring up the subject of our religion. I would speak in such a way that I would be recognized as a Witness. If I had printed matter with me and another person wished to have some of it, I would give it to him.

"If I am asked about my position regarding the government, my answer is that I take no interest in political affairs. I abide by the laws of the government as long as they do not contradict the Bible, since God's Word is above the law of the state. I also reject military service because it runs counter to the fifth commandment.[1] If I were called up to go to the front, I would refuse to go. I am aware that my adherence to this view could cost me my life, but there is nothing I can do about that because life depends on compliance with God's laws."[2]

After Engleitner had made it clear to Dr. Tintara that he was prepared to face the prospect of the death penalty in order to obey the commandment "thou shalt not kill," the judge ended the questioning and had the prisoner taken back to his cell.

---

[1] Exodus 20:13: "Thou shalt not kill."
[2] Translation of an extract from the original transcript of September 19, 1939, recorded at Wels court

Engleitner spent the next few days in terrible uncertainty, wondering whether he would be led out the next moment to be executed. Although he found great comfort and strength in his relationship with God, he was under enormous strain. It did not help that he had to share the cell with a man who constantly ridiculed him. Then, on September 22, 1939, during their daily exercise period in the prison grounds, the two of them noticed a priest from Freistadt, Upper Austria, being released. That supplied Engleitner's cell mate with fresh ammunition, and he jeered: "Look at the priest! He's not as stupid as you, letting himself get locked up just because of the Bible! *He's* allowed to go home!"

Engleitner refused to be drawn into an argument, however, and when he himself was summoned before the examining magistrate just five minutes later, he waved to his mocking cell mate and said with a laugh: "See? Now I'm off as well!" The other was speechless.

On September 22, 1939, Dr. Egon Tintara told Engleitner that the public prosecutor in Wels had stopped the proceedings against him following a general pardon (see following page). Tintara was off the case. Engleitner, greatly relieved, signed the confirmation:

"I hereby acknowledge that the legal proceedings against me have been abandoned under § 3 (1) no. 3 of the general pardon of September 9, 1939, RGBl. I page 1753."[1]

The proceedings against Rosalia Hahn, Pauline Schlägl, and Franz and Emilie Rothauer were abandoned as well.

---

[1] Translation of an extract from the original transcript of September 22, 1939, recorded at Wels court

LANDGERICHT WELS
Eingelangt am 22 SEP 1939 ___ Uhr ___ Mi   1 St 883/39
___ nach ___ ___ Beilagen
Dem   ___ Rubriken   ___   **HAFT**

　　　Herrn Untersuchungsrichter h i e r

mit dem Antrage auf Einstellung der V.U. gem.§ 3 Absatz 1 Z.3
des Gnadenerlasses vom 9+9.1939,RGBl.I S 1753 bezüglich des
Leopold Engleitner und gem.§ 109 STPO. bezüglich Rosalia Hahn,
Pauline Schlägel,Franz und Emilie Rothauer.

Es wird beantragt,dem Leopold Engleitner,der Rosalia Hahn,der
Pauline Schlägel und dem Franz Rothauer einen Anspruch auf
Haftentschädigung nicht zuzuerkennen,da bei Ersterem der lediglich infolge Amnestierung die weitere Strafverfolgung unterblie-
ben ist,bei Letzteren aber gleich wie bei Ersterem der Verdacht
der strafbaren Handlung noch fortbesteht.

　　　Es wird weiters beantragt,Leopold Engleitner an die
Geheime Staatspolizei in Linz zu überstellen und diese zur Zl.
II B 1 5252/39 von dem obigen Ausgang des Strafverfahrens zu ver-
ständigen.

　　　Staatsanwaltschaft beim L.G.Wels,am 21.9.1939.

　　　　　Der Oberstaatsanwalt:

Eingelangt ___
Reingeschrieben ___
Verglichen ___
Abgefertigt ___

*31: Letter from the public prosecutor in Wels, dated September 21,
1939, to Wels court, concerning the abandonment of the preliminary
investigations*

General pardon from the Führer and Chancellor of the German Reich for the civilian population, September 9, 1939, RGBl.[1] No. 1240/1939

§ 3 section 1
Criminal proceedings sub judice which were opened over offenses committed prior to the present pardon coming into force will be abandoned if no higher punishment or overall sentence is to be expected than
1. a fine, for which the corresponding alternative prison term does not exceed three months, or a fine not higher than one thousand Reichsmarks,
2. detention or imprisonment in a fortress,
3. *imprisonment (in the Ostmark,[2] in the Reichsgau[3] Sudetenland, and in the Protectorate of Bohemia and Moravia, also detention) of not more than three months, solely or consecutively, and no reason exists to order some other kind of punishment in addition to the prison sentence with a view to safeguarding or correction, or to order castration. In the instance of No. 3, the case will only be dropped if after committing the offense the offender was not or was only sentenced to pay a fine or to serve a term of detention or of imprisonment in a prison or fortress for a total of six months.*

---

[1] Actually GblÖ (Austrian Law Gazette)
[2] Under the Nazis, Austria was renamed the Ostmark
[3] Administrative district

Imprisonment Instead of Freedom

Instead of releasing Engleitner, the judge handed him over to the police in Wels, who remanded him pending transportation. The policeman in charge was friendly and treated him well. The door to Engleitner's cell was never locked, and he only had to stay in it at night. During the day, he worked in the garden and could pick plums from the trees there; sometimes he was even allowed to eat in the kitchen.

On September 29, 1939, Engleitner appeared before the police superintendent in Wels, who told him: "Herr Engleitner, I would like to release you, since there is no reason whatsoever to keep you under arrest. But if I did, the Gestapo would immediately arrest you again. I think it best to send you back to Linz now." Engleitner spent the following days behind bars in cell number 8 in the police detention center in Linz.[1]

On the day of his arrival, the other prisoners spent hours harassing him about his religion. Then a guard opened the cell door and asked: "Engleitner, what have you been up to?"

"Nothing!" came the answer.

"I've been ordered to put you in solitary!" said the guard.

At this the other prisoners began jeering and gloating: "There you are, you fool! Serves you right!"

He followed the guard to a windowless cell furnished with only a small table and a chair that folded down from the wall. The chair was padlocked, only to be let down at mealtimes. Two steel cables ran the length of the walls so that hands and feet could be fettered, forcing a prisoner to stand all day long with virtually no freedom of movement. Seeing this and imagining that he would be spending the next few days chained to those walls in a pitch-black room, he wondered what he had done to deserve such harsh treatment.

The guard, however, instead of chaining him to the wall, unlocked the chair and told him to sit down. "Get that down you," the guard said as he placed a large bowl of *schinkenfleckerl*

---

[1] Prison records, number 2390

(a warm Austrian pasta dish with chopped ham) on the table in front of him. The guard further explained: "There's no hurry. When you've finished, ring the bell and I'll take you back to your cell. Just don't tell anyone about this." Engleitner's fear gave way to relief as he enjoyed his unexpected feast. The portion was so big that he had trouble finishing it. As he was escorted back to his cell, he struggled to hide his joy over what had just happened without arousing the suspicion of his fellow prisoners. Pretending to have been beaten up, he held his backside and whimpered pitifully. No one suspected a thing.

A man called Paveronschütz,[1] from Bad Ischl, an acquaintance of Engleitner's, was also held at this prison. Rumor had it that Paveronschütz had been a member of the *Heimwehr* and had been involved in a shooting incident with some Nazis at the time of Hitler's march into Austria, which had cost one Nazi his life. In the prison, Paveronschütz had charge of the janitors, and he asked for Engleitner as a janitor, since he knew him to be a hard worker. Engleitner once had to carry a batch of clean laundry to one inmate's cell. The inmate thanked him so politely that Engleitner remarked to a nearby guard: "My, what a refined gentleman!"

"Didn't you recognize him?" asked the guard. "That's the former governor of Upper Austria, Dr. Heinrich Gleissner— in here for political reasons." That was Engleitner's first contact with the man who had once been the most powerful man in Upper Austria, and it would not be the last.

Deportation to the Concentration Camp

On the afternoon of October 5, 1939, the duty sergeant at the police detention center in Linz gave Leopold Engleitner the

---

[1] The identity of this man remains uncertain, since no mention is made of a man called Paveronschütz in the prison records of the police detention center in Linz between 1938 and 1939

most shocking news he would ever hear. "Herr Engleitner,"he said gently, "I'm very sorry to have to tell you that in half an hour you will be transported to Buchenwald concentration camp. Please sign this warrant for your protective custody. You will be brought something to eat before you leave; who knows when you'll be able to eat your fill again! I pity you, but I'm afraid there's nothing I can do about it."

Protective custody—the Gestapo could impose it on anyone, regardless of judicial rulings, according to the February 28, 1933, decree for "the protection of People and State," which was supposedly a "defensive measure against Communist acts of violence endangering the State." This decree deprived the accused of the basic human right to a court hearing before sentencing. The notes of the decree state: "A typical area in which the decree is applicable is, for instance, the prohibition of the Association of Earnest Bible Students in all German countries."

Engleitner's heart skipped a beat and his courage waned momentarily. With trembling fingers he signed the warrant. He had feared this moment ever since the warnings at the convention of Jehovah's Witnesses in Prague, but had always hoped that he would not have to face the horrors of the concentration camp and the direct threat of death. And of all the camps, it was Buchenwald, one of the most notorious of all! His hopes of staying alive began to fade. But he could do nothing about it. The decision had been made. He felt like crying. His refusal to be a part of the barbaric slaughter would likely cost him his life. In a silent prayer he laid out all his feelings before the Almighty, and he remembered the comforting words at Psalm 55:22: "Cast thy burden upon the LORD, and he shall sustain thee. He shall never suffer the righteous to be moved." On pondering these words, he felt renewed confidence and trust and an iron determination never to compromise with the Hitler regime. He resolved always to keep his integrity to God.

Meeting Dr. Heinrich Gleissner

32: Dr. Heinrich Gleissner, circa 1945

After Engleitner had eaten, he was driven to a train that waited at Linz railway station. The train consisted of wagons equipped with two-man cells. As Engleitner's moving prison rumbled off in the direction of Salzburg, the face of the other man in the cell seemed increasingly familiar to him. "Who is that man?" he thought, "I'm sure I've seen him before!" Suddenly it came to him. He was the gentleman Engleitner had delivered laundry to, the former governor of Upper Austria, Dr. Heinrich Gleissner! He asked Gleissner whether he remembered him bringing laundry to his cell. The former governor said that he did, and a lively conversation began. Engleitner asked Dr. Gleissner many questions about the circumstances of his arrest and something about his political background. Dr. Gleissner in turn asked about Engleitner's long record of suffering. When Engleitner explained his position as one of Jehovah's Witnesses, Gleissner sympathetically expressed his displeasure at the way he had been mistreated. Dr. Gleissner asked: "You never had any problems with the authorities concerning your faith during my time in office, did you?"

I most certainly did," Engleitner chuckled. "I can't begin to remember how many times I was picked up by the police for my religious activities and was taken to the police station for questioning. I always explained to them that Austria has freedom of religion and that I only encourage people to read the Bible. They usually let me go after that, but sometimes they did not. I stood trial five times and had to serve some long prison sentences."

Engleitner shared details about the time he had spent behind bars in Bad Ischl, Salzburg, and Bad Aussee and the unlawful decision of the Bad Ischl labor office to disqualify him from unemployment benefits for five years. Dr. Gleissner listened carefully then said indignantly: "That should never have been allowed to happen! As a signatory of the Peace Treaty of Saint Germain, the Austrian State is obliged to grant freedom of religion to all its citizens. Not one of your prison sentences has any legal basis in the constitution."

"Herr *Doktor,*" replied Engleitner, "I cited that Peace Treaty every single time, but the courts ignored my arguments."

"Herr Engleitner," said the former governor, "although I cannot undo the unfair treatment you have suffered, I wish to express my personal apology to you. If you ever need anything, I will do everything I can to help you."

Engleitner appreciated those kind words and the sincere apology from the lips of the man who had been the most senior official in the province. The two men talked about Engleitner's religion for a while. Dr. Gleissner told him that he had met several Witnesses held in "isolation" (particularly "dangerous" prisoners were held separate from all the others) while he was in Dachau concentration camp from March to June 1939 and that he admired their steadfastness. He knew that they could have escaped all the atrocities inflicted on them simply by signing a declaration.

Engleitner enjoyed their conversations immensely; the journey from Linz to Salzburg seemed to fly by.

Following their arrival in Salzburg, the prisoners, about one hundred in all, were chained in pairs and then linked by a long chain. One detainee who had been fettered before the train ride seemed to be missing, causing a guard to swear profusely in a frenzy. Eventually the prisoner he was looking for called out "Here I am!" and pulled his empty manacles out of his trouser pocket.

"Why aren't you in chains?" the guard bellowed.

"I have very small hands," the prisoner replied. "I slipped through the chains, so I put them in my pocket."

Once the excitement subsided, the prisoners were taken to Salzburg prison for the night. When the prisoners' evening meal arrived, one portion was missing. Most of the men protested vehemently that one of them would not have a portion, so Dr. Gleissner stepped up and said: "Calm down. Take my portion; I can go without."

"No, that's out of the question," replied the other men. "Since they have the nerve to lock us up here, they must at least give us something to eat." The prisoners would not settle down until the prison guards brought an additional bowl for the former governor.

The next day most of the prisoners marched off to various *Moorlagers*[1] to do hard labor. Engleitner and the rest of the prisoners were transported to Munich, where they were detained for three more days.

Once again, Engleitner was put together with Dr. Heinrich Gleissner, who soon started an animated conversation with the two other men in the cell. From the legal matters they discussed, Engleitner surmised that the others must be lawyers as well. The terms they used were not familiar to Engleitner, and he did not dare interrupt. All the same, he listened attentively. Dr. Gleissner, ever the gentleman, addressed a few words to him every now and then, and encouraged his colleagues to include Engleitner in their conversation as well. Engleitner took the opportunity to ask them about legal matters relating to his own situation. Patiently the lawyers answered his queries and confirmed that from a legal standpoint, he had

---

[1] Penal camps in which the prisoners had to drain fields

indeed been seriously wronged. Once again the former governor's courteous and obliging manner impressed Engleitner. He esteemed this man of great integrity.

BUCHENWALD
CONCENTRATION CAMP[1]

Arrival

On Monday, October 9, 1939, the detainees were taken from the prison in Munich and put on a train bound for Weimar in Thuringia, Germany. There they were crammed onto trucks and taken up the Blutstrasse (blood road) to Buchenwald on Ettersberg hill. At ten o'clock in the evening, exhausted by the long journey, they finally reached Buchenwald concentration camp.

So now the day had actually come when Leopold Engleitner's steadfastness would be put to the ultimate test. Convinced that he had God on his side and was defending high principles, he, together with his brothers in the faith, was firmly resolved to stand up to Hitler's regime. Even now nothing in the world would stop him from saying a clear "No" to any compromises of his faith, come what may.

Immediately on arrival came the first shock, which some of the prisoners did not survive. The dismal surroundings, the mental and physical stress, the contemptuous shouts of the SS

[1] History: see Appendix II

*33: Main entrance building, with bunker (left) and SS camp
command (right), April 1945*

men together with the constant beatings filled all the camp
newcomers with terror. SS men chased them along the
"Caracho Road"[1] toward the camp entrance, where the camp
command, the garages, and the gasoline stations were situated.
Although the road would have been wide enough, the SS men
preferred to force them to run a gauntlet of guards across the
railway lines that ran parallel to it. Many stumbled and fell,
whereupon the Nazis beat them with the butts of their rifles.
Engleitner did not experience that maltreatment, but soon
afterward he was targeted for many other acts of brutality.

Following this "battue," he was forced into the bunker with the
others, then kicked into a one-man cell that he had to share with
nine other prisoners. The young bunker supervisor, Martin
Sommer, was a notorious tormentor and killer. During his time
in charge of the bunker (1938-1943), more than 160 people

---

[1] Caracho, Spanish for "noisy speed"

CAMP HIERARCHY

SS

Lagerkommandant
(camp commandant)
|
Lagerführer
(camp leader)
|
Rapportführer — Blockführer
(report leader)   (block leader)
|
Wachposten (sentry)

Prisoners

Lagerschreiber ———— *Lagerältester* ———— *Kapo*
(camp secretary)   (camp senior)   (prisoner in charge of a work detail)
|
Blockältester
(block senior)
|
Stubendienst — *Tischältester*
(room orderly)   (table senior)

THE TRIANGLE

Besides his number, every prisoner had to wear a triangle. The color of the triangle showed why the man was imprisoned. Non-Germans also carried a letter indicating their nationality. Prisoners in the penal company also had a black dot sewn on at the tip of the triangle.

Yellow: Jew; yellow triangle with tip pointing upward, overlaid with a second triangle pointing downward, its color indicating the reason for imprisonment.
Yellow/red: Jewish political prisoner
Yellow/blue: Jewish emigrant
Yellow/green: Jewish habitual criminal
Yellow/black: Jewish asocial element
Yellow/white: Jew who had sexual relations with an Aryan

Red: political prisoner
Purple: Bible Student (Jehovah's Witness)
Black: Asocial element, work-shy German, pimp, gambler, marriage impostor, prostitute
Green: Habitual criminal
Brown: Roma or Sinti (Gypsy)
Pink: Homosexual
Blue: Emigrant

died. Opening the peephole he asked each prisoner in turn the reason for his imprisonment. Last of all, he turned his gaze to Engleitner. "And you? Why are you here?"

"I'm one of Jehovah's Witnesses," came the reply.

"What?" yelled Sommer. "They're the biggest idiots of them all! Come on out of there!" He opened the cell door and dragged him out into the corridor, where he began beating him savagely with a switch made of woven willow. Sommer then threw him into the cell on the other side of the corridor and locked the door. Engleitner found himself in a pitch-dark room, and without warning he received a rain of heavy blows to his face.

He had no idea what was happening and could not see his attacker. The unseen tormentor knocked him to the ground and began kicking him in the stomach. Engleitner happened to roll under a bed, where the brutal man could not reach him anymore. Engleitner heard cries of "Ouch! Ow!" as his attacker repeatedly banged his own shin on the edge of the iron bed. Surprised by all the noise, the bunker supervisor came back, unlocked the cell door, and turning on the light, shouted: "What's going on in here?" When Engleitner crawled out from under the bed, he saw that it was another prisoner who had been savagely assaulting him. But he had no time to gather his wits because Martin Sommer grabbed hold of him again and dragged him into the guardroom, beating him all the while.

There Sommer shouted at him: "What do you think of the Brothers Grimm?"

He obviously wanted Engleitner to praise them as masters of German literature, but the latter did not want to do Sommer any favors and replied: "To me, they're just writers of fairy tales."

That was too much for Sommer, and he yelled: "Take that look off your face!" But Engleitner could not hide his revulsion at this man's inhuman behavior. The more violent the ambitious Nazi became, the more contemptible Engleitner found him. The SS man then tried to intimidate him into renouncing his faith using psychological tricks and threats. When those did not work, he ordered Engleitner to bend over a bench. He picked up the switch at the thin end, and he started to lash Engleitner's back with the thick end.

Engleitner winced in pain with every stroke. But because he still refused to yield to the SS man's pressure, the furious Sommer felt he had to resort to the ultimate threat.

"I'm going to shoot you!" he shouted. "But before I do, I'll let you write a few words to your parents to say goodbye!" He handed him a pencil and a piece of card and ordered him to start writing. Engleitner tried to find some words of consolation, but each time he started to write, the brute would jog his elbow so that, in the end, the card was full of illegible scribbles.

Sommer shouted: "Look at that! This idiot can't even write properly! But he's not too stupid to read a Bible!"

After further humiliating and maltreating Engleitner, Sommer drew his pistol, making a great show of it to frighten Engleitner. Pressing the pistol against Engleitner's temple, Sommer said sarcastically: "I'm shooting you now because you're a hopeless case! Are you ready? I'm pulling the trigger now!"

Cold sweat collected on Engleitner's brow; it seemed that he was now staring death in the face. However, in the full conviction that he had remained faithful to his God Jehovah and his just principles to the very end, he replied firmly: "Yes, I am." Then he closed his eyes and waited for the shot that would end his life.

But it did not come.

Instead of pulling the trigger, Sommer took the pistol from his head and yelled: "You're too stupid for me to shoot!"

Engleitner was then taken back to the cell.

In the cell there was a chamber pot, actually just a child's potty, which was filled to the brim with urine. The SS man ordered Engleitner to empty it into the toilet down the hall.

"But don't you dare spill it," he roared. Engleitner tried very hard to carry the stinking pot, but Sommer breathed down his neck and hit him several times on the head so that he could not help but spill the contents. "Look at that pig!" howled the SS man. "He can't even hold a pot straight!"

By the time Engleitner reached the toilet, the receptacle was almost empty. Sommer again inflicted more blows before shoving him back into the overcrowded cell, despite the protests of the other nine prisoners, who said: "There's no room!"

"We'll see about that!" Sommer shouted, kicking Engleitner into the mass of bodies.

He spent the entire night standing up. He would not have been able to sleep anyway after the horrifying experiences of the preceding hours. His body was covered with bruises; even the slightest touch caused him excruciating pain.

Left standing sandwiched among the other prisoners, he pondered his fate and thought: "It would have been better to be thrown to wild animals. At least animals would have killed me by now. Who'd have thought my head could take so many blows? One should have been enough to finish me off. And the only reason that they kicked me and beat me up so badly was that I'm a Witness."

His cell mates teased and mocked him, asking: "What's the point of suffering for such a stupid religion?" Dr. Heinrich Gleissner, who was locked up in the cell next door, commented: "It seems that Christians are being persecuted again."

In the morning, the newcomers were led to the political wing to be registered. Passing the entrance building again, Engleitner saw the ambiguously cynical inscription that dominated the upper part of the huge wrought iron gate: "TO EACH HIS OWN." It seemed to imply that the tortures perpetrated in that place were nothing more than what each one deserved.

The prisoners listened to an intimidating address from an SS officer:

34: Inscription in the upper part of the wrought iron gate, April 1945

"You are being kept here in protective custody to protect society and the state!"

"That's odd," thought Engleitner. "I didn't know I was so dangerous. I love my fellowman and refuse to kill, and so society and the state must be protected from me. Where is the logic in that? Either I'm stupid or there is something wrong with these people!"

The booming voice of the SS officer forced his attention back to the speech. "Buchenwald is the worst of all the camps. You'll be beaten here when you deserve it. You'll be treated in such a way that you'll tear each other apart. The rougher a prisoner treats another prisoner, the greater the service he does us."

Engleitner began to understand what was behind the previous night's incident at the hands of his fellow detainee.

The prisoners were lined up to have their personal details recorded. Engleitner stood in the same row as Dr. Gleissner. Asked what his profession was, Gleissner answered: "I'm a lawyer."

"What? A Jew?" the SS officer bellowed, punching him in the face so hard that he staggered from the impact. Engleitner felt that blow as if he himself had received it. But there was nothing he could do to help him.

Dr. Gleissner was registered as prisoner number 8155 and received a red triangle, which meant he would be sent to the block reserved for political prisoners.

35: *Bear enclosure, 1938*

Then it was Engleitner's turn. When the SS men learned that he was one of Jehovah's Witnesses, they made terrible threats in an attempt to make him renounce his faith. Soon they saw there was no chance of that, so they yelled: "Looks like we'll have

36: *Camp card number 6778*

to throw you to the bears. They'll tear you to pieces!"

Although the idea of being torn apart by bears terrified him, Engleitner did not take the threat seriously. "They have no bears," he thought. "They're just trying to scare me." He was then assigned to work in the penal company in the quarry for three months.

Engleitner later found out that he was wrong in assuming that there were no bears. An enclosure containing several bears, including a grizzly, was part of a small zoo financed by "donations" extorted from prisoners. The caged beasts served as entertainment for the SS and their families.

Engleitner's head and face were covered with cuts and bruises from the beatings he had received. Perhaps for that reason the SS waited a day before moving him to his block.

His hearing had been damaged, and he was plagued with a constant ringing in his ears.

At the penal company his hair was shaved off, and he was given his prisoner's uniform, which consisted of a pair of striped trousers, a jacket, and a hat. He received the number 6778, which he had to sew on to his clothes.

The man Leopold Engleitner had now been reduced to a number, and he bore a black dot that showed him to be a member of the penal company. He also received two purple triangles. One had to be stitched on the right leg of his trousers and the other on the breast pocket of his jacket. This allowed everyone in the camp to see he was a Bible Student. Despite their small number, Hitler had gone to the trouble of giving them a distinct uniform symbol. Hitler expressed his rage with the words: "They will be exterminated in Germany!"[1] Engleitner, the first Witness from Austria to be interned in Buchenwald, took that threat seriously and expected the worst. But he had the unexpected joy of fellowship with at least nine of his brothers in the faith, among them Franz Wimmer (number 7883), Georg Pointner (number 7882), and Wolfgang Mattischek (number 571), all of whom were brought to Buchenwald some time later. At various times they helped each other to withstand the barbaric conditions that prevailed in the camp. But for now, newcomer Engleitner had to work in the limestone quarry under the most adverse conditions imaginable.

---

[1] In October 1934, Jehovah's Witnesses from Germany and the rest of the world sent a letter of protest to the German government. On October 7, 1934, Adolf Hitler clenched his fists and shouted hysterically: "This brood will be exterminated in Germany!"

The Penal Company "Quarry"

The quarry on Ettersberg hill lay about 800 yards outside the camp. It provided the material for the construction of buildings, roads, and pathways in the camp. Work in this unit was one of the severest physical tortures to be endured at Buchenwald. Prisoners crushed, hewed, and transported stones using the most primitive methods, and there were never enough tools available. Each workday began with a rush to the pile of shovels and pickaxes to grab one of the coveted tools. Anyone without one would be forced to toil the entire day using his bare hands. Engleitner's small stature proved to be an advantage, for while the others were busy fighting, he wriggled through the scuffling crowd and always managed to get a tool.

Since the SS wanted to exterminate prisoners, they forced the men to work at breakneck speed. Murder and execution became routine. Almost every evening, the prisoners carried dead bodies back into the camp in wheelbarrows, sometimes as many as ten a day. The often frozen bodies were tipped out

37: Quarry on Ettersberg hill, April 1945

of the barrows onto the roll-call square, like logs tumbling to the ground. Perhaps because of the inhuman labor conditions and the psychological pressures, the hair of many of the fifteen- and sixteen-year-old prisoners went gray within a few weeks of their internment.[1] Raging thirst plagued the men throughout the day, since no water was available to them while they worked. Not until the evening could they quench their thirst in the washroom. They never had enough to eat either. During the marches through the woods on the way to and from the quarry, Engleitner would secretly pull out grass, which he added to the watery stew that he had to eat.

To make matters worse, it poured rain for days on end during the month of October 1939. The prisoners were constantly soaking wet. They had no way to dry their clothes, so the men put them on wet every morning. Engleitner shivered from head to foot and from dawn to dusk. He felt certain that he would not survive his time in this penal company because his health had not been the best to begin with.

The deputy *Lagerführer* Hans Hüttig was a brutal tyrant. His venomous expressions were terrifying. If he lost his temper, he lashed prisoners in their face with his whip.

Engleitner would soon experience his brutality.

The prisoners usually worked in the quarry until two in the afternoon, after which the penal company would be assigned to duties inside the camp. One day Engleitner was part of a 200-man

38: Hans Hüttig, deputy Lagerführer, Buchenwald concentration camp, circa 1938

---

[1] Alfred Vogel, *Der kleine Doktor* (Augsburg, 1993), pp. 400-1

detail assigned to remove a heap of rubble from in front of the
camp and to use it to fill holes in the roll-call square. They
carried rubble on wooden boards similar to stretchers. Engleitner
and another prisoner were hurrying through the camp gate onto
the square with a full load. But Hüttig decided they were moving
too slowly and lashed Engleitner several times across the back
with his whip. Since Engleitner already had lacerations on his
hands from the quarry work, he could not hold the stretcher
anymore, and the two men dropped it. They immediately ran
off as fast as their legs would carry them and quickly mingled
with the rest of the prisoners.

The deputy *Lagerführer* ordered all the men to line up in
rows of five. He closely scrutinized every prisoner. When Hüttig
reached Engleitner, he looked at him long and hard. Engleitner
was terrified at the thought of what would happen to him if
Hüttig recognized him. Silently he prayed to God for assistance
and forced himself to appear calm so as not to give himself
away. Fortunately, Hüttig did not recognize him. But then he
repeated his inspection of the rows of prisoners, looking even
longer and harder into Engleitner's face this time. Again he
moved on to the next prisoner without having identified
Engleitner. When Hüttig had finished his examination and
the officer in charge of the unit had told him that it must have
been a prisoner from another detail, he gave the order to
continue working.

Engleitner heaved a huge sigh of relief, thanking God.
However, the whip had left his back black and blue, and for
weeks afterward he could only sleep on his stomach.

Engleitner happened to meet a judge from the court in
Leoben where in 1938 he had been sentenced to one month's
imprisonment *in absentia*. The judge gave him the following
advice: "Always keep a low profile here. Try never to attract
attention to yourself, either positively or negatively. That's the
way to survive!"

In the early days of his imprisonment, Engleitner often saw Dr. Gleissner. One day he watched as Dr. Gleissner was forced to drag heavy stones for a new road. When he saw that Gleissner's clothes were covered in mud, Engleitner, now on first-name terms with him, good-naturedly exclaimed: "Heinrich, what on earth do you look like? You're absolutely filthy!"

Dr. Gleissner replied: "I'm not used to this kind of work. The stones are so heavy that I have to rest them on my thighs."

This was the last time the two men met in the concentration camp. At the end of December 1939, Dr. Gleissner was released and sent to work for a company in Berlin.

One wet, chilly day, Engleitner and several other prisoners were ordered to collect the parcels that had been sent to the inmates by their relatives. They had to line up in front of a window in the eastern wing of the gatehouse while an SS man handed out the parcels. It was strictly forbidden for relatives to send food, so an SS man inspected every parcel. On this occasion, the SS man discovered that a parcel contained cookies and ripped it open, scattering them in the mud. Many of the famished inmates pounced on the cookies and began devouring them, ignoring the dirt. Since Engleitner did not take part in the melee, the SS man asked him: "Why aren't you fighting for one of them?"

"I'll never be hungry enough to eat muck!" explained Engleitner.

The SS man could easily have forced him to eat them. Instead the man ordered him to present his cap and, filling it with cookies, said: "Eat them out of your cap; you don't have to eat dirty ones." Engleitner thanked the man politely. Just as he was about to enjoy this unexpected snack, he noticed the man for whom the cookies had been sent staring at him in silent anger. When he noticed Engleitner looking at him, he turned on his heels and disappeared into the throng of prisoners. Engleitner set off in search of the man with the intention of giving him what was rightfully his. Try as he might, he could not find him. So he sat down to eat the cookies, but he enjoyed them less than he would have otherwise.

On still another occasion he was once again able to show that he still had his wits about him. He had been called into the camp's orderly room where an SS officer asked him where he was from. "From Upper Austria," replied Engleitner.

"I've never heard of this province," said the Nazi curtly. Following Hitler's occupation Upper Austria had been renamed "Oberdonau" ("Upper Danube"), and it was this name the man wanted to hear.

But Engleitner had no intention of using this new name and replied bluntly: "If you don't know this province, you should have paid more attention before, shouldn't you?"

The SS man was so taken aback by this riposte that all he could do was yell: "Get out!"

The malnutrition, dampness, and bitterly cold conditions in the camp led to an outbreak of dysentery. When the illness also spread to the guards, the order came to isolate the penal company. A fence was erected around the company's barracks in an attempt to prevent the further spread of the disease. The cook had to leave the food by the fence, and the quarantined prisoners could come to collect it only after he had left. The winter temperatures were as low as -33°F. Within ten weeks hundreds of prisoners had died and their numbers had dwindled to about 10,000. The words "Pallbearer to the gate" boomed over the loudspeaker every day.

Engleitner did not catch this dreadful disease. But he had to come to terms with the constant stream of deaths around him as he stayed in quarantine, sitting with the sick inside the unheated barracks on an ice-cold bed.

Only after the death toll had begun to reach alarming proportions did the camp administration decide to build chimneys in order to keep their workforce alive a bit longer.

Contrary to his misgivings, Engleitner survived his time in the penal company, as it was cut short by the dysentery outbreak.

While the penal company was still in quarantine, news arrived that an attempt had been made on Hitler's life on November 8, 1939, in the Bürgerbräukeller in Munich. The attempt had failed, and Georg Elser, the would-be assassin, had been arrested and taken to Sachsenhausen concentration camp. The prisoners in Buchenwald also felt the backlash of Hitler's anger, as the Führer ordered that their rations be stopped. For three days no prisoner had anything to eat; the Jews were starved for six days. There had never been enough to eat, so this additional restriction was an almost unbearable torture. After three days had elapsed, the Jews begged other prisoners for food, but sharing was scarcely possible with the meager rations the prisoners received. This time Engleitner bore the punishment more easily than most. Just before the rations were stopped, hunger had driven him to eat his entire ten-day ration of molasses. He had such a bad stomachache that he could not eat anything anyway.

On November 9, 1939, Engleitner and some other prisoners in the penal company watched through the window of their block as 21 Jews were led out of the camp by SS men. One prisoner remarked. "It's a bad sign if that *Scharführer*[1] is going with them! He's one of the worst!" In the evening they learned that their fears had been justified; the Jews had been shot in the quarry, purportedly another reprisal for the assassination attempt on Hitler.

Engleitner noticed that Jews received particularly bad treatment when they worked. They were often harnessed like draft animals

---

[1] Equivalent to a sergeant

to a heavily laden hay wagon with broad iron wheels and driven
with whips like cattle. He saw how they toiled and labored, how
some of them collapsed from exhaustion, and he felt great pity
for them because the treatment they endured seemed to him to
be the cruelest and most inhuman of all.

Breaks in the Clouds

When the quarantine was lifted, all the prisoners had to line
up on the roll-call square to be reorganized and allocated new
sleeping quarters in the barracks. Engleitner did not hear when
his number, 6778, was called, and worried that he would be
separated from his brothers in the faith. He stood on the square
feeling close to despair. Even under these most adverse
circumstances, the Bible Students did their best to behave in a
Christian manner and display brotherly love. Would Engleitner,
just over five feet tall, physically handicapped with curvature
of the spine, and known in the camp as the "Little Austrian,"
be the only Witness separated from the others?

Fortunately his fears were unfounded; a block senior, an
inmate who was responsible for all the prisoners in one block,
noticed him standing dejectedly by himself and asked him:
"Why are you still here?"

"Nobody called my number," replied the distraught
Engleitner.

"I expect you didn't hear it," said the other.

"That's possible," the "Little Austrian" thought to himself,
"because my hearing has been bad since the beating I got my
first day here." He did not know it at the time, but his left
eardrum had been damaged. When Engleitner entered his
block, he received a delighted welcome from his brothers in
the faith, who had already made his bed for him. His depression
gave way to relief.

Now that the sleeping arrangements had been reorganized,
the much-feared senior *Lagerführer* Arthur Rödl, from Munich,

would rearrange the work details. The Bible Student Fritz Adler (number 1808) worked for Rödl as a secretary. During the evening meal in the day room, Adler sat next to Engleitner and told him: "Tomorrow you'll be presented to the *Lagerführer*. Whatever you do, don't speak High German! He can't stand it. Talk like you do at home."

39: Arthur Rödl, senior Lagerführer, Buchenwald concentration camp, circa 1938

Engleitner went to bed feeling uneasy, thinking: "The prisoners say that the senior *Lagerführer* is cruel and ruthless. Will he be inhuman like the deputy? Who can doubt it, if he even dictates how you speak to him?" The next morning, Engleitner nervously made his way to Block 5, where the orderly room and work-statistics office were housed. As soon as he noticed the figure entering the office, senior *Lagerführer* Rödl asked in an amused tone in the Bavarian dialect of his home: "Hey, where does this come from?"

"From the Salzkammergut," replied Engleitner, likewise using the dialect of his home region.

"What? No kidding! He comes from the Salzkammergut! Now he's going to tell me he's from Ischl, as well!" exclaimed Rödl.

"No," answered Engleitner, "I'm from St. Wolfgang."

"No! Really? He's from Wolfgang, where I went with my friends to the 'Weissen Hirschen' (White Stag Inn) every Sunday and got drunk!"

Engleitner sensed that the senior *Lagerführer* had taken a

liking to him, and began to relax. After some light conversation, Rödl turned to the SS man in charge of assigning the prisoners to their daily labor and asked: "Where shall we put him, then? Let's give him to Walter Schneider. That'll be the best thing."

The *kapo* Walter Schneider supervised a group of prisoners building a huge sewage plant in Buchenwald concentration camp. Following the dysentery epidemic, the camp administration had decided to take steps to improve the sanitation and had hired a construction firm for this purpose.

Engleitner worked in this detail until March 1941, which meant that during the day he was not directly exposed to the maltreatment meted out by the SS. He helped put scaffolding together for a 20-foot shaft, and that brought him into contact with an engineer who had overseen the construction of a bridge in Albania but worked as a bricklayer in the concentration camp. A political prisoner and member of the German Catholic *Zentrumspartei* (Center Party), he expressed great anger at Pope Pius XII, who had, by signing the concordat[1] with Hitler, withdrawn his support of the Center Party.

While laying the bricks for the cable shafts, the engineer gave free rein to his displeasure and found Engleitner an attentive listener. He complained to Engleitner about the Pope's declaring his support for Hitler, saying that the Pope condoned the brutal persecution of Jehovah's Witnesses. He therefore felt that the two of them had suffered much at the hands of these two powerful leaders.

The two inmates discovered that they shared a love for the works of the Austrian writer Peter Rosegger, both having enjoyed reading his works as boys. The engineer and Engleitner had several good laughs sharing anecdotes about the writer and his work. Engleitner very much enjoyed hearing these stories, whether they were true or not, for they took him back to a time long past when he had been free to go on long hikes

---

[1] Concordat between Hitler and the Vatican, signed on July 20, 1933, by Hitler and the secretary of state Eugenio Pacelli, who later became Pope Pius XII

and read the amusing stories of his favorite author. Even little distractions such as this were very important to help them bear the horrors of camp.

Daily Terror

In 1939, *SS-Reichsführer* Heinrich Himmler sardonically described conditions in the concentration camps:

"Concentration camps are a severe and strict measure, it is true. Hard work that creates new values, a regular daily routine, phenomenal cleanliness and hygiene, first-class food, treatment which is strict but fair, guidance in learning new trades and crafts: all these are methods of education. The motto of these camps is: There is a road that leads to freedom. The milestones on this road are obedience, diligence, honesty, orderliness, cleanliness, sobriety, truthfulness, selflessness, and the love of the Fatherland."[1]

In view of the appalling reality of daily life in the camps, these words reveal cynicism of the worst kind.

In Buchenwald around 400 Bible Students[2] were housed in Block 44, a two-story stone building divided into A, B, C, and D wings. The walls of the dormitories were lined by three rows of wooden beds, stacked vertically like shelves and covered

with straw or wood-wool instead of mattresses. In summer the prisoners had to get up before sunrise. But waking up every morning at four o'clock was only the first shock of the day. An SS man would march through the barracks yelling a contemptuous "Get up!" No one was permitted to get out of

40: Foundation walls of Block 44, 1998

---

[1] Guido Knopp, *Hitlers Helfer* (Munich 1998), p. 146
[2] 392 Bible Students on April 30, 1940

bed before this, except the room orderly whose job it was to keep the dormitory and day room clean and distribute the food. For this reason he was exempted from the heavy labor the other inmates did. With a loud thump, hundreds of prisoners would jump down almost simultaneously onto the wooden floor. After making their beds, they washed. Because they made special efforts to keep themselves clean, the Bible Students managed to avoid becoming infested with lice and other vermin. Running, two prisoners had to fetch

41: Dormitory, April 1945

a cauldron containing a brown brew known as coffee, although it was little more than brown water with a slight coffee taste. In the day room, which adjoined the dormitory, the prisoners would sit at their allotted places drinking the "coffee" and perhaps eating a piece of bread if it had been saved from the previous night's paltry rations. This morning ritual had to be performed at top speed and like clockwork to avoid severe punishment. After this, but still before sunrise, the prisoners rushed onto the square for roll call. The square could be very cold, for it had no shelter from the relentless, biting wind.

The area covered about five acres and lay between the camp entrance and the barracks. It was the scene of some of the most brutal maltreatment imaginable. Prisoners received lashings on the whipping stool in front of the other inmates. They sometimes had to stand absolutely still or to sing for hours on end, and many an execution took place there.

Another regular torture was hanging—not by the neck, but by the arms. On the northern side of the square near the timber yard stood tall poles. Prisoners' hands were tied behind their backs, and they were hung for several hours from these poles, until the weight of their own bodies dislocated their shoulder joints. In many cases it took months before a man hung in this fashion could use his arms properly again. These punishments were intended to destroy all traces of individuality, and, ultimately, the man himself.

Every morning the prisoners had to march onto the square, following particular markings, and line up according to blocks. In the presence of the camp commandant or the *Lagerführer,* the officer in charge would then take the roll call. This ritual took place every morning and evening, and sometimes at midday too. It often dragged on for hours and constituted a torture in itself for the inmates, who had to stand to attention the whole time. SS men would stand at the balustrade of the

42: *The roll-call square at Buchenwald concentration camp,
April 1945*

gatehouse or on the watchtowers brandishing their machine-
guns and demonstrating their power.

After the morning roll call, the prisoners went off to work
in their assigned detail. These work details afforded the guards
and the *kapos* the opportunity to give their aggression free rein.
Kapos were inmates who had been put in charge of a particular
detail, and they could earn special privileges from the SS by
mistreating their fellow prisoners; the more they bullied, the
more privileges they could expect. So Engleitner was very
relieved to find that his *kapo*, Walter Schneider, showed great
strength of character and did not let himself sink to the level
of other *kapos*.

One dreaded method of punishment was the whipping
stool. The prisoner had to bend over this wooden construction,
and his hand and feet were tied to it at either end. He then
received lashes or strokes on the buttocks with a cane. The
noise of the blows and the prisoner's screams of agony were

meant to serve as a deterrent to the other inmates and break their will. Victims of this punishment could not sit or walk normally for weeks because of the agonizing pain and bruises.

The SS controlled every little detail of daily life in the camp. Prisoners could not wear jackets, even on cold days, except by special permission. Anyone caught wearing a jacket without permission was tied to the whipping stool and lashed. The same fate awaited anyone who, for example, made himself a warm undershirt out of an old cement sack.

Lunch was served in the day room and always consisted of a watery stew, often with one or two bits of rotten meat or vegetables floating in it, so putrid that it often gave the inmates boils. As time went on, Engleitner and his fellow detainees lost more and more weight, never getting enough food to satisfy their hunger.

After evening roll call, the men again shuffled into the day room, where a meager supper awaited them. At one point, more than a pound of bread was served, but the daily rations decreased steadily until each prisoner had to make do with a few ounces. The rest of the meal consisted of a teaspoonful of margarine, a wafer-thin slice of old ham, and sometimes a tiny onion or a shriveled carrot. Anyone who managed to save any of this meager fare had something for breakfast the next day, but this not always easy to do. In the Bible Students' block, it could be done, but in the other blocks, such leftovers were often stolen. This was so even though each group had a *Tischältester,* a prisoner who was supposed to maintain order in the day room under the supervision of the room orderly. Any man caught stealing would be severely punished. He was sent to the *Kleines Lager* (Little Camp), which had originally been set up to accommodate Polish marksmen but was later used as a prison. This camp, consisting entirely of tents, had no beds, and the prisoners were given even less to eat. Few made it out alive.

On one cold winter's day, the SS ordered Engleitner and
several other Bible Students to take the blankets away from
the prisoners in the "Little Camp" as a punishment and to
hand the blankets in to the SS. Engleitner could not bring
himself to deprive any prisoner of his blanket and so did not
have one to hand in. At least he had kept a clear conscience,
since he did not carry out that heartless order.

The Penal Company's room orderly regularly stole bread
and put the blame on other prisoners. One morning Engleitner
happened to notice him eating stolen food with other inmates.
The victims of the theft tracked the thief down, and the
dishonest room orderly was sent to the "Little Camp" along
with his cohorts.

The unspeakable cruelty and psychological terror
throughout the camp kept it shrouded in a haze of despair
and death. The physical exhaustion from lack of sleep only
heightened the misery. Yet Engleitner found the company of
his fellow Bible Students and prayer to be great sources of
strength and solace.

Forbidden Fruit

On a bitterly cold day in March 1940, the good reputation
enjoyed by the Bible Students in the concentration camp saved
Engleitner from punishment.

He was shoveling snow on the roll-call square when a
truck arrived with a delivery of apples. He and a number of
other prisoners were assigned to carry the crates of apples into
a dark cellar that was normally used for storing potatoes. One
of the crates burst open, and frozen apples rolled out over the
floor. The starving prisoners pounced on them immediately.
Engleitner accidentally stepped on one of the apples in the
dark. Since he had damaged it, he put it in his trouser pocket,
thinking: "Surely no one will mind if I eat this apple later."

But he was very much mistaken. When he came out of
the cellar, SS men were searching prisoners for apples and

anyone with an apple in his pocket was sent to the whipping stool. It now dawned on Engleitner that his actions could be interpreted as theft. But what could he do? It was impossible to throw the apple away without someone noticing, so he had no choice but to get in line. While waiting his turn, he appealed to God: "Please help me so that I don't disgrace my brothers!"

When he was about to be searched, one of the SS men said: "That's one of those Bible Students. We don't need to search him; they never steal anything."

Engleitner breathed a huge sigh of relief—not so much because he still had the apple, which he did not feel like eating anymore, but because his thoughtless act had not damaged the reputation of his brothers.

Secret Signs

Engleitner received help from unexpected sources on several occasions. The truck drivers who worked for the building contractors naturally noticed the appalling health of the starving Austrian and his fellow prisoners and decided to smuggle extra rations in to them. They knew that the guards at the camp gate never inspected the loads of sand they carried in and therefore buried packages of bread and sausage in them. To help the prisoners find the hidden packages quickly, they agreed on a secret sign. The truck drivers always chewed on a matchstick, the position of which indicated where the food was hidden. For example, if he held the matchstick in the right-hand corner of his mouth, the packages would be buried in the sand on the right. Engleitner and the other inmates looked at the drivers very closely when they arrived. After ascertaining the position of the hidden rations, they would jump onto the truck, carefully shovel the sand off it, and put the little packages of food quickly and surreptitiously into their pockets. The prisoners were extremely grateful to the truck drivers, who took a great risk by helping them. It was strictly forbidden to bring food for the prisoners, and if one of the drivers had been caught, he would have been committed to the concentration camp himself.

Contact With the Clergy

On one occasion Engleitner worked with two members of the clergy. One was a Protestant vicar, the other a Catholic priest who had been a close associate of Cardinal Theodor Innitzer, the archbishop of Vienna. Innitzer had made a solemn declaration in support of Hitler. It was Engleitner's job to load soil into their wheelbarrows while a *kapo* constantly exhorted him to load as much as possible to make the barrow extra heavy.

The priest was furious with Cardinal Innitzer. He found it inexplicable that the Cardinal openly demonstrated his support of Hitler, even giving the Nazi salute in public, whereas he himself had been incarcerated in a concentration camp because he refused to follow his superior's example. "If I, a humble priest, refuse to give the Nazi salute," he fumed, "then Innitzer, as a cardinal, has all the more reason to refuse." Engleitner could only express his whole-hearted agreement at the ambivalence of the church's leaders.

Another time he saw two Catholic priests in cassocks subjected to a demeaning lesson in how to perform the Nazi salute. An SS cap was hung on a pole on the roll-call square and the two priests had to approach the cap, raise their arms, and shout: *"Heil Hitler!"* Every day for several days they had to repeat this "lesson" again and again under the supervision of several SS men. Despite the absurdity of this ritual, Engleitner felt sorry for the humiliated men. He remained firmly resolved that he would never give the Nazi salute under any circumstances.

Lightening the Load

One day in the summer of 1940, the senior *Lagerführer,* Arthur Rödl, who liked Engleitner, came to the "Little Austrian's" aid. On Sundays the prisoners usually had the day off, but when one of them had done something that warranted punishment, all of them had to work in the quarry. So it happened on this particular Sunday. With such collective punishments, the Nazis wanted to sow hatred and distrust among the inmates, causing them to maltreat one another.

The SS commanded the prisoners to carry stones into the camp. Two of them loaded an especially heavy stone onto Engleitner's shoulders, whose knees began to buckle under the weight. At that moment the senior *Lagerführer* happened to pass by, accompanied by the camp doctor. Seeing the Austrian groaning under his oversize burden, the *Lagerführer* said to the camp doctor: "Look at that! My Bible mites are having to carry the heaviest stones again!" He then turned to the "Little Austrian" and said: "And just how do you think you're going to carry that great big stone into the camp? It's much too heavy for you. Put it down at once!"

At first, Engleitner thought he had misheard the words, but when the command was repeated, he realized that Rödl was serious and let the heavy stone drop to the ground. Rödl then rolled a much smaller stone toward him with his foot, saying, "Take that one into the camp; it's much easier to carry!" Then Rödl turned to the Bible Students' block senior and said: "They've done enough for today, they can go back to their barracks."

So thanks to senior *Lagerführer* Rödl, Engleitner deposited the stone in the camp and then spent the rest of that Sunday recovering his strength.

On another occasion a spiteful SS man took the evening roll call and kept repeating the count so that the freezing and exhausted prisoners had to stand on the square for hours. Rödl stepped in and told him to stop and to send the men in for their supper.

Engleitner heard about the brutal treatment that the camp commandant, Karl Koch, administered personally. The prisoners also feared Koch's wife Ilse, whom they called the "Hyena of Buchenwald." Rumor had it that she exploited her husband's position to spy on the prisoners who worked near her house. On the basis of her reports, many of them, including some Bible Students, were beaten and tortured.

A Sick Game

One sunny evening, the SS men called a Bible Student out from the line during roll call and held up a letter. It was from his 12-year-old daughter, who was terminally ill and did not have much longer to live. She wrote that she wished more than anything else in the world to see her father one more time before she died. She hoped that this request would get her father released from the concentration camp, if only for a few days. But the SS would grant this request only under one condition—the man would have to sign a declaration renouncing his faith. This he categorically refused to do.

When they realized that he would not compromise, the SS men beat him mercilessly, kicking him repeatedly as he lay writhing on the ground. "You call yourself a father?" they yelled. "You should be ashamed of yourself, not even wanting to see your own daughter! If you really loved her, you'd sign!"

"That's blackmail," he screamed at his tormentors through his tears. "I didn't choose to be here. You brought me here. You're to blame, not me! It breaks my heart to think of my daughter! You think I wouldn't go home now if I could? But I will not sign that paper!"

These words brought him another beating, and his daughter died without seeing her father again.

This incident deeply affected Leopold Engleitner. The spitefulness of the SS men seemingly knew no bounds. Engleitner had never before seen such cruel, barbaric manipulation of the feelings of a human being. That evening, a deeply unsettled crowd of prisoners shuffled away from the square. The heartrending scene he had just witnessed haunted Engleitner for years to come and cost him many sleepless nights.

Secret Spiritual Support and Special Restrictions

Prisoners held in protective custody had to take turns keeping watch in their sleeping quarters at night. They were to raise the alarm in case of fire or escape attempts. Each prisoner had to do a two-hour stint.

Engleitner had sentry duty in Block 44 in Buchenwald only once. He had been allotted the first shift in the day room of B wing. He spent the entire two hours reading. What did he read? Incredibly, the Bible Students hid a copy of the Bible in a secret drawer so that it could be read on sentry duty. Thus this enforced time without sleep could be used to gain spiritual strength. But this was not the only method employed by the Bible Students to strengthen their faith.

One of their brothers in the faith, Wilhelm Töllner, wrote a passage from the Bible every day on a scrap of paper. He always chose passages containing words of encouragement. These pieces of paper were then passed around by the prisoners and used as the basis for discussions in small groups whenever the opportunity arose. One Bible that had been smuggled in was taken apart and divided up among the Bible Students. Engleitner was given the Book of Job, which he carried around with him for three months, hidden in his socks. Of course, he could only read it at night in bed, when the coast was clear. The story of the patient Job, who maintained his faith under adverse circumstances, was a great source of inspiration to the "Little Austrian" and helped him to remain steadfast.

On Sundays, the Bible Students held secret biblical talks on the second floor of Block 44. While these meetings were in progress, one of them had to keep watch at the entrance to the building. Once the job fell to Engleitner. Cleaning the water trough in front of the barracks so as not to appear suspicious, he kept his eyes open for potential dangers so that he could send a warning signal to a second sentry stationed at the window. Suddenly an SS *Scharführer* tapped him on the

Erklärung.

Ich habe erkannt, daß die Internationale Bibelforscher-Vereinigung eine Irrlehre verbreitet und unter dem Deckmantel reli-
giöser Betätigung lediglich staatsfeindliche Ziele verfolgt.

Ich habe mich deshalb voll und ganz von dieser Organisation
abgewandt und mich auch innerlich von der Lehre dieser Sekte
freigemacht.

Ich versichere hiermit, daß ich mich nie wieder für die Internationale Bibelforscher-Vereinigung betätigen werde. Personen,
die für die Irrlehre der Bibelforscher werbend an mich heran-
treten, oder in anderer Weise ihre Einstellung als Bibelforscher
bekunden, werde ich unverzüglich zur Anzeige bringen. Sollten
mir Bibelforscher-Schriften zugesandt werden, werde ich sie um-
gehend bei der nächsten Polizeidienststelle abgeben.

Ich will künftig die Gesetze des Staates achten und mich voll
und ganz in die Volksgemeinschaft eingliedern.

Weiters ist mir eröffnet worden, daß ich mit meiner sofortigen,
erneuten Inschutzhaftnahme zu rechnen habe, wenn ich meiner
heute abgegebenen Erklärung zuwiderhandle.

Konzentrationslager Buchenwald.

Weimar-Buchenwald, den . . . . . .

....
Unterschrift.

Die obenstehende Erklärung kann ich nicht unterschreiben, da
ich nach wie vor überzeugter Bibelforscher bin und meinen
Schwur, den ich Jehova geleistet habe, niemals brechen werde.

Weimar-Buchenwald, den . . . . . .

....
Unterschrift.

43: Copy of the declaration, the so-called "Revers"

Declaration

I have come to realize that the doctrine spread by the International Bible Students Association is heretical and that its aims, which are pursued under the guise of religious activity, are purely seditious.

I have therefore disassociated myself entirely from this organization and have also freed my mind from the teachings of this sect.

I hereby declare that I will never again perform any work on behalf of the International Bible Students Association. I will report immediately any person who tries to persuade me to adopt the heresy spread by the Bible Students or reveals himself to be a Bible Student in any way whatsoever. If the Bible Students send me any literature, I will hand it in at the nearest police station without delay.

I undertake to respect state laws and to integrate myself fully into the community in future.

I confirm that I have been informed that I must expect to be rearrested immediately in the event of my violating this declaration.

Buchenwald Concentration Camp

Weimar-Buchenwald, this .... day of ....

....
Signature

I cannot sign the above declaration because I am still a committed Bible Student and will never break the oath I have sworn to Jehovah.

Weimar-Buchenwald, this .... day of ....

....
Signature

Translation of the declaration, the so-called "Revers"

shoulder from behind. Engleitner froze, fearing that this meant the end of their meetings, with terrible consequences to follow. But the *Scharführer* already knew what was going on and said, "Carry on," indicating that Engleitner should go back upstairs so he did not miss anything. Engleitner lost no time in complying.

The Bible Students were the only prisoners who were not allowed to smoke[1] or receive money from relatives and friends. All the money sent for them went into an account, where it stayed. So the Bible Students could not buy anything to eat in the canteen, something that even the Jews were allowed to do.

The Bible Students also had severe mail restrictions— they could write only once a month, and they were limited to 10–25 words. Every letter carried the stamp of the camp command staff and the following remark: "*The prisoner still obstinately insists on being a Bible Student and refuses to renounce the heretical teachings of the Bible Students. For this reason the freedom to maintain correspondence to the extent usually permitted is forfeited.*" The letters were also censored, so an exchange of detailed information or personal views with family members was out of the question.

Consequently, Engleitner always wrote, "Dear Folks! I am well and steadfast. *Auf Wiedersehen!* Love, Leopold," no matter how badly he was faring at the time. With these words he wished to make it plain to those prying eyes that read his letters that he was not downhearted, would show no weakness, and was determined to maintain his resolute position. This was important, because the SS would have seized on any sign of weakness and used it as an excuse to bully him all the more. He had no intention of doing them that favor. One day in the barracks he discovered that the SS actually approved of his letters. An SS man tore up one prisoner's letter because he did not like what the man had written and read out Engleitner's

---

[1] Although *The Watchtower* had recommended refraining from smoking as early as 1895, it is only since 1973 that all of Jehovah's Witnesses have been nonsmokers.

letter as an example of how it should be done. "*That's* what you should write," he said.

One day, Engleitner and several other Bible Students were lined up on the roll-call square and told they had been selected for deportation to Mauthausen concentration camp in Upper Austria. Engleitner would have had no objection to being taken back to Austria, and secretly hoped that he might receive better treatment in his homeland. But shortly before the transport was due to leave, the assembled Bible Students were told by the *Rapportführer,* the SS man in charge of the roll call, that they had to meet one condition: "Any Bible Student who wants to go to Mauthausen must first sign the declaration!"

"My goodness," thought Engleitner, "he makes going to another concentration camp sound like a privilege we should all be striving for!" Not one of them signed the declaration, and the whole group stayed in Buchenwald.

On one occasion the SS wanted 40 Bible Students to volunteer for work outside the camp on their day off. They wanted Bible Students because they did not have enough sentries. The volunteers had to prepare the beds in the SS building for new recruits. Not surprisingly, no one was eager to give up his day off, so it took a long time for volunteers to come forward. Engleitner volunteered so that the required number would finally be reached, but the SS had become impatient by that time and punished the 40 volunteers by making them crawl over sharp stones the 200 yards up the hill from Block 44 to the camp gate. Engleitner's sleeves were torn to shreds and his elbows were bleeding—some reward for volunteering to help!

Scheming at Home

Engleitner received a letter from his father one day asking Engleitner to transfer certain rights to him. Engleitner did not quite understand what his father meant, so he forgot about it. A little later he had to report to the orderly room in Block

5, where an SS man questioned him: "You got a letter from your father. Do you know what he wanted from you?"

"No," answered Engleitner. "I didn't really understand what he was asking."

"He wants your house," explained the SS man. "He wants you to give it to him."

Engleitner was surprised. "Well," he replied, "I built that house using my own savings. He had a house of his own, which he inherited from his father and could've given to me, except he had to sell it to pay his debts. And now he wants me to give him mine. That's really not fair."

Evidently the SS man held the same opinion, for he said: "Don't worry. Your father can't take it away from you. We've made inquiries at the court in Bad Ischl, and they told us that according to the land register you are the rightful owner of the plot at Weinbach 27. It belongs to you and will continue to do so."

Engleitner left the office feeling disappointed that his own father should try to dispute his right to ownership of the house and land; it was bad enough having to cope with the enormous difficulties he was faced with in the concentration camp without having these depressing schemes hatched behind his back by his own parents.

Reunion With Alois Moser—Sad News

Alois Moser, prisoner number 1286, who had been interned in the concentration camps in Dachau and Mauthausen, was brought to Buchenwald. Engleitner told him about his earlier hopes of being transferred to Mauthausen. Hearing this, Moser explained to his friend the realities of that camp. The conditions in the Upper Austrian concentration camp were even worse than those in Buchenwald, he said. All through the bitter winter of 1939/40, the prisoners had only received cold food because of fire damage in the kitchen. Engleitner was glad that he had not been sent there after all. Engleitner also learned from Moser that Franz Rothauer, his brother in the faith with whom he had been arrested on April 4, 1939, in Bad Ischl, had been transferred from Dachau to Mauthausen and had not survived that harsh winter. This was very sad news indeed.

Medical Examination

One evening as the prisoners ate their meager supper, Fritz Adler, who sat next to Engleitner, told him: "Tomorrow we're being examined to see if we're fit for military service."

This surprised Engleitner, since everyone knew that Bible Students were conscientious objectors. He felt strange about lining up the next day for the examination. Some time later, Fritz Adler came up to him and told him: "You were fortunate. You've been deferred."

Engleitner was relieved; at least the danger of being called up into the army had passed for the time being.

Lethal Dose

While making his bed one morning, Engleitner was overcome by a sudden feeling of weakness and collapsed to the floor. Two prisoners carried him to the sickbay, where they laid him on a bed. He heard one of the orderlies remark: "Well, he's out of it now as well."

Engleitner, fearing he would be killed with a lethal injection, summoned the last of his strength and dragged himself back to his block.

Watch Out—Informers!

One day a former policeman Engleitner knew from Strobl, who had supposedly been interned as a political prisoner, was released. Engleitner asked an inmate who had been in the same block for the reason. The prisoner whispered to him: "I hope you never told him anything. He was a really dangerous man—an informer!"

Engleitner felt relieved that he had never confided in the man or had close contact with him. No methods were too underhanded for the SS when it came to spying on the prisoners.

No Escape?

After some time the camp command began using a new technique to humiliate the prisoners. The inmates' hair, already very closely cropped, was shaved off completely except for two strips, one from the forehead to the back of the neck, and one from the left ear to the right ear. Now any man who managed to break out could easily be identified as an escaped concentration camp prisoner. Some of the prisoners found this new humiliation particularly depressing, but the Bible Students did not find it as disheartening, since they had no intention of trying to escape anyway.

Nevertheless, Engleitner once had a golden opportunity to escape. One day before morning roll call, he had to go to the goods station in Weimar and load cement onto tractors. At the same time, a group of soldiers were preparing a military transport of field kitchens, and they asked the SS men guarding the prisoners for help. The SS men answered: "What's that got to do with us? Do your work yourselves."

Engleitner found this retort amusing. "When it comes to working, it's every man for himself. But when it's a question of waging war, they willingly join in," he thought to himself.

One of the SS men then pointed at Engleitner and called to the soldiers: "You can take Shorty here; he'll help you."

One of the soldiers explained to Engleitner: "I've got a nice little job for you. Get a hammer and a box of nails and wedge the field kitchens so they don't roll about. And since I don't have time to watch you," he added, "I'll leave you to it. And I know you won't run off, will you?" Engleitner assured the soldier that he had no such intentions and buckled down to his task.

It was a strange feeling to be able to move freely between the wagons with no one watching him. It would have been easy to run away, but if he had his fellow prisoners would have been severely punished with food deprivation or extra work.

In March 1941 the rumor began to spread in Buchenwald that several Bible Students would be transferred to another concentration camp. Although Engleitner was not sure whether to believe it, he would have been glad to move to another camp without having to renounce his faith. He had now spent 17 months in Buchenwald, and the prospect of a change represented a glimmer of hope. Maybe conditions elsewhere were better than in Buchenwald, where the deplorable conditions continued to deteriorate.

During one morning roll call, the number 6778 was called. Engleitner was told that he and 81 other Bible Students, including Alois Moser, Wolfgang Mattischek, Georg Pointner, and Franz Wimmer, had been chosen along with eight political prisoners to be transferred to Niederhagen concentration camp in Wewelsburg.

NIEDERHAGEN
CONCENTRATION CAMP[1]

SS-*Reichsführer* Heinrich Himmler had ambitious construction plans for Wewelsburg and the surrounding area. His architect, Hermann Bartels, had drawn up the plans. The immense scale of the project required a huge workforce of prisoners. After several inmates had been shot trying to escape, Himmler decided to use Bible Students because of their reputation as hard workers who would not try to escape. Hence, Bible Students from concentration camps all over Germany were deported to Niederhagen.[2]

On March 7, 1941, Engleitner and the other deportees were squeezed into cattle trucks wrapped in barbed wire and were taken from Buchenwald to Niederhagen concentration camp near Paderborn. At Wewelsburg, in Westphalia, Germany, his humiliation would continue for two more years.

---

[1] History: see Appendix III

[2] The camp in Wewelsburg was originally an external command post and later a subcamp of Sachsenhausen concentration camp. On September 1, 1941, it became a concentration camp in its own right. Although it was officially called Niederhagen, the prisoners always referred to it as Wewelsburg.

44: Heinrich Himmler (right) with his architect Hermann Bartels (left); behind them, the building contractor, Scherpeltz

When he arrived there, only four barracks, looking more like stables, had been completed. Engleitner was housed in Block 2 with the other Bible Students and had prisoner number 46. It quickly became apparent that his hopes for better conditions had been illusory. The Bible Students worked hard and always did their best, but they received harsh treatment in return. Oddly, the habitual criminals enjoyed the greatest respect.

Franz Wimmer and Georg Pointner worked in the carpenters' workshop. Alois Moser had many different jobs: working in the storage areas, for example. After working as a bricklayer in the camp for a while, Engleitner was assigned to the "Wewelsburg" unit, helping to build drains and cable shafts. Following that he worked for a short time in the *"Waldsiedlung"* (wood settlement) unit under the supervision of the *kapo* and habitual criminal Brosowski. This unit built houses for members of the SS and their families. His next assignment was in the *"Stabsgebäude"* (staff building) unit, whose task was the construction of a new staff headquarters beside Wewelsburg concentration camp. There he first experienced the brutality

45: Wewelsburg, with camouflage, looking west, 1944

of Max Schüller, one of the most feared *kapos* in the entire camp. Schüller wore a black triangle (asocial element) and performed the tasks entrusted to him exactly as the SS wished. He had a long criminal record and treated the prisoners under his command with unthinkable cruelty. His outbreaks of extreme violence generated fear among the other inmates. The Bible Student Friedrich Klingenberg saw such an incident:

Several prisoners had to carry bottles of wine into Wewelsburg. One of them stole a bottle. When Max Schüller discovered the theft, he beat the prisoner to a pulp before tossing him off the top of a 20-foot-high wall. The prisoner's body smashed to pieces on the stones at the bottom.

During his time in this unit, Engleitner and his fellow inmates frequently had to carry dead bodies back to the camp in the evening. Schüller sometimes threatened to beat Engleitner to death if he did not work faster. Weak as he was, Engleitner always did his best. But he could never please his brutal taskmaster. Schüller regularly beat the "Little Austrian" with a stick or aimed a kick at him with one of his heavy boots.

The prisoner Franz Renner from Salzburg saved Engleitner's life by managing to arrange his transfer to the tree-felling unit for a few weeks. Shortly after this Engleitner was assigned to the electricians' unit, supervised by Max Gartenschläger, a Bible Student. What a relief to be out from under the violent *kapos!* As the camp underwent expansion, the electricians had to erect an electric fence topped with barbed wire. While work on the fence was in progress, the electricity had to be switched off. Only the sentries posted on the lookout towers could prevent prisoners from escaping. For this reason the SS only used Bible Students for this work. The harvest units, which worked outside the camp, also consisted entirely of Bible Students. The mayor of the town of Wewelsburg had asked the camp commandant whether any of the prisoners could be spared to help the local farmers. Because he had worked as a farmhand in the past, Engleitner was often assigned to such details.

In other areas too the SS displayed great trust in the Bible Students. They were among the few detainees assigned to shave the SS men because they could be trusted with razors.

Besides the houses for members of the SS and their families, the Bible Students worked on constructing a memorial hall in honor of leading SS functionaries. It would be built in the castle's north tower. Engleitner sometimes had to carry cement up to this building site. But until the winter of 1942/43, he worked mainly with the electricians' unit. After that he was assigned to the *kapo* August Kaiser, a Bible Student, who had charge of the "Burghof" work detail, which performed various jobs in and around the castle. This gave him the opportunity to spend time with his brothers in the faith during the day.

As in Buchenwald, Bible Students in this camp had no access to their money. Their accounts remained frozen, and Engleitner had to resort to a ruse to obtain some cash. The camp senior, Willi Wilke, a Bible Student, had access to the cashbox and subscribed to the newspaper the *Westfälische Zeitung* in Engleitner's name. Since the camp commanders had no objection to this, Wilke was able to pay for the subscription from Engleitner's account, who then charged other prisoners a couple of pfennigs to read the paper. Thus Engleitner managed to collect some money to buy himself something in the canteen now and then.

Schüller the Tyrant

Although Engleitner no longer worked in Max Schüller's unit, the *kapo* took every opportunity to bully the "Little Austrian." One day Engleitner was working in the tree-felling detail in the woods nearby. The prisoners had to use ropes to pull trees out of the ground. The branches were then removed and the felled trees cut to size. Max Schüller was supervising excavations for a rifle range, but he suddenly stormed up to the tree-felling unit and began a tirade of abuse: "You lazy dogs! Can't you work any faster? I'll show you how to work properly!" To Engleitner's horror, the raging Schüller stopped right in front of him. In his fright, the Austrian dropped his tool. Schüller's eyes fell on the rain-filled holes that remained after the crew had torn out the roots of the beech tree. Grinning maliciously, he yelled at Engleitner: "Jump into that hole! Now!"

Engleitner did not want to catch cold and knew that Schüller was not in charge of his unit. So deciding to take a chance, Engleitner retorted: "No way! I'm not jumping in there!"

"Then I'll throw you in, you good-for-nothing little fool!"

"Go ahead and try," replied the undaunted Engleitner, "but I wouldn't advise it."

That was too much for the bully. Never before had a prisoner dared argue with him. As Schüller shoved Engleitner into the hole, the "Little Austrian" quickly grabbed Schüller's jacket, pulling him in as well. As the two of them splashed in the water, the grin was now on Engleitner's face.

Schüller snorted with rage, his face turning crimson. He clambered out of the hole, grabbed the broken-off handle of a shovel, and began to bludgeon Engleitner over the head with it. "I'll kill you, you treacherous dog!" he bellowed, beside himself with fury. His victim warded off the blows as best he could, shielding his head with his arms.

One of the sentries had seen what had happened and hurried over to save Engleitner from further injury. "Max! Stop it! Stop it at once!"

"Do you want to protect an enemy of the state?" snarled Schüller, turning to the sentry. "I'll report you for this!"

Hearing the commotion the other sentries came running up, and a melee of pushing, shoving, threats, and accusations ensued. Only the arrival of the captain of the guard restored some kind of order. Engleitner, shocked and badly bruised, could only thank the sentries for their timely intervention, and despite his great pain, he went back to work.

Schüller's hatred of Engleitner was now greater than ever, and he waited for a suitable opportunity to get rid of his adversary. It was not long before the two clashed again.

Engleitner was working on the fence when Max Gartenschläger received a call to do a job elsewhere. He told Engleitner to take charge of the prisoners until he returned. He asked the sentry to remind his workers to begin putting their tools away five minutes before the trumpet signaled the end of the workday. On several occasions previously the electricians had stopped work too late and had left things lying by the fence. As a result, when the current came on again in the evening, the tools caused a short-circuit, and the foreman was punished with 25 lashes. From then on, five minutes before the trumpet sounded, the sentry would order the electricians' unit to put their tools away. Engleitner and his brothers in the faith hurried to be finished in time, so that they could dash off as soon as the signal was given. When the time arrived, the sentry gave the order, but strangely, the signal did not come.

Max Schüller and his prisoners were excavating the foundations for a new prisoners' kitchen nearby. Before long he noticed that Engleitner and his group had stopped working. "Hey!" he shouted to them, "Why aren't you working?"

The undaunted Engleitner replied: "That's none of your concern, Max. See to your own men!"

Schüller was furious. Tearing off part of the fence, he charged towards Engleitner, seething with rage: "Now you're going to get it!" he yelled. "I'm going to kill you this time!" Engleitner had only one chance to save himself—he quickly retreated toward the safety zone, the area between a coil of barbed wire running along the ground and the barbed wire fence a few yards further on. Only prisoners working in the electricians' unit were allowed to enter. Any other prisoners who crossed the line would be shot by a sentry. Engleitner dashed toward the barrier and leaped into the safety zone, but Max Schüller was evidently determined not to let his adversary escape and made as if to follow him. Suddenly the voice of one of the sentries rang out from the watchtower: "Max! Stop right there, or I'll shoot!"

This warning finally brought Schüller to a standstill, and he stood cursing and foaming with rage in front of Engleitner. "Just you wait," he screamed. "I'll get you alone one day, and then no one will be able to help you!"

Just then the trumpet sounded, and Engleitner hurried back to camp with his brothers in the faith for the evening roll call. "That was a close shave," he thought to himself. But he knew that it was only a question of time until Schüller carried out his threat. From that moment on, he lived in constant fear of Schüller, and his life was all the more unbearable. The next day, Engleitner went up to the sentry who had saved his life and thanked him for intervening.

"You know what?" remarked the SS man. "I would really have liked to shoot him, but I had to warn him first. If he

46: The roll-call square at Niederhagen concentration camp, 1946/47

hadn't stopped, I'd have gladly pulled the trigger." Even the SS man knew how evil Schüller was.

On another occasion Max Schüller tormented about 100 prisoners on the roll-call square with a punishment drill. Engleitner was among them. Schüller was in his element, giving free rein to his violent temper. He made the prisoners crawl along the ground until their sleeves were in tatters and their elbows were bleeding. Then he made them stand up and lie down at double-time. Engleitner, who was in the middle of the group, could not keep up and collapsed exhausted on the ground. The others continued trying to follow Schüller's near impossible commands. Fortunately for Engleitner, Schüller did not notice him lying there.

The SS eventually rewarded Max Schüller for his brutal behavior by granting him early release from Niederhagen concentration camp. Following his release there were no more deaths in his former work detail.

The Execution

Some time later the prisoners received the order to form a semicircle around a gallows located behind the timber yard near the roll-call square. They would be forced to watch the hanging of a young man who had tried to break out of another concentration camp. The horrible sight at close range was meant to serve as a warning of what happened when prisoners tried to escape. As the noose went around the man's neck, Engleitner could not bear to look and turned his head to one side. An SS man noticed this and grabbed Engleitner's head in both hands, holding it firmly in place toward the gallows. Engleitner shut his eyes so that he would not have to look, but he could not close his ears to the dreadful sounds of the lynching.

Following the execution, the camp commandant and sadist, Adolf Haas, warned the inmates that the same fate awaited anyone who tried to escape. Engleitner was too distressed by what had just happened to hear what Haas said. It was the first time he had been present at an execution, where a young man was alive one moment and dead the next. That the SS could make a spectacle of death convinced him that it was futile to hope for fair treatment at their hands. He went to bed that night filled with deep sadness and the memory of the terrible sounds of the execution, and sleep would not come. The incident gave him nightmares for years. The constant conflict between his belief in humanity and the continual

47: Adolf Haas, camp commandant of Niederhagen concentration camp, circa 1940 (reproduction)

disappointments he suffered weighed heavily on him. Racked with uncertainty, torn between hope and fear, he carried an enormous psychological burden. Every single prisoner was completely at the mercy of the moods and whims of the SS.

A Close Call

Engleitner continued to be a conscientious worker so that no one had cause for complaint. One of the sentries found his attitude laudable and gave him the following advice: "If you carry on at that rate, you'll never make it home. You're working yourself to death!" The SS man then took Engleitner's shovel and showed him a less strenuous way to use it. He hardly moved the shovel, and the Austrian thought: "If that's the way I should work, no problem!"

During roll call one morning, the camp commandant, Adolf Haas, said: "We need more firewood. Do not come back from the woods empty-handed. From now on I want each one of you to bring a dry tree with you to use as firewood."

Engleitner took this order very seriously. After he had finished his work in the woods the next day, he went off to look for a suitable tree. After a while he found a small, dry beech. "That'll burn well," he thought. "I'll take that one."

He made his way toward the tree and was just about to uproot it when suddenly the voice of one of the sentries stopped him in his tracks. "Stop! Where do you think you're going?"

Engleitner froze. With a shock he realized that he had accidentally crossed the cordon. "I'm so sorry," he said. "I was concentrating too hard that I didn't notice where I was."

Fortunately the sentry accepted Engleitner's explanation and reminded him that he could have shot him without warning, since the crossing of the line could be considered an escape attempt. The SS man warned him to be more careful in future. Engleitner thanked the man for this act of consideration and then asked him: "What good would it have done you to shoot me?"

To Engleitner's dismay the SS man replied: "The camp commandant grants 14-days' leave to any sentry who shoots an escaping prisoner!"

This made Engleitner realize how close he had been to death. A sentry had shown a glimpse of humanity after all. Had he been wrong to lose all hope of fair treatment in the wake of the execution? Perhaps. But before long he experienced the other side of the coin again.

Murder for a Fortnight's Leave

One cool September day in 1941, Engleitner had another close call. A fellow Bible Student gave him the easy job of filling up the water tanks at the building site for the SS houses. But he reminded Engleitner that he had to ask the sentry's permission to go down to the stream, which lay on the other side of the cordon. Every time he headed down the path to the stream, Engleitner asked the SS man for permission to do so.

Eventually the man said: "You don't have to ask permission every time you cross the line. I know you're not going to run off." From then on he filled his containers without requesting permission from the friendly sentry.

The changing of the guards took place at midday, and a different sentry stood watch over the path by the stream in the afternoon. This one hoped for an opportunity to earn himself extra leave. Engleitner failed to notice the change at first. When he did, he asked: "Permission to fetch water from the stream, sir!" The SS man did not reply, and simply turned his back on him. Engleitner went round the other side where the man could see him and repeated his request: "Permission to fetch water from the stream, sir!" But again, the sentry ignored him. Engleitner was at a loss. He could not cross the line without permission, so he decided to try once more, walking over to look the sentry in the face. "Permission to fetch water from the stream, sir!" But this third attempt also failed to produce a reaction. "Well," he thought, "he obviously doesn't want me to report to him all the time either." So he picked up his bucket and began making his way down to the stream. Suddenly he heard an ominous click behind him. Someone was loading a rifle. He spun round and saw the sentry pointing his gun at him.

Dropping his bucket, he thrust his hands into the air, his mind racing. What should he do now? Was this the end?

With his finger on the trigger and the "Little Austrian" in his sights, the SS man barked: "You have crossed the sentry line without permission!"

"But I asked you three times for permission!" replied Engleitner desperately.

"You did not," replied the sentry, settling his rifle against his shoulder ready for the fatal shot. At that moment the Bible Student who had given Engleitner the job of fetching the water came running up and began remonstrating with the SS man. "I don't take orders from prisoners!" shouted the sentry, and once more adjusted his sights.

The noise alerted *Sturmführer* Rieger, an Austrian SS from Graz, who had charge of the construction workers at the site. He hurried to the scene and, although he had watched the entire incident, asked the sentry what the commotion was all about. The sentry told him his version of what had occurred, not knowing that Rieger had seen everything. He hoped that Rieger would side with him and give him permission to shoot. His superior told him: "You seem to be forgetting something. I saw with my own eyes that the prisoner did ask you for permission, and not just once, but three times. You turned your back on him every time and ignored his request. So leave him alone!"

Engleitner, his knees still shaking with fright, could hardly believe that an SS officer had just saved his life. He thanked him for his fairness and carried on with his work. But he could not stop thinking about what had just happened. "What made the sentry ignore my requests for permission? Why did he want to shoot me?" He puzzled over the man's motives for some time. Then he remembered what the sentry had told him by the beech tree. This guard wanted extra days of leave—what a reason to kill a man!

Reality had caught up with him once more. Nothing could be taken for granted.

Looking at Death

A short time later, Engleitner and some 100 other prisoners had to dig up squares of turf in a field next to the camp. As they carried the turf back on their shoulders, a Dutch prisoner made a break for it through a forest plantation. He broke ranks about five yards ahead of Engleitner and had only gone about ten yards when he was shot dead by a sentry. The other prisoners had to put their hands behind their heads and prostrate themselves on the ground. The dead body lay at the side of the road waiting to be taken into the camp by a work detail. At midday roll call, the prisoners had to file past the body. The man had been shot in the back of the head, blowing his brains out. Engleitner could not bear to look. The labor supervisor Ludwig Rehn saw him averting his gaze and pushed him right on top of the corpse. In disgust, Engleitner picked himself up again as quickly as he could, horrified at Rehn's inhuman behavior. At the same time he remembered his own experiences and how close he himself had come to death.

A few days later, Engleitner was working in the camp next to the timber yard when Rehn drove to the rifle range with two prisoners. Engleitner wondered why he had taken them with him. The rifle range could only be used for target practice. A little while later, Rehn returned to the camp and ordered Engleitner and another inmate to load two coffins onto the truck. He then drove to the rifle range again, and on his return ordered Engleitner and the other prisoner to carry the two coffins into the mortuary. Engleitner climbed onto the back of the truck, holding on to the side. As he did so he felt something warm on his hand. Looking down, he was not particularly surprised to see blood. "They've killed the prisoners at the rifle range," he thought. So now it was clear that the range was not only being used for shooting practice; men were being used as targets and were being executed there.

Courageous Individuals

Toward the end of September 1941, Engleitner went with his unit to help a local farmer bring in the potato harvest. Naturally, the sentries escorted the harvest unit to prevent escape. Each sentry was responsible for two prisoners.

The farmer was so pleased with the work and so shocked by their emaciated bodies that he said: "This afternoon my wife will give you coffee and plum cake so you can keep your strength up."

The prisoners looked forward to the snack and kept glancing eagerly toward the farmhouse in anticipation. Eventually the farmer's wife and daughter appeared carrying two baskets of plum cake and a large flask of coffee. The prisoners' mouths started watering, but one obstacle remained: the sentries.

"Come and get it!" called the farmer's wife to the prisoners. "Sit down here on the ground and eat up!"

The sentries objected. "It is strictly forbidden to give the prisoners food," they said firmly.

"Well, that's a pity," replied the farmer's wife. "I'll just have to take everything back indoors, then."

"No, no!" said the sentries. "You don't need to take it away again. Just leave it here, and we sentries will take care of it!"

"Out of the question!" retorted the farmer's wife. "If the prisoners can't have anything, you won't get anything either. Either you let the prisoners eat, or nobody eats!"

These brave words could easily have landed her in the concentration camp, but her boldness so astonished the sentries that they gave the order: "Everybody sit down and eat." The prisoners obeyed straight away, amused at the bravery of the farmer's wife. They gratefully ate the delicious cake and savored the marvelous aroma and taste of real coffee, which they had not experienced in a very long time.

Another farmer found a way to smuggle food to the starving prisoners during the potato harvest. His horse and cart, which he used to transport the potatoes, had a false bottom, and he hid sandwiches in it. "When you load the potatoes on the cart," he told the prisoners, "take a few sandwiches. But for heaven's sake, make sure the guards don't see you!"

Besides these humane and courageous civilians, several SS men also had a sense of justice and would at times intervene on behalf of the oppressed.

One day Engleitner and another prisoner had to shovel a load of coal into the cellar. As they worked, the other man constantly made fun of him on account of his faith and kept up a barrage of derogatory remarks. Among other things, he accused Engleitner of being unwilling to defend his fatherland. A guard who was watching over the two workers eventually told the man to leave Engleitner alone. But the mocking prisoner ignored the reprimand and continued harassing his colleague. At last the guard had had enough and went up to the two men. "What do you keep pestering him for?" he demanded.

"Because he's too cowardly to defend his fatherland," came the reply. "That's why he's here." Expecting the SS man to agree with him, the prisoner was surprised to hear him retort: "And you're here because you're too lazy to work!"

That brought the verbal attack to an abrupt halt, and Engleitner could work in peace.

The starving and emaciated Engleitner one day experienced another demonstration of human kindness. A guard surreptitiously slipped a piece of bread into his trouser pocket then quickly walked away.

On one occasion *Sturmführer* Rieger also came to the aid of the Bible Students. In an attempt to force them into a military unit, 26 of them were taken from Niederhagen at the beginning of 1941. A few weeks later they returned because they had refused to put on the uniform. The camp commandant, Adolf Haas, flew into a rage over their refusal to do military service. He called the foremen of the construction workers' unit to the roll-call square and said: "In four weeks' time I want to see grass growing over them!" Labor supervisor Ludwig Rehn then proceeded to make them do "sport"; he forced them to run for hours on end until their clothes were in shreds. They were then put into a "penal unit" in which they were tormented in the most cruel and savage ways imaginable.

In the woods at the top of a steep hill, houses for the SS men and their families were being built. Every day for a week a particularly vicious *kapo* forced the prisoners by means of repeated blows with a stick to run up the makeshift steps to the building site carrying sacks of cement and other building materials. Engleitner's heart ached as he watched this torture. But one afternoon *Sturmführer* Rieger stood waiting at the top of the steps until the last of the 26 prisoners had stumbled past him, gasping for breath. He then placed himself firmly on the top step, barring the way for the foreman, who was hurrying up after the others. As soon as he was within reach, Rieger smashed his fist into the foreman's face, sending him flying back down the steps.

A few days earlier the *kapo* Brosowski had ordered Engleitner: "Go join the 26 in their running. Jump to it!"

Engleitner ran over to them and started carrying the heavy building materials on the double just as they were doing. After an hour a guard noticed him and asked: "What are you doing in this group? You don't belong here!"

"Brosowski sent me here!" explained Engleitner.

Hearing this the guard took Engleitner back over to Brosowski and told him: "Look after this man, and give him a proper job!" Engleitner heaved a sigh of relief and thanked the SS man for his assistance.

All 26 Bible Students survived the appalling treatment in the "penal unit," thanks to their brothers in the faith who tended their wounds in the evenings and saved up a little food for them.

Soon there was another medical inspection for conscripting new recruits for the army. Engleitner again received a deferment on medical grounds, meaning he would be spared the fate of his 26 companions.

Growing Pressure—Differing Reactions

One prisoner, Georg Pointner, could stand the pressures of incarceration no longer and agreed to sign the declaration renouncing his faith. Prior to his release he had to appear on the roll-call square in front of all the other prisoners and answer the question put to him by the SS: "Are you still one of Jehovah's Witnesses?" He had to answer with a loud "No!" to be released.

Engleitner felt sorry for Pointner but was more determined than ever not to give up. Of course it saddened him to see a friend with whom he had endured so much now abandon his resolve. But Engleitner was determined not to budge an inch from his position. He would sooner die than give up his faith. Besides, every signature the SS wrested from a Bible Student was a major triumph, strengthening their belief that further pressure would bring this group to its knees.

Some time later Engleitner and a fellow Bible Student in the electricians' unit were discussing the Bible while digging a hole for a mast. A guard hurried over and said: "Aha! Now I've caught you! You were talking about the Bible, weren't you?"

Engleitner's companion fearfully tried to deny it, but Engleitner looked straight at the guard and said: "Of course we were. What else should we be talking about?"

This honest reply took the SS man aback, and he let Engleitner go unpunished, whereas he ordered the other man to do extra chores after evening roll call.

Get Lost!

Engleitner repeatedly cut his hands while working on the barbed wire fence. He felt constant pain from the swelling and the open gashes that would not heal because of lead poisoning. That winter, Max Gartenschläger again assigned him to dig a hole for a mast, but he could not do it—the pain was just too much. "Just look at my hands," he said to Gartenschläger. "How am I supposed to hold a shovel?"

"Yes, I see," said the foreman. "Well, you'd better come with me to the workshop. You can prepare the spools of wire instead." Engleitner followed Gartenschläger into the workshop and watched attentively as the foreman showed him how the job was done. Before leaving him alone, Gartenschläger issued him a warning: "Whatever you do, make sure no one finds you. I'm not really supposed to let you work in here. If anyone comes, hide behind this diesel engine."

The diesel engine was of paramount importance to the camp command because it supplied electricity in the event of a power failure. If power to the barbed-wire fence around the camp were cut off for any length of time, the prisoners could stage a mass breakout. Engleitner gazed at the machine for a few seconds, and then began to work. It felt good to have an inside job, away from the cold. The work was easier on his hands too. He knew where to hide should the need arise, but felt certain that there would be no visitors.

Suddenly, though, he heard the sound of approaching footsteps and voices; the commandant, Adolf Haas, was showing visitors round the camp! Engleitner dropped the wire and ducked behind the diesel engine. But of all things it was the generator that Haas wanted to show his visitors so they could see that no one could escape from his camp. As he showed the group the various parts of the engine, he noticed the prisoner cowering behind it.

"What are you doing here, you miserable wretch? Get lost!" he yelled. Engleitner rushed past him as fast as his legs could carry him. The commandant made as if to kick him, but slipped on the snow he had brought in on his shoes, falling against some uninsulated wiring. This caused a short circuit, and the lights went out.

The commandant could easily have gone up in flames, but fortunately for him and for Engleitner, he escaped with nothing worse than a shock. He even forgot to punish the prisoner with the customary whipping.

The Biter Bit

In Niederhagen concentration camp, the SS trained German-shepherd dogs to attack any prisoners who attempted to escape. The dogs also guarded large groups of detainees on external working expeditions.

The animals were supposed to attack only prisoners and to respect anyone in uniform. But two of the dogs had become progressively uncontrollable until they no longer differentiated between prisoners' clothing and that of the SS. If anyone approached their cage, the dogs would hurl themselves at the bars, growling ferociously and baring their fangs. Eventually the dog-handlers could no longer control them and refused to work with them any longer. Camp commandant Adolf Haas decided to show the SS men that there was nothing to fear. He opened the door of the cage and went inside. The dogs pounced on him, sank their teeth into his upper arm, and ripped his uniform almost to pieces. Haas saw no other way of saving his skin than to shoot his assailants, killing both of them outright.

Unimaginable Hunger

From May to August 1942, the internees in Niederhagen concentration camp suffered a drastic reduction in their food rations. The midday meal now consisted of nettle soup–nothing else. Had the cooks used younger, more succulent leaves, the soup would at least have had some nutritional value. But the soup only had large, old leaves.

The tiny portions could not fill their stomachs even temporarily, and the feeling of hunger that followed eating was even more terrible than the one before. Engleitner found the constant gnawing hunger harder and harder to bear. When the rations eventually increased again and the prisoners were given stew, it did not make much difference to Engleitner. One of the kitchen assistants told him that they only had 44 pounds of meat per day for the hundreds of prisoners. No wonder that Engleitner's bowl of "stew," only half full in any case, contained only a few strands of sinewy meat. One day he was fortunate enough to find half a pig's ear in his bowl. It took some chewing, but at least it satisfied his hunger for a time. Sometimes the desperation drove him to rummage in the bins in search of bones, which after they had been boiled, were soft enough to chew.

On one occasion camp commandant Haas canceled the rations for an entire day, alleging that a prisoner had committed some offense. Haas ordered the prisoners' rations to be fed to pigs he kept for his own use. But the *Lagerältester* made sure the cauldrons of food were hidden in the barracks, so the prisoners were secretly able to eat without Haas noticing.

The longer Engleitner's incarceration wore on, the thinner and weaker he became. He contracted scurvy. His teeth fell out. He suffered from festering boils that made every little movement intensely painful. The camp doctor prescribed a yeast cure that did the boils no good, but at least he had a little something to ease his hunger.

Singing

Whitsunday 1942 was a sunny day. After the evening roll call, the *Lagerführer* announced to the prisoners, who were all standing in line: "As today was such a beautiful day, I would like to top it off with a song from a Tyrolean. I would like to hear the song *Erzherzog Johann Jodler* (The Archduke Johann Yodel)." He waited for a prisoner to step forward to carry out his order, but none felt in the mood to sing. When it seemed that no one was going to volunteer, he lost his temper and yelled: "If somebody doesn't start singing immediately, you will spend the entire night standing here! I'll give you five more minutes, otherwise you'll stand to attention until tomorrow morning!" Engleitner's feet hurt at the thought of this punishment, but he was sure that if he started singing, the *Lagerführer* would punish him for inflicting his singing voice on him in public. He fervently hoped that someone else would volunteer.

To everyone's great relief, a man stepped forward and began to sing. He yodeled brilliantly, hitting the high notes to perfection. The *Lagerführer* was visibly pleased. When the man finished, the *Lagerführer* asked him what part of the Tyrol he was from.

The yodeller replied: "I don't come from the Tyrol. I'm from Berlin. I'm a painter and decorator by trade and have traveled about a great deal in the course of my work. So I also had the chance to learn to yodel."

Whenever the prisoners were marched out of the camp to do jobs outside, they had to sing the Wewelsburg hymn. This song had been written by prisoners in Buchenwald concentration camp, but the words were adapted for Wewelsburg.

Muselmänner

In the spring of 1942, Engleitner was one of a team of four prisoners who had to dig a large ditch for pipes that were to run under a road outside the camp.

The *Lagerführer* appeared and stood watching them. After a few minutes, he turned to the foreman and said: "You'll never get the job done using these *Muselmänner!*"

A *"Muselmann"* (plural *"Muselmänner"*) was a man whose spirit had been broken by life in the camp. The permanent hunger led to the muscles' wasting away. The pulse and respiratory rate slowed, blood pressure and temperature dropped, and the body shivered with cold. The voice became little more than a whisper, and every movement required enormous effort. Such a man could no longer lift his feet and walked with a characteristic shuffle. Everyone knew he would soon die.

Engleitner was not about to allow himself to be compared to a man at death's door. "Herr *Lagerführer,*" he said, "just you leave it to us. We'll be finished on time, don't you worry." The *Lagerführer* walked off, annoyed at this retort. But when he returned to the building site in the evening, he was surprised to see that the prisoners had indeed managed to finish the job and had even put away their tools. Turning to the foreman, he said with an approving glance in Engleitner's direction: "See to it that he gets double rations tonight."

"You've got some nerve, saying what you did!" said the foreman to Engleitner after the SS man had gone. Engleitner ate his double portion that evening with delight.

Freedom Within Reach

Toward the end of 1942, Engleitner was again assigned to a harvest unit. The small group consisted of four prisoners and two guards. A farmer needed help bringing in the potatoes, but before they could start digging, the prisoners had to cut down the shoots of the potato plants with scythes. Engleitner, an experienced farmhand, was in his element, working efficiently and rapidly. The farmer noticed the prisoner's skill and made himself comfortable at the edge of the field from where he watched the prisoners toil along with his own

"Oh Wewelsburg, ich kann dich nicht vergessen!"

1. Wenn der Tag erwacht, eh die Sonne lacht,
die Kolonnen zieh'n zu des Tages Müh'n
hinein in den grauenden Morgen,
und die Steine sind hart, aber fest unser Schritt,
und wir tragen die Picken und Spaten mit,
und im Herzen, im Herzen die Sorgen:

Oh Wewelsburg, ich kann dich nicht vergessen,

weil du mein Schicksal bist.
Wer dich vertieß, der kann es erst ermessen,
wie wundervoll die Freiheit ist.
Doch Wewelsburg, wir jammern nicht und klagen.

Und was auch unsre Zukunft sei,
wir wollen trotzdem ja zum Leben sagen,
denn einmal kommt der Tag, dann sind wir frei!

"Oh Wewelsburg, I Can't Forget You"

1. When the day breaks, before the sun smiles down
The columns trail to their daily toil,
Off into the gray dawn
Over stones that are hard, but our steps are firm
As we carry the picks and spades in our hands
And our woes in our hearts, in our hearts:

Oh Wewelsburg, I can't forget you,

Because you are my destiny.
Only who has left you can truly judge
How wonderful liberty is.
But Wewelsburg, we neither wail nor moan.

And no matter what the future brings
We will always say yes to life
For the day will come when we'll be free!

<table>
<tr><td>

2. Und der Wald ist schwarz und der Himmel rot,
und wir tragen im Brotsack ein Stückchen Brot,
und im Herzen, im Herzen die Liebe,
und die Sehnsucht brennt heiß
doch das Mädel ist fern, und der Wind weht leis,
doch ich hab' sie so gern,
wenn treu sie, wenn treu sie nur bliebe:

Oh Wewelsburg, ich kann dich nicht vergessen

3. Und die Nacht ist so kurz und der Tag ist so lang,
doch ein Lied erklingt, das die Heimat sang,
und wir lassen den Mut uns nicht rauben.
Halte Schritt, Kamerad, und verlier nicht den Mut,

denn wir tragen den Willen zum Leben im Blut,

und im Herzen, im Herzen den Glauben:

Oh Wewelsburg, ich kann dich nicht vergessen

</td><td>

2. The wood is black and the sky is red,
In our packs we carry a small piece of bread,
And love in our hearts, in our hearts,
And a powerful yearning
But my girl is so far away, and the wind sighs so low
But I love her so dearly
Oh, will she stay true, will she stay true:

Oh Wewelsburg, I can't forget you...

3. And the night is so short and the day is so long,
But a song rings out that was sung at home,
We won't be discouraged.
Keep in step, comrade, don't be down-hearted

For we have the will to live in our blood,

And faith in our hearts, in our hearts

Oh Wewelsburg, I can't forget you..."[1]

</td></tr>
</table>

[1] Kirsten John, *Mein Vater wird gesucht* (Essen, 1996), p. 85

farmhand. Usually a farmer would lend a hand in the harvest, but this one exploited the prison labor to have a lazy day. Later that evening, one of the guards told Engleitner: "You're going to be released."

"Why?" inquired the apparently fortunate man.

"The farmer has asked for you. He wants you as a farmhand."

Engleitner pondered the prospect of escaping the treadmill of horror in the camp, but he doubted that there would be no strings attached to this opportunity. Besides, he had not been very impressed with the farmer's apparent laziness. He went to bed with mixed feelings that night.

Immediately after morning roll call, he received a summons to the political wing, where a friendly-looking SS man greeted him and said: "You can be released. The farmer has asked for you. He wants you to work for him as a farmhand."

"On what condition?" Engleitner wanted to know.

As if it were the most natural thing in the world for a Bible Student to renounce his faith, the SS man pushed a piece of paper across the table toward him that bore the heading "Declaration."

"All you have to do is sign the declaration and you're a free man!" he said.

A choice between God and freedom: Engleitner had expected as much. Compromise for him was utterly out of the question. Without even stopping to read the declaration, he replied firmly: "I do not refuse the work offered me, but I refuse to sign this paper."

Not only had he passed up a chance for release, but he could have been subject to punishment for his refusal, just as he had been in Buchenwald. The SS man's eyes darkened, but he made no move to administer corporal punishment. He merely said: "Well, you'll have to stay here, then."

"Right," said Engleitner calmly, "I'll stay here." The SS

man made some notes, placed the papers into a file, and dismissed him.

Engleitner left with a clean conscience, as determined as ever to remain faithful to his Creator. He would take no easy way out.

Blind Faith

A short time after that, another farmer asked the camp administration for prisoners to help him bring in the turnip harvest. Engleitner and three other Bible Students were chosen for this harvest unit, which had two guards.

The two SS men had spent the previous night drinking, and it showed. They asked the prisoners, who had already worked in several harvest units, whether the camp commandant normally sent out patrols to check up on the external work units. "Of course!" they answered, realizing immediately the reason for the question.

"We didn't get to bed until four o'clock this morning," explained one of the guards.

"If you decide to take a nap, we won't run away," one of the prisoners assured them. "If we see any other SS men coming from the camp, we'll wake you. They always come by bike, so you'll have plenty of time."

The guards knew that they could end up as camp inmates themselves if the prisoners did not keep their word. But they decided to trust the Bible Students' reputation for honesty and made themselves comfortable in a bed of clover in a barn, laying their rifles next to them. This was most extraordinary— the prisoners harvested turnips and kept watch over the slumbering guards! The SS men slept through the afternoon. When the prisoners had finished their work, they roused the two guards. Refreshed, pleased, and grateful, the SS men accompanied them back to the camp. Engleitner was sure that he would get no ill treatment from either of those two. But it came from another quarter.

A Vicious Kick

Engleitner received another assignment outside the camp. He and two other Bible Students had to pack tools at Wewelsburg railway station. Because their guard had to leave them early, the three prisoners had to join up with another group for the march back to the camp. But the men in that unit marched so fast that Engleitner fell a little behind. One of the guards noticed this. Without warning he came up behind Engleitner and angrily kicked him between the legs with his heavy jackboot. Engleitner doubled up in pain, writhing on the ground. He had to be carried to the camp and onto the roll-call square by the other prisoners. During the evening roll call, he could not stand, so the others laid him on the ground and afterward carried him to bed. The brutal guard had crushed one of Engleitner's testicles, causing him agonizing pain for a long time to come. He still had to report to work the next day as usual and was not even allowed to have his injury seen to by the camp doctor.

The Face of Death

Ever since the start of the Russian campaign,[1] it became common knowledge among the prisoners that hangings regularly took place in the bunker area of Niederhagen. The victims were Russian partisans and forced laborers, including three women. The SS went so far as to hang a 15-year-old Jewish boy, Günther Ransenberg, for alleged "illicit relations with an Aryan." During a snowball fight the boy had hit the daughter of a high-ranking SS official.[2]

One day Engleitner and several other prisoners were ordered to carry coffins to the bunkers, which were surrounded by a high wall. On the other side of the wall they saw a long gallows from which four bodies in civilian clothing were still

---

[1] June 28, 1941: Operation Barbarossa
[2] Kirsten John, *Mein Vater wird gesucht* (Essen, 1996), pp. 103-6

48: The bunker building with Belgian military vehicles, 1946/47

hanging. The *Rapportführer* Josef Kuhn shouted impatiently at the prisoners to get a move on or they would be hanged as well.

Engleitner was crossing the square one day when he came across a dying prisoner lying on the ground. At that moment labor supervisor Ludwig Rehn happened to pass by. Glancing distastefully at the figure on the ground, he said to Engleitner in irritated tones: "What's he lying here for? Take him away!"

Engleitner carried the still groaning fellow inmate to the sickbay. When he went in, however, the officer on duty barked: "What are you bringing him in here for? He's already dead! Take him to the mortuary at once."

Some time later Engleitner was working on the fence when Rehn came up to him. He took the rope the Bible Students used with their pulley and disappeared with it towards the bunker area. A few minutes later, the screams of agony from the bunker made it plain to Engleitner that another victim had been hanged.

The increasing number of executions eventually led the camp administration to build the camp's own crematorium; there were now so many corpses that the local funeral parlors could no longer dispose of them without arousing suspicion.

At the beginning of November 1942, Engleitner was one of about 100 prisoners assigned the task of putting potatoes into winter storage. The potatoes, which were grown to feed the prisoners, came from the garden next to the crematorium. The potatoes were to be stored in a hole in the ground, about 20 inches deep and lined with straw. Engleitner and the others had to dig this hole, put the potatoes in the straw, and then cover them with earth again. The job took them all day. For once the SS did not supervise them.

The majority of the prisoners took advantage of this "freedom" to eat some of the potatoes. Engleitner did not eat any, but he noticed that the prisoners had roasted the potatoes and he wondered how they had done it. Just then the crematorium assistant, a fellow prisoner, came out of the building. Seeing the pensive Engleitner, he said: "If you want to know what the others are doing, go in and see for yourself." Engleitner hesitated at first, but curiosity got the best of him. Inside he saw the starving prisoners putting potatoes next to the naked corpses that were covered in ulcers and purulent boils. He felt sick at the sight and the pungent smell that pervaded the room.

The crematorium assistant showed Engleitner how the bodies were cremated. He closed the door of the oven then flicked a switch to turn it on. With a loud blowing noise, the oven heated up. After only a few minutes, the process was over. The body had been reduced to a pile of snow-white bones. He then removed the tray from the oven and tipped the bones into an iron tub that already contained many others. Next he took an iron rod and ground all of the bones into a powdery

49: The crematorium, post-war

mass. The urns were then filled indiscriminately with the combined remains. Another prisoner, Oskar Krieg, engraved the names of the deceased onto the urns, which were then sent to the relatives—in return for a fee, of course. So it was that Engleitner discovered that the urns sent to the relatives did not contain the ashes of their loved ones. "The SS do not even respect the dead and deceives the bereaved families," he thought to himself.

In the evening two SS ordered Engleitner and four other "Aryan" prisoners to search the others for stolen potatoes. Engleitner carried out the task halfheartedly, not wanting to see anyone punished. But while he found nothing, the other four searchers did. Engleitner expected to be disciplined for his show of mercy. But in a surprise move, the SS then searched the four others and found their pockets also stuffed with potatoes. Without frisking Engleitner, the guards sent him and the others back to camp without punishment, presumably feeling that the prisoners were harming themselves.

A Trick Question?

In the winter of 1942/43, Engleitner was shoveling snow on the roll-call square when he was summoned to the guardroom. There an SS man gave him two pairs of warm, knee-length felt boots and told him to take them to one of the lookout towers. Engleitner only had a pair of wooden clogs that offered little protection against the cold. He looked at the boots enviously and went to the lookout tower. Standing at the bottom, he called up to the guards: "I've got two pairs of boots for you. I'm putting them by the steps."

As a prisoner he was not allowed to climb up a lookout tower. The only prisoner permitted to do that was the Bible Student Joachim Escher, whose job it was to keep the towers clean and take the guards their meals.

50: Joachim Escher, 1935

51: A lookout tower at Niederhagen concentration camp, circa 1947

Despite this, the guards called down to him: "Bring them up! We can't come down."

So he tied the boots together, slung them over his shoulder, and climbed up the steps, feeling uneasy because he knew the rules and wondered what ulterior motives the guards might have. At the top of the tower, he handed the boots to the guards, who thanked him. Unexpectedly, one of them said: "Tell us something about the Bible. When is Armageddon[1] coming?"

Engleitner could not believe his ears. Here was an SS man not only asking him about the Bible but also using a word that showed some knowledge of it! Was it a trick to get him talking about the Bible, which was forbidden? What should he do? On the one hand, he did not want to provoke the guard by refusing to answer him. On the other hand, answering the question posed a real danger too. He decided to keep his answer short. But the guard wanted more information.

Engleitner explained: "The Bible says that only God knows the day and the hour."

The SS man then sent the "Little Austrian" away again. Engleitner could only wait and see whether he would be reported and whether he would receive a punishment. But nothing of the kind happened.

Spies?

Some time later Engleitner and another Bible Student had to do some electrical wiring in the attic of the camp command office, directly over the office belonging to Adolf Haas, the feared camp commandant.

Suddenly the two prisoners were hauled down from the attic by the *Rapportführer* Josef Kuhn. The commandant had been hearing suspicious noises coming from above, and he sent Kuhn to investigate. Kuhn marched them into Haas' office,

---

[1] In the Bible, Armageddon is described as being God's day of judgment.

where the commandant bellowed at them: "You're spies, aren't you? *Rapportführer,* give them six lashes each. At once!"

Engleitner was given no chance to defend himself and fully expected the aggressive *Rapportführer* to carry out the unfair punishment without delay. But the *Rapportführer* said: "Get back to work. Perhaps the commandant will forget about it."

Why would the commandant have assumed that they were spies? Perhaps, he thought, he feared that the two Bible Students had seen his aerial in the attic and concluded that he had been listening to prohibited foreign radio broadcasts.

Before midday roll call, Kuhn said to Engleitner's block senior: "Tell those two prisoners not to step forward at roll call of their own accord. It could be that the commandant has already forgotten the incident."

Roll call was duly taken, and the camp commandant made no move to order the two to step forward out of the line. Engleitner was beginning to feel that Haas really had forgotten about the punishment. At the end of the roll call, the *Rapportführer* reported the number of prisoners to the commandant, and everyone waited for the order to dismiss.

52: Whipping stool, reproduction

But to Engleitner's dismay, Haas shouted: "Where are those two criminals from this morning? Step forward!"

"So we're going to be whipped after all," thought Engleitner, bowing his head dejectedly. But as he stepped forward in his oversize clogs, he tripped and fell flat on his face right at the commandant's feet. Haas burst out laughing and could hardly stop. The prisoners found it highly amusing too. Haas eventually managed to regain his composure and said, still chuckling: "Dismiss!"

That afternoon *Rapportführer* Kuhn said to Engleitner and the other Bible Student: "If it hadn't been for me, your backsides would be black and blue by now."

"No, Herr *Rapportführer,*" replied Engleitner. "It was my oversize clogs that saved us!"

A Terrible Ritual—Reallocation

On one icy winter's day, Engleitner had to install wiring for electric lighting under the roof of the washroom in the sickbay. From there, he saw two naked Bible Students being hosed down with cold water. One of the two was already coughing up blood because of a bad case of pneumonia. He died the next day. Engleitner told the other Bible Students what he had seen. This got back to the prisoner who had ordered the hosing, and he threatened Engleitner with the same fate if he spread such stories again.

It was not unusual for malicious SS men and *kapos* to force prisoners to jump into the water reservoir near the roll-call square when the weather turned cold. If a prisoner refused to jump in, he was thrown in. The tormentors took twisted pleasure in watching the shivering victim. Labor supervisor Ludwig Rehn and the *kapo* Brosowski were two of the ringleaders of this vindictive ritual.

That winter, camp commandant Haas had all the prisoners in Niederhagen concentration camp line up on the roll-call square. He announced: "It has come to my attention that fewer Bible Students die than any other group of prisoners. Only one Bible Student dies each month,[1] whereas in the other groups it's more than 20 a week."[2] Haas then added: "This only goes to prove that conditions in our camp are not so bad after all. So I have decided to reorganize the groups. The 'Bible mites' will no longer form a group on their own but will be divided up among the other groups. I am convinced that in this way fewer will die."

These words shocked Engleitner. He well knew what conditions were like in many of the other blocks. He had often witnessed the thievery and fighting himself. Engleitner went to Block 9 with about fifty other prisoners, and it was not long before he experienced unpleasantness from his new roommates.

He had managed to save a morsel of the evening meal and had hidden it under his pillow to go with his coffee the next morning. Before going to bed, he had to go to the toilet. By the time he came back, his piece of bread had disappeared. And his brothers in the faith suffered far worse things. One Bible Student, for instance, was petrified of going back into his block at night. The room orderly stole everything he could lay his hands on and blamed other prisoners, who he then proceeded to beat up.

Table Senior

The reorganization of the prisoners brought Engleitner a position of responsibility from the camp administration. He became *Tischältester* (table senior) of tables One and Two. As such he had to make sure that 19 Russian detainees kept their day room neat and tidy and did not steal food from each other.

---

[1] According to the report made by the former *Lagerschreiber* (camp secretary), Ewald Wettin Müller, also a Witness, only 19 of them died during their entire time in Niederhagen. This has been attributed to the strength they drew from their faith and the great care and support they gave each other.

[2] 385 deaths in the fourth quarter of 1942

53: Prisoners' barracks in Niederhagen concentration camp, postwar

Once he caught one of them stealing bread from a prisoner who had bent down to tie his shoelaces. Engleitner could have ordered punishment, but he simply had the thief stand in a corner until all the others had finished eating. Then he allowed the man to carry on with his meal. Engleitner did not resort to tyranny, because he did not want to make anyone's life harder than it was already, and he knew that the stealing was an attempt to satisfy the terrible hunger everyone felt.

The other prisoners tried to take advantage of his good-naturedness. Every time the 19 came back from work, their boots were covered in dirt. It was Engleitner's responsibility to see that the boots were clean for the next day's work. So every day he reminded them to clean their boots, even saying it in Russian *("Patinki viemiet!"*[1]) so there could be no misunderstandings. Despite this they pretended not to understand him and shoved their dirty boots on their lockers. Engleitner wanted to avoid any complaint about the conditions

---

[1] "Wash your boots."

in his day room and therefore cleaned all the boots himself. He did this until one evening the orderly said to him: "There's a block inspection tonight, did you know that? Make sure everything's shipshape."

"That suits me fine," replied Engleitner.

"Now, now," said the orderly. "Don't do anything stupid."

"You should've helped me before," retorted Engleitner, "but you didn't. You just stood and watched me cleaning the Russians' boots for a fortnight. I know what I'm doing."

That evening he did not clean the boots and went to bed earlier than usual. Suddenly he heard the sound of loud footsteps. The SS men had arrived to carry out their inspection, stamping on the floorboards with their heavy boots to intimidate the prisoners. The *Blockführer* could not fail to notice how dirty and untidy the men were and yelled: "Where is the table senior of tables One and Two?"

Engleitner knew that he was in for a rough ride, but he saw no other way to remedy the situation. He got out of bed and went to the connecting door between the dormitory and the day room. As soon as he poked his head through the doorway, he was greeted by a rain of blows from a stick. "Why haven't these boots been cleaned?" yelled the block captain.

Engleitner, his head spinning from the onslaught, began to explain: "Herr *Blockführer,* I tell them every day to clean their boots, but they pretend not to understand me. So every evening for the past two weeks I've cleaned all the boots myself. Today the orderly told me that you were coming, so I purposely didn't clean them."

This candid explanation placated the SS man. The men were beaten and ordered to clean their boots themselves in the future, or there would be more penalties.

Despite the beating he had received, Engleitner was glad not to have to do this dirty work anymore. He was also relieved of his position as table senior on the grounds that he could not exercise authority. He should have beaten the disobedient prisoners, something he would never have dreamed of doing.

Under the new table senior, things changed. He had the men show him their boots every evening after they had cleaned them. If he was not satisfied, he sent them away to do it again.

In April 1943, the SS closed down Niederhagen concentration camp. All the prisoners except for 42 men with special skills were transferred to other concentration camps. Before their deportation, every single detainee had to submit to a medical examination. Those in need of "convalescence" went to Dachau, where they were used as human guinea pigs for medical experiments, a sure death sentence. A few prisoners, including Wolfgang Mattischek, were sent to Buchenwald. Together with fellow Bible Students Franz Wimmer and Alois Moser and 200 other internees, Leopold Engleitner found himself on the way to Ravensbrück concentration camp.

RAVENSBRÜCK
CONCENTRATION CAMP[1]

In the spring of 1943, Engleitner was taken by train from
Wewelsburg to Ravensbrück, near Fürstenberg, Germany.

Ravensbrück concentration camp was originally built for
women prisoners who performed heavy manual labor in the
workshops there. Rosalia Hahn, who had been arrested along
with Engleitner in Bad Ischl in 1939, died there in 1942. From
1941 onward, the camp was enlarged to accommodate male
detainees in new barracks next to the existing buildings.
Horrific conditions prevailed in these new blocks.

Engleitner had prisoner number 3523. He slept in the
Bible Students' block, and was assigned to the construction
detail. He had seen many terrible things during his internment,
but what he experienced here exceeded his worst fears. The
overcrowded conditions left the new prisoners with nowhere
to sit. They had to eat their watery soup standing outside in
front of the barracks, whatever the weather. Engleitner's whole
body had been covered in festering ulcers for months. The
jostling of the crowd caused him great pain.

One time he lost his spoon and had to carve a makeshift
spoon from a piece of wood using broken glass. Later a fellow

---

[1] History: see Appendix IV

54: View of part of the barracks in Ravensbrück women's concentration camp, 1940/41. Taken from the SS propaganda book

Bible Student, who worked in the metalworking shop, forged him a new spoon out of a piece of iron. It was permanently rusty, but better than his wooden one, and Engleitner always carried it with him. His bowl broke as well, forcing him to eat his stew out of a cardboard box; most of the stew dripped out.

In Buchenwald and Wewelsburg, the Bible Students had been able to keep themselves scrupulously clean and had thus avoided being plagued by lice and other parasites. But conditions in Ravensbrück made cleanliness impossible; their clothes were threadbare and permanently dirty. Blood and pus stains could no longer be washed out of them. In the other concentration camps, they had been able to change clothes once a week, but here they were given clean uniforms only every two to three weeks. Nevertheless, the Bible Students did their best, washing their clothes themselves in the cold water in the washroom whenever the weather allowed. But this did not kill the lice. The bodies of many prisoners were completely covered with bites.

While Engleitner was working in the construction unit, he
noticed a prisoner who seemed to be in unusually good physical
condition. "I don't suppose he's been here very long," he
thought. One day he overheard a truck driver, who recognized
the prisoner as a former guard, ask him: "What are you doing
in with the prisoners?"

"I was caught giving a prisoner a piece of bread," answered
the former guard, "so they've put me in the concentration camp
as well."

The terrible hunger of the prisoners made for hostility among
them that was worse than that from the SS. The Bible
Students often bore the brunt of the harassment because other
prisoners feared that their good reputation would earn them
privileges from the SS. Prisoners took every opportunity to
harry and bait the Bible Students. They put gravel and dirt
in the Bible Students' lockers. Spiteful *kapos* forced Engleitner
and his brothers in the faith to do extra chores every evening
as punishment for imaginary offenses. These things often
occurred without the knowledge of the SS, making it seem
to Engleitner that it was the prisoners who really ran the
camp, and one day they played a mean trick on him.

Spiteful Prisoners

During the morning roll call on Whitsunday 1943, all the
prisoners at Ravensbrück were told that they would not have
to do any work that day. Instead, they were to wash their dirty
uniforms and hang them up to dry. In addition, everyone had
to stay in bed until four o'clock that afternoon, and no one
would be allowed to leave the barracks before then. Accordingly,
Engleitner set about washing his jacket and his new trousers,
which he then hung on the clothesline to dry, just as the other
prisoners had done. He then returned to his barracks and slept

until four o'clock. But when Engleitner and the other prisoners went to collect their now clean and dry uniforms, he could not find his trousers. Evidently they had been stolen. Engleitner went straight to the room orderly and reported the loss. Instead of receiving another pair, he was given a hefty whack to his head and was sent back to his block.

What on earth was he to do now? In a few minutes, he would have to appear for roll call. He explained his predicament to his brothers in the faith who advised him to line up in his underpants. Engleitner hesitated to do this, however, because he had heard about an SS man who had been given fourteen days' detention simply because the band of his underwear showed above his trousers. What, then, would they do to a half-naked prisoner?

In the end, though, he had no other choice. The other Witnesses tried to encourage him, saying: "Don't worry, Poidl. We'll put you in the second row. Maybe the *Rapportführer* won't even notice."

He stood in his underpants, nervously awaiting the start of the roll call. Several prisoners had a good laugh at his expense. When the camp commandant appeared, their laughter died away. Engleitner's heart sank. Today of all days the camp commandant would take the roll call personally! This occurred because of a shortage of guards in the camp on this public holiday.

"Oh no. That's all I need!" thought Engleitner. "Why today? If he sees me, there'll be big trouble."

Engleitner became more nervous as the count proceeded. The commandant went along the rows of men, sternly scrutinizing each one from head to toe. He then noticed the "Little Austrian" standing there with no trousers.

"What's this?" he bellowed. "Come on out! What do you think you're doing, standing there in your underpants?"

Engleitner stepped forward and explained: "Someone stole my trousers, Herr *Kommandant*. I washed them and hung them up, as ordered, and when I went to fetch them this afternoon, they were gone!"

The commandant, who obviously found the prisoner's appearance quite comical, asked him: "Why didn't you report it to the room orderly?"

"I did!" replied Engleitner. "He just boxed my ears."

The camp commandant had the room orderly step forward, slapped him in the face in front of the assembled prisoners, and barked: "When I order the clothes to be cleaned, I expect it be done without things like this happening! Is that clear? If this prisoner's trousers have not turned up by tomorrow morning, there will be no food for the whole camp for the entire day! I hope I have made myself clear."

Engleitner was thankful that the commandant had personally expressed his disapproval of such a mean trick and had not punished him. The next day, Engleitner's trousers were once again hanging on the clothesline. But they were wet, and his number and purple triangle had been torn off.

A Life in Agriculture

In the last week of June 1943, Engleitner labored in the pine forest bordering the camp. The prisoners had to march several miles every day to and from their place of work. They had been told that a housing estate would be built there for families from Berlin who had lost their homes in the war. The woods had therefore already been cleared, and the prisoners were busy excavating the foundations. Engleitner had been assigned a particular plot, which he was working on together with Paul Jeschke, a fellow Bible Student. They had worked together in the electricians' unit in Wewelsburg.

The two men found a tangle of roots in the soil, making it extremely difficult to dig down very far. They toiled away with their spades, trying to remove the roots at the same time. But progress was slow. Engleitner said to Jeschke: "Look how much the others have done! We're miles behind already. If we get further behind, we'll have to do extra chores as a punishment. Let's go get a pickax from the warehouseman so we can cut through the roots." Although Jeschke was bigger and stronger than Engleitner, he was afraid of the aggressive warehouseman.

So the "Little Austrian" went himself, preparing himself for some rough treatment. When he reached the shed, however, he was surprised to be greeted by a friendly face and the words: "Go on in!"

Engleitner obeyed and went into the toolshed, wondering what was going to happen next. "Are you hungry?" asked the warehouseman.

"Who isn't?" replied Engleitner. "But I've only come for a pickax."

"Here's a bowl of stew," answered the other, placing a steaming portion on the table. "Sit down and enjoy it!"

Engleitner, taken completely by surprise, did as he was told, even though he had to get back to work as quickly as possible. Watching him eat, the warehouseman said: "You could've gone home a long time ago, you know that?"

"Oh, I know!" replied Engleitner. "I hear that every day. They offered to release me when I was in Wewelsburg, but I refused to sign the declaration. I won't sign it here either. May I have the pickax? I have to get back to work."

The warehouseman was not to be put off so easily. "You don't need to sign the declaration. All you have to do to get released is promise to work in agriculture."

This seemed too good to be true, and the "Little Austrian" was skeptical. "If that's true, the camp commandant will tell me, and not you," he said. Then he took the tool he had come for and returned to work. He had only gone a few paces when he heard a voice call out: "Prisoner number 3523 to the guardroom immediately!"

Engleitner's heart skipped a beat. "That's my number!" he thought. He turned on his heels at once and made for the

guardroom. "Was the warehouseman telling the truth?" he
wondered as he hurried along, "or did he play a trick on me?
Will they punish me now for eating that stew?"

He entered the guardroom with no idea what lay in store
for him. But then he overheard two Bible Students in front of
him refusing to sign the declaration. He was now sure that he
would be confronted with that wearisome topic again.
Engleitner was just about to tell the SS man to save himself
the trouble when the guard said: "You're being released."

"But you know that I will never sign the declaration," he
replied firmly.

"I know that," said the SS man. "Let me finish. You need
only agree to work in agriculture for the rest of your life."

Now Engleitner had to think very carefully. "I can't see
any objection," he reflected. "I can live with having to spend
the rest of my life working in agriculture. Besides, rejecting
this offer would be virtually the same as refusing to work. I
can't reject something that doesn't conflict with my beliefs."

Engleitner said: "If it's how the warehouseman told me it
is, I have no objection. And if I don't have to sign the
declaration, I am willing to accept this offer."

"It is exactly as the warehouseman said," confirmed the
SS man. "However," he continued in threatening tones and
with a reference to Wewelsburg, "if you don't sign this offer
either, you've had it!"

"I have nothing against work," explained Engleitner. The
SS man placed a piece of paper on the table in from of him
and said: "Good! Write your first name and your surname
here."

Engleitner wrote his name where the SS man indicated
and went back to work. As he walked along, many thoughts
raced through his head. "Am I really going to be released? Are
the horror, the hunger, the humiliation really over? Will the
suffering, the pain, and the fear soon to be things of the past?
If so, I could go home to my family and friends! I would see
them again! I would have survived this madness and still have

remained true to my faith! I would be free again! Freedom—
how lovely the word sounds! But after more than four years of
incarceration, I'm not sure I still know what it really means.
What if I've been deceived and it was all a cruel joke? Maybe I
just dreamed it!"

When he arrived back at the pine forest, he told Paul
Jeschke what had just happened. Jeschke, too, was skeptical,
and did not think things could change as easily as that. It took
some considerable time before they received confirmation.

Subcamp Comthurey

Several miles outside the main camp at Ravensbrück stood
the subcamp Comthurey, which was on the farm belonging
to the head of the *Wirtschafts-Verwaltungshauptamt*
(Central Office for Economy and Administration), SS
Obergruppenführer[1] Oswald Pohl. At first all categories of
prisoner were held there except Bible Students, but this
arrangement led to enormous difficulties. The prisoners joined
forces with the SS to carry out raids on neighboring farms,
even stealing and slaughtering lambs for meat. They would
then tie the skins together, weigh them down, and throw them
into a nearby pond. When the camp administration found
out about this, it decided to reorganize the camp and have
only Bible Students on this large area of meadows surrounded
by woods. One of the first things the Bible Students had to do
after their arrival was to dive for the sheepskins and try to fish
them out.

Engleitner was transferred there, causing him to doubt
the promises of release made by the SS. The Bible Students
had to build garages and erect fences around enclosures for
cows and pigs. Women Bible Students were also held there,
working principally in the stables and gardens. In the evenings,
when the day's work was done, the men did not have to return

---

[1] Equivalent to Lieutenant General

to the camp but spent the night in caravans. The quality and quantity of food improved markedly, which did Engleitner a lot of good. There was only one SS man on guard, and after a while he came to trust the Bible Students so much that he even allowed them to move around freely during the day. On Sundays they could wander into the woods unsupervised to pick bilberries. Engleitner, who usually stayed in the camp to keep an eye on things, did not go without.

One day a group of prisoners arrived that included Alois Moser and a political prisoner. When the camp commandant found out, he was furious and yelled at the guard responsible: "I don't want any politicals here! How many more times do I have to say that I'll only tolerate 'Bible mites'!"

55: Alois Moser, 1945

RELEASE

In the afternoon of July 15, 1943, two SS men arrived at the subcamp Comthurey in a truck. They found Engleitner and said: "Come on! We've got to take you to the main camp for the release formalities."

Engleitner climbed into the back of the truck and they drove off. "So I really am going to be released!" he thought as they jolted along.

The first of the formalities was a visit to the camp doctor. Engleitner had to undress and present himself stark naked to the medical man, who remarked on seeing him: "Wait a minute. You're still one of those Jehovah's Witnesses, aren't you?"

Without a second's hesitation, Engleitner responded: *"Jawohl,* Herr *Hauptsturmführer,*[1] "deliberately using the doctor's official title to butter him up a bit.

"We can't release you, then, can we?" replied the doctor.

"I wouldn't know about that," said Engleitner. "That's your responsibility."

The doctor stared at him a moment and remarked: "Still, we'll be glad to be rid of such a wretched creature as you." He then told the medical orderlies to put plasters on the prisoner's boils and ulcers.

---

[1] Equivalent to Captain

Although Engleitner found the description "wretched creature" insulting, he could not deny that he was in terrible health. From head to toe he was covered with lice bites and festering ulcers, and one of his testicles had been crushed. After forty-six months of permanent hunger and hard labor, he was nothing but skin and bones. His weight had dropped to less than sixty-five pounds!

Following this makeshift medical treatment, he was taken to the orderly room and given his civilian clothes. He was just about to put on his shirt when one of the SS men barked: "That's a prisoners' shirt. That stays here."

"Now you even want the shirt off my back?" asked the exasperated Engleitner. "Look. I've embroidered my name in here. Is that proof enough that it belongs to me?"

After the SS man had inspected the garment and satisfied himself as to its rightful owner, Engleitner finished dressing. He was then given the money from his account.

Two young SS privates began to make fun of him, and threatened: "We'll have to chase this dog through the sentry line!"

An *Oberscharführer*[1] put a stop to the abuse. "Leave him alone, you two," he said. "He's going home today." This was the last potentially dangerous situation Leopold Engleitner experienced in a concentration camp. If he really had been chased through the sentry line, he would likely have been shot as an escaping prisoner. The secretary gave Engleitner a piece of paper containing the last order he had to carry out: "Report to the office of the Gestapo in Linz, Langgasse 13, Room 13, at 1600 hours on July 16, 1943." Clutching this piece of paper, he went into the day room in the barracks one last time to clear out his locker. An inmate passing by hit him in the face. Engleitner had no idea why. It would be the last time he received a blow in a concentration camp.

An SS man then led him out of the camp. "You can count yourself lucky that you've escaped from this hell," said the officer on the way out. The officer stopped a passing prison

---

[1] Equivalent to Staff Sergeant

truck and asked the driver to take them to the railway station. Engleitner had to climb into one of the cells in the back, and they set off. At the station the SS man bought him his ticket and even accompanied him into the carriage. Before departing he warned Engleitner sternly not to look out of the window. Of course, the warning only made him curious. So as soon as the SS man had gone, he peered cautiously out. What he saw was a small group of Bible Students in civilian clothing, some of whom were personally known to him from Buchenwald and Wewelsburg, being loaded into prison trucks.

The train moved off, and Engleitner began to roll homeward. But he simply could not believe that he was free. He glanced continually about him to see whether a guard might be watching him. After the long years of oppression and incarceration, it felt strange to be able to move freely. The humiliation he had suffered in the concentration camps had become so ingrained in his mind that freedom felt entirely foreign to him.

The important thing now was not to make any mistakes changing trains because his timetable had been worked out to the minute. Woe betide him if he did not get to Linz on time! Approaching Berlin he became anxious because a fellow passenger, a soldier from the Tyrol, had told him that the train would not actually enter the city but would stop on the outskirts. How was he supposed to find Anhalt station, from which his next train left, in this sprawling, unfamiliar metropolis? The Tyrolean, who thought he recognized Engleitner from his visits to Bad Ischl, introduced him to a soldier from Leipzig who knew his way around. After Engleitner agreed to help him carry his heavy cases, the soldier took him via the underground to his connecting train.

There was another stop in Nuremberg. By this time Engleitner was really hungry, so he went to the dining car and asked for a meal, even though he did not have any coupons.

The waitress said she would have to see if there was anything
left over. One of the passengers had ordered a meal and then
not eaten it. Engleitner was therefore able to buy it and at
least take the edge off his enormous hunger.

"Guten Tag!" instead of *"Heil Hitler!"*

The rest of the journey passed without incident. On Friday,
July 16, 1943, at four o'clock in the afternoon, he arrived at
the much-feared Gestapo office at Langgasse 13, the very place
where he had been interrogated on April 5, 1939, more than
four years earlier. He knew that the Nazi salute could present
a problem, but was absolutely determined not to perform it,
come what may. So he entered Room 13 with a loud and
cheerful *"Guten Tag!"*

The officer on duty was evidently taken off guard and
automatically returned the greeting, forgetting that he should
have said *"Heil Hitler!"* Six Gestapo officers then entered the
room, registering his presence there with obvious surprise.
However, they quickly regained their composure and remarked:
"Oh, it's old Engleitner," as if they had been expecting him.

One of the policemen turned to him with the air of a
haughty schoolmaster about to impart some pearl of wisdom
to one of his pupils. "Well, well, Engleitner," he said, "the
only thing that counts is the . . ."

Engleitner interrupted before the policeman could say the
words "Hitler regime." "Strange. Abraham was promised
something else."

"What? Don't give me that rubbish about that wretched
Jew!" shouted the Gestapo man.

"But, gentlemen," answered Engleitner, "Abraham wasn't
a Jew. Remember that he came from what is now Iraq. He was
an 'Arab.'" This calmed things down, since the Nazis were great
admirers of the Arabs, as Engleitner well knew.

He continued: "The term "Jew" only came into use after
Abraham's great-grandson Judah. His descendants were called
Jews."

One of the men remarked: "See, you have to ask a 'Bible mite' to find out things like that."

"Give him here!" said another, obviously less impressed by Engleitner's explanation. "I'll give him a good thrashing. That'll shut him up."

"No you won't," objected the others. "We don't want any of that here!"

Engleitner was relieved to be spared another beating but could not help thinking that the Gestapo's last remark was a sheer mockery, bearing in mind the methods of interrogation he had experienced himself in this very place on April 5, 1939. He well remembered the resounding blow that Alois Moser had been dealt. As the atmosphere became tense and aggressive, Engleitner had to listen to more threats: "If you think you've been released so that you can go back and resume your Jehovah's Witness underground activity, you've got another think coming! We had better not catch you preaching. We'll be watching you all the time."

But now Engleitner had had enough: "Well, if you don't like what I do, you can always send me straight back to where I've just come from!"

This daring reply could have been his undoing, since it made it perfectly clear that he had not budged an inch from his convictions and had practically told them that he was prepared to return to the concentration camp of his own free will. It could quite easily have landed him in very hot water again. But fortunately one of the SS men defused the situation by saying: "All right, everybody. Calm down!"

Engleitner started to pick up his release certificate, which had been lying on the table the whole time, but one of the men stopped him. Engleitner said: "I need that. How else am I to prove that I've been released?"

"Just say that we know all about it. We'll help you if you encounter any difficulties."

"No, that won't do. What if you're not working here anymore? Then nobody will know anything about it. I can't leave without that certificate!"

"My God, you're stubborn," groaned the SS man. "All right. Take it and go!"

Engleitner picked up the release certificate (see 56 and 57) and made for the door.

The Gestapo officer who had greeted him wanted one more chance to expound the merits of the Nazi regime. However, he was interrupted by the man who had just given Engleitner his release certificate. "Forget it!" he said. "If four years in a concentration camp have had no effect, you're hardly going to be able to change his mind in five minutes. Besides, if he doesn't hurry up he'll miss his train from Ischl to Aigen-Voglhub; the last one goes at seven, and if he misses it he'll have to walk."

Engleitner went to the door and took his leave, not with the Nazi salute, but with a friendly *"Auf Wiedersehen!"* The Gestapo man who had just tried to persuade him to embrace National Socialism forgot his duty again, and responded: *"Auf Wiedersehen!"* Engleitner had already closed the door behind him when the man suddenly leaped up, jerked open the door, and shouted down the corridor at the departing figure: *"Heil Hitler!"*

But Engleitner was hurrying to the station and did not answer.

Coming Home

As the train moved along from Linz to Bad Ischl, Engleitner watched the countryside flash by and reflected on all the suffering he had seen and endured, but he was now determined to leave this horror behind. He simply could not believe that he had been released despite his defiant attitude. It all seemed so unreal; how long would his freedom last? It was not until the mountains of his home came into view, the Traunstein, the Hohe Schrott, and the Katrin, that he finally knew for sure that this was really happening. Nevertheless, he still kept

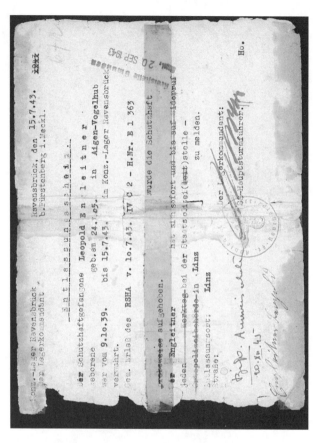

56: Certificate of release dated July 15, 1943, (the decree issued on July 10, 1943, by the Reichssicherheitshauptamt [RSHA, Reich Security Central Office, the central SS department] could not be traced in the archives in Berlin)

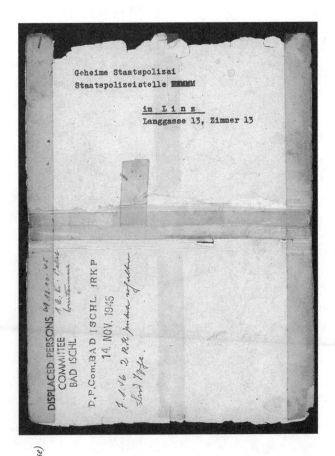

57: *Certificate of release*
dated July 15, 1943 (reverse)

glancing involuntarily to one side, just in case there was an SS man sitting beside him. Although both his hopes and his fears were great, this was the most pleasurable and wonderful homecoming he had ever experienced.

At last the train pulled in to the station at Bad Ischl, and he heard the announcement: "Bad Ischl, all change!" He felt a warm glow in his heart. Now he was really and truly home again.

He traveled the last six miles to Weinbach on the "*Kleinbahn*," arriving at his house at half past seven in the evening.

His parents had already gone to bed, so he announced his arrival by knocking loudly on the bedroom window. Engleitner was overjoyed when his father opened the door. His mother was surprised to see her son standing on the doorstep. Only a few days earlier, they had received a letter from Ravensbrück concentration camp that carried the same stamped remark as all the others: "*The prisoner still obstinately insists on being a Bible Student and refuses to renounce the heretical teachings of the Bible Students. For this reason the freedom to maintain correspondence to the extent usually permitted is forfeited.*" His father was evidently less surprised to see him, and the welcome he received was, all in all, rather subdued. His parents likely felt that he had brought all the suffering on himself by having refused to change his religion.

But what really hurt Engleitner was the fact that they showed no sympathy for his terrible state of health and, after his four years in concentration camps, did not even give him anything to eat. He had to wait until the next morning, when everyone would sit down at the table and eat together. Although he was ravenously hungry he did not say anything. He sat down in the kitchen and began to tell his parents about the dreadful suffering he had seen and experienced, from the brutal way he was received in Buchenwald to the work in the quarry, the countless deaths, the execution in Wewelsburg, the horror of being pushed onto the body of the murdered would-be escapee, the brutal guard who had crushed his testicle, the many times he himself had escaped death by the skin of his teeth, and the appalling conditions he had encountered in Ravensbrück.

But one thing he could not tell them was that he had refused to sign the declaration in Wewelsburg; they would not have understood. He did not mention his father's attempts to take his house from him while he was in Buchenwald, either; he made no allusion to it then or at any time thereafter. But it became apparent to his parents that what he had written in his letters bore no relation to the reality of the situation. Engleitner mentioned his obligation to work solely in agriculture from now on, commenting that he was unsure why he had been released without having to sign the declaration.

At this a knowing smile stole across his father's face. "Poidl," he said, "you don't know what I've been doing here. I've been going to the council offices in St. Wolfgang practically every day, begging the mayor and the GP Dr. Franz Xaver Rais to help you! I said to him: 'You know what Poidl's like. He's a hard-working lad, and I desperately need him. I'm getting too old to do all the work myself. I can't carry the timber the state allows me out of the woods on my own anymore. Heinrich hasn't got the strength. Please do what you can for Poidl!' The mayor promised he'd do everything in his power to get you out of the concentration camp. Besides, the Nazis in Wolfgang still remember how you didn't betray the farmer Alois Unterberger during the Schuschnigg[1] era when the police asked you if he was a Nazi. They also promised to help get you out!"

When Engleitner heard this, the circumstances surrounding his release seemed to make more sense. He had, of course, known nothing about any intervention by people

---

[1] Kurt Schuschnigg, Austrian Chancellor from 1934-1938, was vehemently opposed to the rise of National Socialism in Austria.

in his home district, and now he realized why he had been treated as a special case in Ravensbrück and had been released without having to sign the declaration.

It was with a feeling of deep calm and contentment that he then retired to his room.

Engleitner also had no idea at the time of the developments that were taking place at higher levels that made it possible for Bible Students like him to be released. SS *Reichsführer* Heinrich Himmler decided as early as the beginning of 1943 that a new strategy was required regarding the treatment of Bible Students. He seemed to realize that not even the most brutal methods would break their religious will. He began to consider the "Bible Student problem" less from an ideological point of view and more from a practical one, and to this end he issued new instructions:

"I request that Bible Students be put to work more in areas in which they will not come into contact with war—for example, in agriculture. If appropriate tasks are chosen, no supervision will be necessary, since they will not try to run away. They can be left to work on their own and will prove themselves the most efficient administrators and workers."[1]

Himmler even specified that in such cases a written renunciation would not be required. Some of the concessions made to Bible Students included release from concentration camps without a declaration of renunciation, allocation to work units outside the camps, privileged positions, and exemption from work in the armaments industry. These "privileges" were not granted on humanitarian grounds, however; the SS wanted to exploit the Bible Students' positive characteristics for the good of the German Reich. The decision to release a prisoner without a declaration of renunciation lay with the *Reichssicherheitshauptamt,* the head of which was

---

[1] Detlef Garbe, *Zwischen Widerstand und Martyrium: Die Zeugen Jehovas im Dritten Reich* (Munich, 1997), p. 463

Dr. Ernst Kaltenbrunner from Ried in Upper Austria. He, however, was not enthusiastic about Himmler's suggestion, and only allowed releases of that kind in exceptional circumstances.

Himmler also planned to make use of the Bible Students for his geopolitical activities after the war.[1]

In his room Engleitner found everything exactly as he had left it more than four years earlier on April 4, 1939. Even his Bible was still lying open on his bedside table. Although the Gestapo had confiscated his gramophone and records when they had searched the house following his arrest, they had not found any forbidden literature that he had hidden. An indescribable feeling of joy came over him as he said a fervent prayer of thanks for his survival and for having been given the strength to remain true to Jehovah. Then for the first time in many years, he was able to lie down in his own bed without the humiliating and oppressive atmosphere of the concentration camp around him. He fell into an untroubled slumber.

On Saturday afternoon he went to the local inn, Gasthaus Leitner, in Aigen-Voglhub. He wanted to get out and mix with the villagers again, to show them that he was not ashamed of being a former concentration camp prisoner. Other former prisoners were afraid of going out, but Engleitner knew that his suffering had been for a good cause. He sat down in the inn's garden and told the villagers about the hard times he had gone through in the various camps. Most of them showed a great deal of interest in his stories. They then began discussing the war, wondering how much longer it would last. Suddenly, a man nudged Engleitner and whispered into his ear: "Be careful what you say. There's an informer sitting over there, and he has already pricked up his ears." Engleitner changed the subject immediately and began talking about current events of a more general nature, but the damage had been done. The informer wasted no time in reporting what he had heard to

---

[1] See Appendix V

the mayor in Strobl, who said: "Engleitner must be called in immediately."

Forced Labor in Agriculture

Since Engleitner had received strict instructions from the Gestapo to complete all official formalities within six days, he went straight to the labor office in Bad Ischl on the following Monday morning and spoke to the manager, Josef Nöstlinger. It was Nöstlinger who had been responsible for the unjustified stoppage of Engleitner's unemployment benefit in the 1930s. Engleitner informed him of the conditions under which he had been released and said: "It is essential that I work in agriculture."

"What?" exploded the manager. "You think you can pick and choose, do you, after you've spent four years hanging around in a concentration camp? I'm sorry, but there'll be no special treatment for you. You'll work in the limestone works in Bad Ischl."

Disappointed, Engleitner went home and told his father what had happened. His father protested: "You can't work there! It's a state-owned enterprise. It'll only be a matter of time before your attitude toward the Nazi salute gets you into trouble, and then you'll be arrested again. Anyway, you have to work in agriculture or, at the very least, in forestry. Go see your cousin this afternoon and ask him if he's got a job for you at the sawmill in Weissenbach."

As soon as he had finished his dinner, Engleitner set off for Weissenbach to ask his cousin whether he could work for him as a tree-feller. That way he would at least be working in forestry. But his cousin considered it too risky to employ a former concentration camp prisoner. He told Engleitner he would have to think about it and would let him know the next day. The following day, he received a message from his cousin saying that he had no work for him. Then his father had an idea: "What about that Johann Unterberger over in Windhag? He's a friend of yours, isn't he? You've helped him a lot in the past. He's taken over the farm now and has often

58: Franziska and Johann Unterberger, wedding photo, 1939

asked about you. Why don't you ask him if he needs a farmhand?" Engleitner thought this was a marvelous idea, and set out immediately to visit his old friend and hiking companion.

Johann Unterberger and his wife, Franziska, were delighted to see him, and unlike his parents made no secret of their indignation at the appalling physical state he was in. Shaking their heads in dismay and offering many words of sympathy and consolation, they immediately set about preparing a sumptuous meal for him. It was an enjoyable reunion for Engleitner, who, after having told them what he had endured, put his problem to Unterberger. Without a second's hesitation, the farmer suggested: "Would you like to stay with me?"

"Yes, please," replied Engleitner.

"Of course I'll keep you here, Poidl," said Unterberger. "You'd be a great help to me. But first I'll have to write to the local farmers' representative. He has to ask for you at the labor office, you see." Unterberger sat down to write the letter immediately. Engleitner took it with him on Wednesday morning when he cycled to Schwarzenbach to see the local farmers' representative, Johann Raudaschl, a fervent Nazi.

When Raudaschl had finished reading Unterberger's letter, he said to Engleitner: "I am in complete agreement. We've got no farm workers in Wolfgang as it is. I'll write you the application, and you take it to the manager of the labor office in Ischl. But whatever you do, don't let him see how much you want to work for Unterberger or he won't agree to it!"

He then wrote the application and gave it to Engleitner, who cycled off at once towards Bad Ischl, wondering how on earth he was going to hide his excitement and delight from the manager.

By the time he entered Josef Nöstlinger's office, he had already worked out a plan. He put the letter from the farmers' representative on the table and waited while Nöstlinger read it, evidently without much enthusiasm. "I see," he sighed when he had finished. "He wants you to go to Unterberger, does he?"

That was Engleitner's cue to put his plan into action. Wringing his hands, he complained: "Herr Nöstlinger, I have heard it said that Unterberger is an out-and-out Nazi!"

Nöstlinger went for the bait immediately, saying: "Well, then, I can think of no better place for you!" Engleitner hung his head in mock dejection and shuffled out of the room. With a light heart, he mounted his bicycle and rode home.

Engleitner started work for Johann Unterberger on Thursday, July 22, 1943. He told his friend and employer about the trick he had used at the labor office. Both men laughed long and loud about the ruse. Engleitner then began his job assisting Unterberger and his wife, who had three small children to look after. They also had a Polish prisoner-of-war working for them, but he was not much help. The rest of the household was made up of a Ukrainian girl who helped in the kitchen and Johann Unterberger's father, who had been badly wounded in World War I.

Unterberger had a profound knowledge of his profession. Before fertilizing the soil he would put a little cake of earth in his mouth and chew on it. He could tell by the taste what nutrients were most necessary; if the earth tasted too sour, for example, it needed more phosphorus. He would then spread a layer of beech shavings over the ground, which provided it with the necessary nutrients. As a result of this unique method of checking the soil, Unterberger had highly productive fields every year.

Engleitner had nothing but admiration for the farmer's extensive knowledge and learned a lot from him. He was very happy for the work and tried to do as much as he could. Unterberger paid him a small wage even though he was not required to do so.

On Unterberger's farm he was no longer directly affected by political pressures and slowly but surely began to recover from the consequences of the years of malnutrition. Although Unterberger was a Catholic, he had allowed Engleitner to hide his Biblical literature on his farm before the war. Now, taking all the necessary precautions, Engleitner could use that material to build up his spiritual strength, as well.

The Army Persists

It was too good to last. In mid-August, after only a few short weeks of tranquillity and contentment, he was summoned before a military medical board for examination with a view to conscription into the army. This came as a complete shock to Engleitner, who had hoped that the military authorities would finally leave him alone. His steadfastness would be put to the test again. His first thought was simply to ignore the summons, but he decided it would be more advisable to take the train to the army registration office in Gmunden and go from there to the medical board. He hoped that he would be exempted from military service, having been deferred twice already in the concentration camp.

When he arrived, the MO took a good look at him and remarked: "You don't really want to be in the army, do you?"

"You're right, Herr *Doktor*. I don't."

"Why's that?"

"I'd like to tell you something. When I was a boy I stood in front of my teacher just as I stand in front of you now, with a stoop. I've always had pains in my back whenever I try to stand up straight. At school I wasn't even allowed to play games."

After the doctor had inspected Engleitner's back, he said: " You're right. You have curvature of the spine and should be exempted from military service."

Engleitner was greatly relieved. He took the train home, stuffing his ticket into his jacket pocket without really thinking what he was doing. That he did so saved him from a difficult situation a week later.

Engleitner quite naturally assumed that with his deferral he would hear no more on the subject of military service. But in this he was mistaken. It was clearly an illusion to think that the Nazi regime would leave him alone at last. A week after his medical inspection, he was summoned before the medical board a second time. He traveled to Gmunden again, hoping that there had been a mistake.

As he entered the army registration office, he met with a frosty reception. "Why did you fail to appear for your inspection last week?" barked the clerk.

"What?" asked Engleitner. "Who says I wasn't here? The MO examined me personally and deferred me on medical grounds."

"Don't lie to me, Herr Engleitner. We have no record of your having been here. Why weren't you here?"

Engleitner could not prove that he had been there, and the army clerk began threatening him with punishments for his alleged refusal to obey a summons. Just then, Engleitner happened to put his hand in his jacket pocket. His fingers felt a small piece of paper. He took it out and saw that it was the train ticket from the previous week. He lost no time playing his trump card.

He held the ticket up and said: "Here is the train ticket I bought last week to come here. Will this do as proof?"

The clerk took the ticket and inspected it. "So it is," he murmured.

Despite this Engleitner had to report to the office where the second medical inspection was to take place, which was about a 30-minute walk away. Engleitner went as slowly as he could so as to arrive as late as possible. He arrived just as the MO who had examined him the week before was leaving. When he saw Engleitner coming along the corridor, he pulled a piece of paper out of his jacket pocket and said: "Herr Engleitner, you're just in time. Here's your medical report: Fit for active service at the front lines, reserve No. 1. Here you are!" Knowing it was pointless to argue, Engleitner took the paper without a word. "I don't believe it," he thought to himself. "Now I'm suddenly fit for active service. And to make sure they finish me off this time, they're sending me straight to the front." Disappointed, but determined not to lose heart, he went back to the railway station and took the train home. He remembered what the mayor of Strobl had said: "Engleitner must be called up immediately." Was the mayor behind all this? Engleitner had no proof, but it certainly looked that way.

A week later his service record book and stand-by papers were sent to him. Without telling a soul, he immediately burned them. He fully expected to receive further ominous mail from the army, but since nothing more came initially he continued working hard on the farm. Occasionally his employer even gave him days off, which he used to transport the timber out of the woods for his parents on an oxcart and to construct a better entrance to the cellar, because his parents could not open the trapdoor leading down to it in winter when it was covered with snow. He heard nothing more from the military.

In the spring of 1944, Johann Unterberger received his call-up papers. As a farmer he should have been exempted. Engleitner was now in charge of the farmwork, and worked as hard as he could.

Unterberger lost his left leg during the Allies' invasion of Normandy. He would be treated at several military hospitals before returning home just before the end of the war.

Engleitner did his utmost to keep the farm running. But in June he had a serious accident. While repairing a rotten beam in the roof of the stable, he slipped and fell eight feet to the hard floor below, landing on his shoulder and head. When the Polish prisoner-of-war came into the stable to feed the cattle, he noticed that the bull did not charge up to the trough as usual. It was then that he saw his colleague on the ground near the bull's trough. Engleitner was just starting to come to. He felt a sharp pain in his right shoulder and was bleeding from a cut on the head. Accompanied by the fourteen-year-old son of a neighbor, he took the train to a "bone-wrencher" (chiropractor) in Ebensee. His right collarbone was broken. This presented a huge problem for Engleitner because the hay would soon have to be brought in. The work had to be done somehow, so Engleitner did as much as possible with only one arm.

Two weeks later he returned to Ebensee for a check-up. A group of prisoners from Ebensee[1] concentration camp were digging along the side of the road in the town, closely watched by several guards. The work caused traffic to back up. As Engleitner made his way past the emaciated detainees, the SS men watched him suspiciously to make sure he did not slip any prisoner a morsel of food. At that moment the feelings of oppressiveness came flooding back; only a year before he himself had been in a similar situation. A wave of sympathy washed over him, but there was nothing he could do to help them.

One day he took a cow to the butcher's. He wound the rope several times around his left hand to control the animal. But all of a sudden something frightened the cow and it bolted, pulling Engleitner over and dragging him 30 yards along the road. Now Engleitner not only had a wounded right shoulder but an injured left hand as well. The butcher tended to his badly skinned and bleeding hand.

At the end of December 1944, an envelope addressed to Leopold Engleitner bearing the stamp of the Wehrmacht was delivered. Inside was a request for him to send in his certificate of invalidity, but he had no such certificate. Shaking his head at the chaos that evidently reigned at the army office, he ripped up the letter and simply ignored it. Two weeks later Engleitner's father told him that his brother Heinrich had received a sharply worded letter from the army rebuking him for having failed to send in his certificate of invalidity as required. His father was very surprised about this, since he had seen no sign of the letter requesting that it be sent in. Engleitner did not mention the letter he had received, although it was now clear to him that the letter had actually been meant for his brother. "It's a good thing I didn't write back," he thought, "because I'd only have drawn attention to myself."

---

[1] Ebensee concentration camp: subcamp belonging to Mauthausen concentration camp (11/18/43 to 5/6/45) 27,000 prisoners

The army was still hot on his trail, though. Every Sunday afternoon the male population of St. Wolfgang had to assemble on the square to take part in a roll call and military exercises. Participating in such a gathering was out of the question for Engleitner on account of his beliefs, so he never went. As long as Johann Unterberger regularly took part, no one seemed to care that his farmhand was not there. But after Unterberger's call-up, Engleitner was visited the next Saturday by neighbors who told him that he would now have to take part in the roll call. Engleitner ignored the demand.

One evening, though, in the spring of 1945, he crossed paths with Hans Stadler, who led the roll call. Engleitner had been to the sawmill in Radau to fetch some planks and was on his way home in the oxcart. As he reached the main road, he saw Stadler but quickly looked the other way, as if he had not seen him. Engleitner started to drive faster, but Stadler shouted after him: "Poidl, stop! I need you!"

"I'm in a hurry," replied Engleitner.

"Why don't you come to the roll calls?" asked Stadler in threatening tones.

Engleitner, never at a loss for words and knowing Stadler very well, answered sharply: "Are you mad? I have to work on that huge farm day and night. I haven't time for that sort of thing. I have more important things to do."

"But Johann always used to come," objected the Nazi.

"Yes, and I'll tell you why. He was afraid of you Nazis and didn't want to get on the wrong side of you. But I'm not scared of you." With that, Engleitner went on his way, leaving Stadler standing open-mouthed by the roadside.

"Just you wait," he shouted after the departing Engleitner. "We haven't finished with you yet!"

Later, when Engleitner recounted the episode to Franziska Unterberger, she reproved him sternly: "Why did you have to say that? Now they'll come and take you as well, and I'll be all alone here with the farm!"

Engleitner, too, feared that the altercation could have consequences for him. On April 17, 1945, those fears were realized.

A NARROW ESCAPE—Part 2

Franz Kain sees only one possibility to prevent Engleitner's being found and executed. He plants himself firmly in the way of the leader of the Nazi patrol and objects: "I'm not going down to that hut in this fog! It's much too dangerous!"

The leader of the patrol is taken in by his guide's ruse and says: "Well, if it's too risky, we'll have a look at it some other time."

That was a close call for Engleitner. Franz Kain's quick thinking has saved Engleitner's life, because this is the last search.

It is now the morning of May 5, 1945, and Engleitner is awakened by a loud droning. When he gets up from his bed of hay and looks out of the window in the roof, he sees a sight that will remain engraved in his memory for the rest of his life: Allied aircraft, flying low over the Attersee, a sign that the Allies have defeated the Nazi regime. Engleitner thinks to himself: "At last! The war must be over! I've made it." He lies back on his bed of hay and offers up a prayer of thanks and indescribable joy.

Suddenly he hears a series of explosions and once more peers out of the hut. In the distance he sees huge clouds of smoke billowing up and concludes that the Allies must be

destroying the Germans' ammunition. He decides to go down
to Unterberger's farm to find out whether his assumption is
correct. Although he would prefer to start out immediately,
he considers it prudent to wait until dusk, just in case there
are still some fanatical soldiers abroad who could cause him
trouble.

He makes use of the time to melt some snow on the stove
for a shave and a thorough wash, which he hasn't had in three
weeks.

When evening falls he sets out, choosing a route that passes by
Haleswies and crosses four alpine pastures. He moves with
caution through the protection of the woods. When not far
from the Toffenwald near Radau, he sees a long convoy of
German military vehicles. He disappears back into the woods
and continues to the farm by another route. As he crosses a
field, he hears shots! Thinking that soldiers have spotted him,
he dashes for cover in a panic. When he thinks he must be out
of range and looks behind him, he realizes that it was soldiers
shooting at burning gas cans on the backs of the trucks.

When Engleitner arrives at the Unterbergers' farmhouse
and cautiously peers through the window into the parlor, he
gets another fright. Sitting in the room are soldiers in German
uniforms. "Don't tell me I've run from my hut straight into
their arms!" he thinks, and hurries next door to the farmer's
uncle, Franz. He asks him breathlessly: "What's going on?"

"Don't worry!" answers Franz. "The war is over! You can
stay here now."

"What about the soldiers in the parlor?" demands
Engleitner. "What are they doing there?"

"Oh, don't worry about them. They're Russians who went
over to Hitler and now have to disappear."

At this, Engleitner immediately heads back to the
farmhouse. When he flings the door open, the first person he
sees is his old friend Johann, who has been released from

hospital and is now back home. Johann Unterberger is overjoyed to see Engleitner again, and cries out: "Look who's here! Poidl's back at last!" His delight at the reunion knows no bounds, and he is full of questions about how his friend has fared. He also tells him that St. Wolfgang will surrender to the Allies the next day.

While Engleitner is telling him all about the turbulent events of the past few weeks, the Russians begin to scoff at him in their own language, saying: "When the Germans catch him they'll cut his head off!"

Engleitner does not understand what they are saying, but the Ukrainian girl does, and she leaps to his defense, angrily rebuking the Russians. "How dare you speak about this brave man like that! You should be ashamed of yourselves! Although he is a 'Teuton,' he didn't fight for Hitler, whereas you Russians did! So shut up and leave him alone!"

Following this altercation the Russians get up to leave, and Engleitner finishes describing his adventures in peace.

Engleitner goes to bed that night happy in the knowledge that he has been able to maintain his integrity and keep a clean conscience. He did not let himself be ground down under the cruel Hitler regime, something that he knows was only possible with the support of the Almighty God. So he thanks God for having once again fulfilled the promise made in the Psalms: "He will never let the righteous fall." (Psalm 55:22) Next morning Engleitner goes to Weinbach and pays his parents a visit, and they give him a rather cool reception. The next day he returns to the Meistereben hut to collect the blanket and the pots and pans. Only two days ago, he had to creep around like a hunted animal, but today he can move freely and therefore enjoys his hike.

When he arrives at the hut, the terrible memories of his accident when he and his clothes were burned, and the sense of relief he felt when he saw the Allied planes heading towards him, pass like a film in his mind's eye. Only now does he really and truly realize that he is a free man again.

He reaches for the key, opens the door, and stops petrified at the scene before him. The terror that was his constant companion during the past few years overcomes him once again. The floor is strewn with SS uniforms! He realizes with a sickening jolt that it was by a hair's breadth that he escaped death. "These SS men must have fled from Ebensee concentration camp[1] and changed into civilian clothes in the hut. If I had stayed here any longer, they would have found me and that would have been the end." Relieved and deep in thought, he walks slowly back to the farmhouse.

---

[1] Ebensee concentration camp was liberated by the Americans on May 6, 1945. The SS personnel fled at around midday on May 5, 1945.

LIFE AFTER THE WAR

After the end of the war, Leopold Engleitner continued to work for Johann and Franziska Unterberger as a farmhand, helping them to clear the work that had mounted up. Although offered lucrative work with the road maintenance department in Bad Ischl, he declined it, saying: "I can't leave Johann to do all the work on his own now that he only has one leg!"

But an incident on April 10, 1946, caused him to change his mind. He was having a hard time plowing one of Unterberger's fields because one of the oxen was still young and not yet broken in. As a consequence, the young animal kept pulling the more experienced ox to one side, resulting in furrows that were anything but straight. When the farmer came down to the field to inspect his farmhand's work, he was furious to see the crooked furrows. "What do I keep you for, if you're so useless?" he yelled hysterically.

Engleitner felt the criticism to be unfair. "Johann," he said, "if you really feel that way, I'll go. I wouldn't want you to keep me for nothing!" Engleitner turned on his heel to walk away, hoping that the farmer would come after him and apologize. But Unterberger said: "You crook! That's just what you've been waiting for, isn't it?"

That did it. Engleitner left. The next day, Engleitner went to the labor office in Bad Ischl and was assigned to another farmer, but he had had enough of working as a farmhand, and said so. The clerk told him: "When you were in the concentration camp, you promised to work solely in agriculture for the rest of your life. And that's what you will do."

Engleitner disagreed. He replied: "That was a promise made under Hitler. You can't expect me to be bound for the rest of my life by a promise from that terrible time. That's no longer valid." The clerk did not share this view, and sent him away.

Engleitner's father, who was secretary of the construction and forestry workers' union, wrote a letter to the American military authorities now responsible for the area, asking for their support in this matter. The Allies instructed the labor office in Bad Ischl to cancel this ruling, as it was no longer applicable. As a result, Engleitner was immediately offered the post of night watchman at the Kollontay soap factory in Weinbach, just the sort of thing he was looking for.

After the war, Jehovah's Witnesses in Bad Ischl and the surrounding area began meeting again. Their religious visitation work would resume with new fervor. Engleitner enjoyed this activity during the day as he traveled around Bad Goisern, Hallstatt, and Obertraun as far as Gosau, and at night he worked as a watchman.

On February 5, 1949, Engleitner married the divorcée Theresia Kurz, née Limberger, from Obertraun. Her previous husband had lived with another woman for many years in Vienna and left Theresia with two small children, Ida and Heinrich. Engleitner, his wife, and her daughter Ida moved into an apartment near his house so that his parents and brother could continue living there.

After his marriage, he changed jobs. From January 2, 1951, he worked as a laborer for the road maintenance department in Bad Ischl (see page 238), where he stayed until his retirement on September 1, 1969.

59: Leopold
Engleitner, 1949

60: Theresia
Engleitner, circa 1960

His wife, Theresia, suffered from acute diabetes and, after being lovingly cared for by Engleitner for seven years, died in 1981. Since then, Engleitner has been living alone. Although now in his ninety-ninth year, he still spends his time and strength proclaiming the "good news." He is more convinced than ever that it is only the Kingdom of God that will be able

61: Ida, 1943

62: Leopold Engleitner (second from the left) with colleagues from the road maintenance department in Bad Ischl, 1968/69

to satisfy mankind's yearning for peace and happiness on a permanent basis.

Despite his advanced years and physical disability, he continues with undiminished joy and fervor to follow the way he first embarked on back in 1932. That path may have brought him enormous suffering, but it has also given him tremendous zest for life, immense satisfaction, and great contentment.

INTERVIEW

You survived the horrors of three concentration camps. Were there moments during your incarceration when you longed for death?

Now and then I went through phases when I thought death would be a welcome release from all the suffering. Remaining

63: Leopold Engleitner with Bernhard Rammerstorfer, February 1998

alive was punishment enough because of all one had to go through. But whenever I had thoughts like that, I immediately said to myself: "You coward, pull yourself together; be strong."

As a concentration camp survivor, how were you received by society?

When the war was over, I imagined I would be welcomed with open arms. But the very opposite occurred. We were regarded as asocial elements and were treated like lepers. We were not supposed to talk about it. People wanted to hush up the horror and the atrocities and pretend they never happened. A lot of people were bothered by their conscience because they hadn't spoken out against what was going on or had even been actively involved in it. There were even people who claimed that concentration camps never existed. This was very hard for us former prisoners to come to terms with. It was almost as if we were the culprits instead of the victims.

What do you think about the way Nazi atrocities have been dealt with since the war?

It has given me great satisfaction. We [Jehovah's Witnesses] were always treated as second-class citizens and lumped together with the work-shy and criminal elements. That hurts. So it's very satisfying to be able to talk openly about all the things that for so many years were regarded as taboo. The analysis of these terrible times highlights the fact that we were fighting for a noble cause, that we were committed to high moral standards and to peace. I find it very encouraging when I hear that people often express appreciation for what we were willing to go through in those days. I am particularly pleased that so many young people are interested in my life, and I would like to advise them to support noble principles during their lives as well. I can say from experience that it's worth it.

Did you have any more confrontations with the tyrants from the concentration camps?

Yes, in 1970 in Paderborn, Germany, when several Nazi criminals were tried by jury. Shortly before the trial, the prosecuting attorney and a detective came to St. Wolfgang from Cologne and questioned me at the police station there. When the prosecuting attorney wanted to know about Max Schüller's crimes, I asked him: "What? Is Max still alive, then? Word had it in the concentration camp that he'd been killed after his release."

"I'm afraid he is alive," said the lawyer, "although, to be honest, we'd be glad if he weren't."

At the trial the defendants were Labor Supervisor Rehn, another SS man, and two *kapos*. Max Schüller was charged with grievous maltreatment of prisoners and manslaughter, which, however, could not be proved, and he was acquitted.

It was known that the *kapos* had often pushed prisoners into cold water. So the judge asked me: "Were you ever thrown into cold water?" When I told him I had been, he asked: "By whom?"

"By him," I replied, pointing at Max.

"And did you get very wet?"

"Yes," I said. "But so did he."

"How did that happen?" asked the judge. When I told him how I'd held on to him and pulled him into the hole with me, he burst out laughing. Max Schüller laughed as well.

When did you find out about the changes at top levels regarding the release of Bible Students—an important factor in securing your release from Ravensbrück concentration camp without your having to renounce your beliefs?

I had always thought my release was because of the efforts of the Nazis in St. Wolfgang. It wasn't until you started your intensive research for this book that I discovered the whole story. I am very pleased that this book has cleared up all the points that were still unclear, because for many years there were a lot of people who did not understand the reasons for my release. Even my brothers in the faith, those still in the concentration camp and those at home, could not explain why I'd been released without complications, because, like me, they didn't know anything about Himmler's instructions.

How do you account for your falling out with your friend Johann Unterberger?

After his leg had been amputated, he suffered aftereffects from the anesthetic and was very irritable, which is not surprising. There was also talk in the village that he'd only been called up because he'd allowed me, a conscientious objector, to work on his farm. This talk was so persistent that after the war he began to believe it himself, and this put a great strain on our relationship. We made up with each other some time later and remained friends right up until his death.

Did you have any more contact with Hans Stadler, the man who took the roll calls in St. Wolfgang?

I met him a few times. Shortly after the war, he suffered a stroke and spent most days sitting on a bench in front of his house. I often saw him when I bicycled past in the course of my preaching activity. He would call out to me like an old friend. But I always had to smile when I remembered that it was thanks to him that I had my "narrow escape."

Your flight into the mountains began with your call-up to the base in Krumau. Do you know what would have awaited you there?

Certain death. I found out later that the Czechs had attacked this base and that there had been no survivors.

What lasting effects did incarceration in concentration camps have on your health?

It aggravated my back problems, which have got steadily worse. In the 1980s I had to start using crutches, and now I need a wheelchair because I can't walk at all anymore. The beating I received on my arrival at Buchenwald permanently damaged my left eardrum and my hearing has been bad ever since. The kick to the groin I received in Wewelsburg left me sterile, and the other physical hardships I endured have left their mark. My wife and I were unable to have any children of our own. Those are the physical side effects. Psychologically, I also had a fair amount to cope with after the war. I had recurring nightmares about the atrocities I'd witnessed. An uninterrupted night's sleep was a rarity, and I often woke up bathed in sweat. If a scene on television showed a slave receiving a beating, I would have to leave the room because it was as if I were being beaten. Bible study and prayer have helped me overcome these difficulties, and I no longer have the nightmares.

How have you as a former concentration camp prisoner been treated by the authorities?

I can't complain. Because of my internment I was issued an official certificate protecting me from dismissal. Since 1951 I have received a small pension granted to victims of the war from the War Victims Trust. I get a small annual allowance from Dr. Josef Pühringer, the governor of Upper Austria. The Ministry for Health and Social Affairs grants me a generous subsidy every year toward my heating costs. In addition, I received a considerable sum from the same ministry to mark a

particular anniversary relating to the war. I remain very grateful
to these authorities for the support they have given me, since
I only get a small pension and have to watch every penny.

In Spring 2003 I received generous compensation from
the National Fund of the Austrian Republic for the
gramophone that the Gestapo had confiscated in 1939. In
September 2003 I received financial compensation from the
Austrian Reconciliation Fund for my years of forced labor in
the concentration camps. I am very grateful to the Republic
of Austria for this sum.[1]

*After he had been reinstated as governor of Upper Austria, did
your fellow detainee Dr. Heinrich Gleissner keep the promise
he made when you shared a cell on the train?*

Yes! In 1949 I applied to the War Victims Trust for a pension
because of the physical injuries I had suffered as a result of my
imprisonment in the concentration camps. The doctor at the
local government office in Gmunden, a former army doctor,
could not—or, more likely, didn't want to—find any handicap.
Even though I appealed the decision, the result was still
negative. It looked as if I was once more the victim of the
whims of officialdom. I saw no other course but to contact
the governor directly, since I knew that he would see that justice
was done. However, I wanted to write to him at his home
address. So I went to Matthias Hödlmoser, who was later to
become president of the Landtag (state parliament) and who
also lived in Weinbach, and said to him: "Hias, did you know
I was with Heinrich Gleissner in the concentration camp? I'd
like to write him a letter. Can you give me his home address?"
He gave it to me without asking too many questions, so I

---

[1] Voluntary payments by the Republic of Austria to former slave and forced
laborers of the Nazi regime on the territory of present-day Austria.

wrote a letter to the governor. I mentioned a few things from our time together in the concentration camp, said I was delighted to be able to write to him, and only hinted at the problem I had without begging him outright for assistance. Dr. Gleissner immediately ordered an additional medical examination at Linz general hospital. My physical handicaps were fairly and objectively assessed, were confirmed as being a direct result of my imprisonment, and were judged as curtailing my ability to work by 40 percent. As a result, I started receiving a small war victims' pension in 1951.

Wolfgang Mattischek, another victim, also contacted Dr. Gleissner after he had been refused the retirement pension to which he was entitled. Dr. Gleissner also helped him so that, in the end, he received it.

What did Dr. Eduard Pesendorfer do for you?

After the war, Dr. Pesendorfer went back to work at the local council offices in Gmunden. In the late 1940s, he inquired through the council secretary in St. Wolfgang whether I was being paid the annual allowance that had been granted to former concentration camp internees. I explained that I had received nothing of the kind. He then saw to it that I was paid a sum of between fifty and a hundred Austrian schillings.

What became of Alois Moser, Franz Wimmer, and Wolfgang Mattischek?

Alois Moser was interned in Ravensbrück concentration camp and various subcamps until the end of the war, returning home in August 1945. One of the first things he did was come and visit me, and we compared our experiences. We saw a great deal of each other after that and remained good friends right up until his death in 1995. It was important to him to speak about his time in the concentration camp, and he did so on many occasions. We shared the desire to make our sufferings known even when the general public didn't want to hear anything about it. In 1992 we both took part in a meeting of concentration camp survivors in Wewelsburg.

In 1943, Franz Wimmer was sent from Ravensbrück concentration camp to work as a carpenter on the estate belonging to Dr. Felix Kersten, who was personal physician to *SS-Reichsführer* Heinrich Himmler. Dr. Kersten was a good man and secured the release of many of Jehovah's Witnesses, including Friedrich Klingenberg. He made sure they had enough to eat, had them build a hunting lodge for him, and thus saved their lives. He even arranged for copies of *The Watchtower* to be smuggled out of Sweden for the brothers and sisters in the faith to study. Franz was therefore able to recover physically before the war ended. I had regular contact with him, too, until his death in 1981.

Wolfgang Mattischek was held in Buchenwald concentration camp until the end of the war. We met a few times after that. He died in 1965.

What happened to Georg Pointner after his release?

We met once after the war. He told me that he hadn't realized the full implications of signing the declaration. His signature was forced out of him under false pretenses. Shortly after his release, the army summoned him, but he was deferred because of a serious heart condition. He regretted the step he took in the concentration camp very much and later rejoined the fold. I tried to console him and had a long discussion with him, but he never forgave himself for what he did. He died in 1958.

What became of the farmhand you spoke to in 1934 in St. Nikolai im Sölktal?

At the time I had no idea what consequences that meeting would have. Thirty-two years later, I happened to be chatting with a man at a congress in Linz who introduced himself as David Meissnitzer. He told me that he had worked as a farmhand on a farm in St. Nikolai in the 1930s and had once had a conversation with one of Jehovah's Witnesses. When he found a tract on the farmhouse door with the address of the Watchtower Society on it, he ordered more literature, eventually becoming baptized as a Witness himself. He too had to maintain his integrity during the war in concentration camps, as so many others had had to do. When I told him that I was the one he had spoken to all those years ago, we were absolutely delighted.

Is there a love story from your youth you can tell us about?

Girls never really took any notice of me because I didn't meet their expectations. But there was one nice girl who liked me. After the First World War I went to work for the first farmer in St. Wolfgang. On holidays I sometimes went to a neighboring farm where some of the young people met to dance and sing in the hayloft. I was 15 years old at the time. One day I went for a walk with the farmer's youngest daughter, who was about 14. We talked about all sorts of things. I could see she liked me, and I thought she was very nice too. Suddenly she put her arm round my shoulder. I immediately pushed it off, saying, "Don't do that! If someone sees us you'll be in big trouble at home. You're a farmer's daughter and I'm only a poor farmhand."

Later, when I was working for Moabauer, we happened to meet on the way home from church in St. Wolfgang. She asked me whether we could go some of the way together. I was extremely pleased because others ignored me completely and would have been embarrassed just to be seen with me. As we walked we had a very pleasant chat.

In the mid-1920s, a friend and I went on an excursion to an alpine hut on Schafberg, where the farmer's daughter worked temporarily as a herdswoman. We were delighted to see each other again. She had to fetch water for household chores from a spring about a mile and a half away. She was holding four buckets and asked me to help her. So I went with her, telling her on the way that I had saved assiduously so I could buy a plot of ground to build a house on. That impressed her a lot. She told me she didn't like working on the farm and had to marry her brother-in-law, who was over twenty years older than her. He was the husband of her sister, who had died young. He had a farm and two children to support. She found the prospect of marrying him anything but agreeable, but her parents had left her no alternative. When we arrived back at the hut, her fiance was there. That night he slept with her in her room. I spent the night with my friend in the loft. I found out that she had really liked me when, after her death in the 1980s, I met her stepdaughter in the Bad Ischl spa park. She said: "My stepmother often talked about you!"

How did your relationship with your parents develop after the war?

Unfortunately they refused to accept my religious views right up until their deaths. They also tried to take my house again. This is shown very clearly by something that happened in 1950. Following my marriage I moved into an apartment especially so that my parents and my brother could stay in my house. In the spring of 1950, my wife wanted to do some gardening there. When my father saw her he shouted at her: "Get lost; you have no right to do anything here!" With that he had made it clear to us that he regarded the house as his own. So I had to do something about it. I went to see the judge Dr. Klimesch at Bad Ischl court, who had often questioned me in the 1930s regarding the various charges brought against me. I

64: Leopold Engleitner's house, Weinbach 27, 1998

explained the problem to him, asked for his support, and made it plain that I did not want to take any legal action against my father. The judge told me he would have a look at the land register and would invite my father and me for an interview. During this conversation Dr. Klimesch informed my father: "I've had a look at the land register, and the owner is given as Leopold Engleitner junior. Why, then, are you claiming ownership?"

My father replied: "Because I've spent a lot of money on the house!"

"Bring me the receipts, and your son will reimburse your expenses," answered the judge.

But of course, my father didn't have any receipts, because I'd paid for everything myself. The judge also added: "I can't understand you. Your son lets you live in his house, yet you insist on claiming ownership of it?"

My father's response to this hurt me very much. He said: "My son's spent most of his life in jail! He's a concentration camp internee!"

Then even Dr. Klimesch lost patience with him, and came to my defense, saying: "Your son has a very good reputation. The sentences he received were not for criminal offenses. He has suffered for a just and good cause and would not even abandon his principles under Hitler. A lot of fathers would be proud of such a courageous son!" That silenced my father, but despite that he never once offered a word of gratitude to me. My wife and I made additions to our house up until 1953. We moved in with our daughter Ida, whom I had adopted, and lived with my parents and my brother. Following my mother's death in the spring of 1955, we looked after my father until his death in October of the same year. My brother Heinrich died in 1960 following a stroke.

What can you tell us about your wife?

She suffered greatly as a result of the family problems that she experienced with her first husband, who lived in Vienna with a girlfriend. She put her six-month-old son Heinrich into the care of her sister because she worked as a washer-woman in order to care for her little daughter Ida. During World War II she had to have her gallbladder taken out. Unfortunately the military doctor who performed the opera-tion was addicted to drugs, and the opera-tion left her in constant pain afterward. Then she began to suffer from diabetes. I looked after her for the last seven

65: Leopold and Theresia Engleitner, circa 1955

years of her life. During this time she hardly slept a single night through, and some nights I had to go with her to the toilet up to ten times. After her death a post-mortem discovered that a surgical instrument had been left inside her during the gallbladder operation. That was the reason for her terrible pains!

How have you coped since your wife's death?

I live alone and manage very well. In 1987 I was able to fly to the United States. I visited South Dakota where I spoke to Sioux Indians for the first time in my life. I was able to learn a great deal about their fascinating culture. They were delighted to meet a former concentration camp prisoner face-to-face. After that I lived in Hermagor in the province of Carinthia for six months, and from September 1989 to February 1991, I was in Meran in South Tyrol, helping my brothers in the faith there.

After all the suffering you have been through, why are you not bitter? What is the secret of your happiness and your continuing enthusiasm for life?

I have no reason to feel bitter. When I decided to follow this path in 1932, I was well aware that it would mean a hard struggle. But I knew that I was fighting for a noble cause. Of course there were difficult times, times when all the problems began to get me down. But

66: Leopold Engleitner in South Dakota, USA, 1987

my intimate relationship with our Creator always helped me to overcome them. No matter how much one suffers or is tormented, no one can take away the right of a human being to come closer to the Lord. I want to make it quite clear that it is not my strong personality that got me through those trials; it is, if anything, in spite of my personality, being of limited education and treated as inferior since I was a boy.

67: Leopold Engleitner, 1997. Photo by Hofer, Bad Ischl

I was very shy and had very little self-confidence. The person who went through the trials described in this book was transformed by thorough Bible study and an intimate relationship with Jehovah. Leading a life true to God and his principles while keeping a clean conscience can only result in great joy and contentment. I have expressed my optimism by writing the words to a song called *"Gerechtigkeit auf Erden"* (Justice on Earth).

Are you still a committed Witness of Jehovah?

Yes, and I'm happier and more content than ever. I am firmly convinced that it is only the Kingdom of God, for which millions of people pray in the Lord's Prayer, that will solve the problems of mankind. Because I have been unable to walk very far the last few years, I decided to offer Biblical literature in the spa gardens in Bad Ischl and in front of my own house and to talk to people about this Kingdom. I enjoy it very much, and I've been able to hold many pleasant conversations.

What is your view of the book "Unbroken Will"?

This book summarizes my experiences exactly as they happened. When reading the manuscript, I sometimes felt as if I'd been transported back to those times. I can assure the reader that this is no work of fiction, but an account of what really took place. Having read and discussed the manuscript many times, I can say that the finished product fulfills my expectations and describes my life as it really was.

I would never have thought it possible that one day a book would be written about me, since all my life people have hardly taken any notice of me. I was afraid that my experiences would be completely forgotten once I had died. But with this book a dream has come true. You see, I think it's very important that those difficult times and especially the suffering that individuals had to endure are not forgotten. I hope that coming generations never experience a time like it. That's why I think it's vital to show mankind that problems cannot be solved with violence, because violence breeds violence, and I had the misfortune to experience personally what that leads to. Instead we should follow the path that Jesus Christ shows us and love

69: Leopold Engleitner reading the manuscript, February 1998

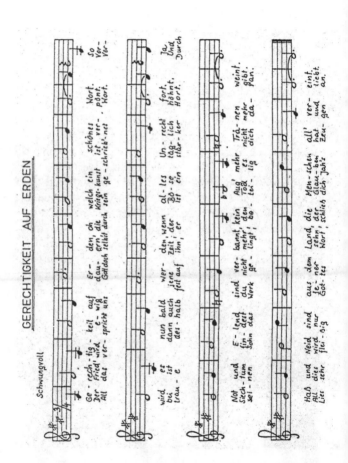

GERECHTIGKEIT AUF ERDEN

JUSTICE ON EARTH

Justice on Earth, O what lovely words
Soon it will be so, when all wrongs are cast out
Need and suffering banished be, no eye will shed a tear
Hate and envy found no more, all humankind as one

Peace will last forever, war be frowned upon
Gone the time when evil jeers and mocks each day
There'll be no more infirmity, death no more will strike
And only he will see all this who loves and has belief

God himself promises this in his own written Word
So trust in him, have faith in him, he is a haven safe
His work is done through his own son, join in and play your part
Read God's Word with zeal and love, and join Jah's Witnesses.

68: Song, *"Gerechtigkeit auf Erden"* (Justice on Earth), words: Leopold Engleitner, music: Peter Esser

our neighbors. I have always done my best to apply just
principles and respect the rights of others. That's why no one
was ever able to force me to raise a weapon against my
fellowman. When I look back on my life, it fills me with great
joy that I am able to say: "I lived according to noble principles."
What I did is, in my view, a natural duty and no more than
anyone else would have done. But I know, too, that a great
many of my generation had to go to war against their will and
had to suffer a lot because of it. This book is not meant to be
a condemnation of those who took part; its intention is merely
to show that there is another way.

What is your opinion of Adolf Hitler?

I never met him, and he never interested me particularly. It
goes without saying that he committed the greatest of crimes
against humanity. He was ruthless in his persecution of
Jehovah's Witnesses. He had a free will, just as everybody else
does, and used it as he wished. And as history shows, that
turned out to be enormously damaging to mankind. Therefore
we should use our own free will for the good of others.

What feedback has there been since your biography was published in 1999, and how has it affected you?

I have been overwhelmed by everything that has happened
since the book came out. I never for one moment imagined
that people would react so positively. The huge interest shown
in my life story fills me with great joy.

      People from all over the world and from all walks of life,
from ordinary people to university professors, have written to
me to express their admiration. In my immediate vicinity, where
people had barely taken any notice of me before and where I
was always something of a pariah, the book has brought about
a great change in people's attitudes. Whereas they used to make

derogatory remarks about me, people now tell me how much they admire and respect what I did.

The large number of positive press articles was also a complete surprise to me. Nearly fifty articles have appeared so far, and even contributors to church publications have praised the book. Both the book and the video have been recommended for use in schools by the Upper Austrian education authority, and they received a glowing review in the Education Yearbook in Germany too. Without doubt the thorough research and neutral style have helped the book gain such wide acceptance.

I am especially delighted by the enormous interest shown at the various book and video presentations. The first presentation, in Puchenau, near Linz in Upper Austria, was attended by 350 people. The atmosphere was marvelous, and I signed many books. I very much enjoyed the lively discussions with students at the presentations at the universities in Salzburg, Vienna (Austria) and Bern (Switzerland) and with high school students in Bolzano (Italy). The presentation in Wewelsburg

70: Bernhard Rammerstorfer and Leopold Engleitner present the Italian-language version of the video in Milan, Italy, 2003

(Germany) in 2002 was a particular highlight. Even though I was out of action with a severe flu as the date approached, I made sure I did everything I could to get better so that I would be able to return to Wewelsburg nearly 60 years after my internment in Niederhagen concentration camp. I was happy to undertake the 500-mile journey to see some of my former fellow internees and to talk to many inhabitants of Wewelsburg, including several students, who gave me a wonderful welcome.

The presentation of the Italian-language version of the video in Milan, Italy, in January 2003, was a marvelous experience, too. Some 400 people attended it. Afterward I stayed for a week for the exhibition "The Nazi Regime's Forgotten Victims." The exhibition attracted 5,000 visitors, and 35 school classes from Milan asked me to give an eyewitness account of what I had experienced. The enormous interest that was shown in my history and the warm-heartedness of the Italians made those days in Milan among the happiest of my life.

But the absolute highlight was May 5, 2003, in Vienna, 58 years to the day after my return home following my flight from the military authorities. I was able to take part in a remembrance gathering called "A Letter to the Stars" and talk about my life before an audience of 15,000 young people. It was a truly wonderful experience. I also met the Hollywood actor Leon Askin, who fled to the United States from Austria to escape the Nazis. I was particularly impressed by the speech given by Austria's President Dr. Thomas Klestil. Afterward the President received me in the Hofburg, the presidential palace, and I gave him a copy of my book and the video for a gift. He was very pleased about that and made a point of expressing his gratitude to me. For me, a simple man who used to be held in contempt, it is a great honor to have been received by the Austrian head of state, especially since it means that I have been granted rehabilitation that I would never have believed possible. For me it is a belated acknowledgement that I was right to live my life by the principles of justice.

On June 6, 2003, I was invited to the Austrian parliament in Vienna as a guest of honor by the Chairman of the Austrian National Assembly, Prof. Dr. Andreas Khol. In parliament Prof. Dr. Walter Manoschek from the University of Vienna and head of the research project "Austrian Victims of National Socialist Military Jurisdiction" presented the findings of the two-year project, which aims to rehabilitate every single victim of National Socialism. The project was commissioned by the Ministry of Education.

Dr. Andreas Khol, the Chairman of the Austrian National Assembly, underscored the importance of the research project with the words: "If the present is unaware of the past, it cannot shape the future. And it is important that this research project places the facts on the table about what happened." Afterward I gave Dr. Khol a copy of my book with a dedication to thank him for the invitation. He was pleased to accept it and said: "Thank you very much. I will certainly read your book."

I was very happy that another high-ranking representative of the Republic of Austria had shown interest in my biography in this way and publicly stated his support for the rehabilitation of the victims of National Socialism.

I see the visit to parliament as a magnificent gesture of rehabilitation and a significant step toward a change of attitude, so that we conscientious objectors are no longer regarded as criminals but as men with high principles.

Then on June 16, 2003, the governor of Upper Austria, Dr. Josef Pühringer, awarded me the "Silver Order of Merit of the Province of Upper Austria" in recognition of all the talks I have given at universities, schools, and international memorial sites on the subject of my experiences during the Nazi regime. This award came as a complete surprise to me. That I, an ordinary man, should receive such a great honor at my age is something I would never have thought possible.

I am very grateful that I lived to experience all that and that my life story has made a small contribution to an objective historical analysis of our country and my faith. It is a matter

71: Leopold Engleitner on the Leonsbergalm, September 2001

of great importance to me to show how important it is for peace that we live according to the principles of justice. That has given me renewed strength in the last few years, and I am looking forward to attending further events in the future. It goes without saying that I hope that the people who read my biography in translation will also find it interesting and useful.

I think the best way to answer the second part of the question about how the book has affected me is to recall an incident from 1932, the year I left the Roman Catholic Church. At that time I was treated with contempt by my neighbors, who refused to have anything more to do with me; some people even spat at me as they went by. Thanks to the book, there has been a complete turnaround. As I already mentioned, this has gone so far that I was received by the Austrian President, Dr. Thomas Klestil, was invited to parliament, and was even awarded the Silver Order of Merit of the Province of Upper Austria. These honors have transformed me from a persecuted, despised concentration camp internee and a cowardly conscientious objector to a completely rehabilitated man who is even regarded as an example to others. In the past this would have been altogether unthinkable. People now stop to talk to me in the street and tell me how much they admire what I have done. That people's attitudes should change so dramatically is something I would never have believed possible.

In the light of your life's experiences, what advice would you give the readers of this book?

I can only advise each one of them to take a thorough look at the Holy Scriptures, the book that God caused to be written for mankind. It has had a deep effect on me and has helped me to deal with all the problems in my life. My personal experience has left me absolutely convinced that the Bible is still the best guide for a happy and full life. It can help everyone to solve the problems he or she is confronted with, whatever their nature.

Show true wisdom of heart by keeping your conscience intact—for your own good and for the good of the people around you.

APPENDICES

Appendix I

Was Leopold Engleitner a pioneer of freedom of worship, speech, and the press? What has changed?

The prevailing social attitudes toward people with "unorthodox" religious views at the time of Leopold Engleitner's clashes with the authorities can best be summed up by referring to two rulings of the Supreme Court which show how the concept of "libel on a legally recognized church" as laid down in § 303 of the Penal Law was interpreted:

72: The cover of the publication "Intolerance," Watchtower Bible and Tract Society, Brooklyn, NY, USA 1933, facsimile

Supreme Court ruling of 15/02/1892, collection 1512: Any remark which injures the dignity of a minister of religion constitutes an offense. The words, "Reverend Father reproves everyone. But what if everyone were to start reproving Reverend Father?" contain an offense.

Supreme Court ruling of 18/04/1891, collection 1426: The misdemeanor need not reach the degree commonly deemed to be injurious to honor; therefore an accusation made against the minister of religion that he is disobliging is sufficient to constitute the offense.

Accordingly, one did not even have to make a disparaging remark about a religious minister to have "offended" him. All it took was a remark such as "you are disobliging towards me," or "you have something against me." In the light of this interpretation of § 303 of the Penal Law, it is hardly surprising that the authorities took action against people who uttered or made available the kind of direct criticism contained in the Bible Students' publications in the 1920s and 1930s (see following page). Conversely, under Section V, Articles 62 and 63 of the Peace Treaty of St. Germain, Austria was obliged to guarantee free and unhindered public worship. However, a number of different court rulings indicate that a change was under way; the courts and authorities were beginning to realize that their treatment of the Bible Students in the past was incompatible with a modern, liberal state form. In the case of Leopold Engleitner, this was shown once by the dismissal of legal proceedings against him by the Austrian president, once by an amnesty, and once by allowing extraordinary extenuating circumstances under § 266 of the Penal Law. Despite this, efforts were still being made to maintain the old order and satisfy the requirements of the legally recognized churches and religious communities.

People like Leopold Engleitner were pioneers of freedom of speech, worship, and the press in Austria because their unwavering convictions forced the authorities to look to the future and consider freedom of speech and human rights although the legal interpretation of these laws was still very much dominated by past conventions.

They were pioneers of basic rights that are today taken for granted. It is partly thanks to such courageous people that we can now voice criticism openly without having to fear the legal consequences. At the time, this was not possible, resulting in great suffering for people like Leopold Engleitner. But it was they who paved the way, and today we are more tolerant; these basic rights are, generally speaking, respected. Every one of these pioneers has thus done our society an enormous service.

Appendix II
History of Buchenwald Concentration Camp

Buchenwald concentration camp was established on Ettersberg Hill near Weimar in Thuringia in July 1937. The first detainees were political opponents of the Nazi regime, convicted criminals, Jews, Jehovah's Witnesses, homosexuals, and so-called asocial elements. When World War II broke out, an increasing number of prisoners were brought in from other countries. At the time of the camp's liberation, 95% of the detainees were non-Germans.

Particularly after 1943 the prisoners in Buchenwald were mercilessly exploited, being forced to work in the armaments industry in Buchenwald and its 136 subcamps. In 1944 they were joined by women as well. Although the camp was not one of those where systematic genocide was carried out, prisoners-of-war were massacred in large numbers, and many other detainees met their deaths in the course of medical experiments or at the hands of despotic SS men. Buchenwald was fully integrated in the National Socialists' program of mass extermination, selecting prisoners to be sent to the death camps. At the beginning of 1945, the camp was chosen as the final destination for prisoners evacuated from Auschwitz and Gross-Rosen concentration camps. Shortly before its liberation, the SS tried to evacuate Buchenwald, sending 28,000 people on death marches. Around 21,000 others, including over 900 children and adolescents, remained in the camp.

On April 11, 1945, units of the American 3rd Army reached Ettersberg Hill. The SS fled, and prisoners of the underground resistance movement opened the gates from inside. From 1937 to 1945, over 250,000 people were interned in Buchenwald, of which more than 56,000 died.

Source: Buchenwald Memorial Site

Appendix III
History of Niederhagen Concentration Camp

The concentration camp in Wewelsburg was established in 1939. The purpose of the camp was to assemble workers for the ideologically most important construction project of the SS at a time when there was a severe shortage of personnel. The fortress itself had been built in the style of the Weser Renaissance, and its location and unusual triangular form attracted the interest of *SS-Reichsführer* Heinrich Himmler as early as 1933. Himmler's idea was to make Wewelsburg the center of the pseudo-scientific work supposed to corroborate the National Socialist ideology, and at the same time create a shrine for dead SS leaders there.

Building work on the extension of Wewelsburg fortress began in 1934 with around 100 workers from the *Reichsarbeitsdienst* (Reich labor service). In 1939 a 100-strong group of prisoners from Sachsenhausen concentration camp was sent to Wewelsburg to begin the conversion of the north tower, of which only a shell remained standing after it had been struck by lightning in 1815. The cellars were converted into a "crypt," and there were plans to turn the former chapel into a memorial hall for *Obergruppenführers.* Soon not only the fortress itself but the whole village was included in Himmler's construction plans; a sumptuous villa was built for his head architect, Bartels, as was a staff building for the SS, a housing development for SS leaders, etc.

During the first period of the concentration camp's existence, the number of internees rose, reaching 480, in August 1941. In mid-1940 the prisoners began constructing a new camp on a site which had been cleared of trees and bordered Niederhagen wood. On September 1, 1941, the subcamp Wewelsburg, which had previously belonged to Sachsenhausen concentration camp, became a camp in its own right. In January 1940 the escape attempt of two prisoners caused such anxiety in the town that the entire group of workers was deported back to Sachsenhausen, to be replaced in February by seventy prisoners with purple triangles: Jehovah's Witnesses, otherwise known as Bible Students. For religious reasons, this group would not attempt to escape, and the SS regarded them as hardworking and disciplined. In the months that followed, more Bible Students arrived at Wewelsburg from other concentration camps. In the following years, the 300 Bible Students formed the real nucleus of the workers in Niederhagen concentration camp at Wewelsburg, of which there were around 3,900 in all.

Death certificates are known to exist for at least 1,285 prisoners who met their end from malnutrition, overwork, poor sanitation, and despotic punishments meted out at the whim of the SS. But there were also deliberate killings. Prisoners were shot or their thoraxes crushed beneath heavy army boots. Other methods included dousing with cold water. Niederhagen concentration camp was selected by the inspector of concentration camps for the operation Aktion 14 f 13. Codes of this kind were used for the "euthanasia" programs. From April 1941, medical commissions began selecting prisoners who suffered from serious mental and physical illnesses or were in a weakened condition for deportation to clinics where they were murdered with poison gas.

In April 1943 construction work was temporarily stopped and Niederhagen concentration camp closed. All the prisoners except for 42 were transferred to other concentration camps.

In order to prevent the capture of Wewelsburg by the Americans, Himmler ordered the entire complex, in the middle of the village, to be blown up. However, this was only partially successful. Two days later, on April 2, 1945, US soldiers liberated the remaining prisoners from Wewelsburg.

Source: Wulff E. Brebeck/Karl Hüser, *Wewelsburg 1933-1945 Das Konzentrationslager*, (Münster, 1998)

Appendix IV
History of Ravensbrück Concentration Camp

In November 1938 the SS had prisoners from Sachsenhausen concentration camp and elsewhere build a concentration camp for women in the Prussian village of Ravensbrück. This installation, near the former health resort of Fürstenberg in what had previously been Mecklenburg, was the only major concentration camp on German soil that was intended solely for women.

In the spring of 1939, the first thousand women prisoners were taken to Ravensbrück from Lichtenberg concentration camp, and in April 1941 a men's camp was added to it. In the summer of 1942, the Uckermark Youth Concentration Camp was opened close by.

The women's concentration camp was constantly expanded; more and more barracks were added, as was an *"Industriehof,"* an area of workshops for jobs traditionally done by women. Adjacent to the concentration camp, the firm of Siemens & Halske constructed twenty factory buildings, where the prisoners had to work as forced laborers. As the war went on, more than 70 subcamps of the main camp in Ravensbrück were established all over the German Reich. The women were exploited primarily by the armaments industry.

Between 1939 and 1945, some 132,000 women and children, 20,000 men, and 1,000 female adolescents (in Uckermark) were registered as prisoners. The people deported to Ravensbrück were of over 40 different nationalities, and included Jews, Sinti, Roma, and Jehovah's Witnesses. Tens of thousands were murdered, some dying of starvation or illness or as a result of medical experiments. Following the construction of a gas chamber at the end of 1944, the SS gassed between 5,000 and 6,000 prisoners in Ravensbrück. In addition to this, many women, mostly Jewish, were murdered during the operation Aktion 14 f 13 in pursuit of its aim to "destroy life unworthy of life" or were killed with injections of phenol.

Shortly before the end of the war, about 7,000 prisoners were taken to Switzerland and Sweden with the help of the International Red Cross, the Swedish Red Cross, and the Danish Red Cross. Tens of thousands of women who remained in the camp were forced by the SS on "death marches" toward the northwest. On April 30, 1945, the Red Army liberated about 3,000 sick prisoners who had been left behind. But even after their liberation, the suffering for countless men, women, and children was not yet over. Many died in the weeks following the liberation, while others are still suffering today from the consequences.

Source: The Brandenburg Memorials Foundation / Ravensbrück Memorial Museum

Appendix V
Himmler's Post-War Geopolitical Plans for the Bible Students

Although *SS-Reichsführer* Heinrich Himmler had initially singled out the Bible Students for particularly severe treatment, his point of view underwent a dramatic change as the war progressed. Since he held a diploma in agriculture, Himmler was very impressed by their conscientious attitude toward work. This is shown by a letter he wrote to a farmer in Upper Bavaria on June 26, 1943, in which he suggests using a Bible Student to help with the harvest. Despite describing them as "members of a crazy sect," he considers them decent people. "On the whole they are people who work hard," he writes in the letter, "but who are 'cranks' when it comes to this one subject."

He was fascinated by the strength of their faith, which he stressed on many occasions. On the basis of those characteristics of the Witnesses that Himmler held in high regard, he hatched the absurd notion of involving them in his post-war geopolitical plans. He wrongly assumed that over the next few years Germany would win back large areas of Russian territory. In a letter to the head of the *Reichssicherheitshauptamt, SS-Obergruppenführer* Dr. Ernst Kaltenbrunner, dated July 21, 1944, Himmler presents his ideas on how Russia is to be kept under control and at peace:

"Any thought of introducing a kind of National Socialism is sheer madness. What the people need, however, is a religion or a philosophy of life. To support and resuscitate the Orthodox Church would be wrong, because it will always be the institution of nationalistic rallying. To allow the Catholic Church in would be at least equally wrong; there is no need for any explanation of this view. . . . We must support every form of religion and sect that promotes pacifism. Of all the beliefs of the Turkish peoples, the teachings of Buddhism can be considered; of those of all other peoples, the teachings of the Bible Students. The Bible Students have, as you well know, characteristics which are, to us, extremely positive: apart from the fact that they refuse to do military service or any work relating to war—or any other 'damaging' activity, as they describe it—they are bitterly opposed to the Jews,[1] the Catholic Church, and the Pope. Moreover, they are extraordinarily moderate in their habits, neither drink nor smoke,[2] and are very hard-working and upright; they always keep their word. In addition they are excellent farmers. They do not strive for riches or prosperity, since this is detrimental to them in respect of eternal life. All in all, these are ideal characteristics and it is generally evident that the most fervent and idealistic Bible Students possess good and very praiseworthy characteristics. . . . For this reason, I wish that the Bible Students in the camps who are known to be genuine be scrutinized again by examining bodies so that those of them who only professed to be Bible Students after they had been committed to the camp or did so shortly before their committal for reasons of expediency are removed from the group. This will also prevent characteristics of the Bible Students being exploited in a communist manner and will prevent people calling themselves Bible Students who do not possess the quality of diligence and are lazy, as I have already experienced here and there on farms, for instance in Fridolfing, Upper Bavaria. Thus the possibility is opened up of placing the genuine Bible Students in positions of trust in the concentration camps where temptations of a monetary or other material nature exist, and of treating them particularly well. This in turn provides us with the starting point for deploying these German Bible Students in Russia in the future and with the missionaries through whom we can pacify the Russian people by spreading the teachings of the Bible Students."

---

[1] This is not true, since Jehovah's Witnesses condemn anti-Semitism.
[2] Although this was true of most Jehovah's Witnesses, there were still a number of smokers among them at that time.

The *SS-Reichsführer* wanted to take advantage of the fact that Jehovah's Witnesses always remained neutral. Although there were certain requirements of the National Socialist regime that they did not fulfill, they never took part in any subversive activities. It is almost unbelievable; one of the most powerful and influential men in the Third Reich suddenly considered the Bible Students, who, as supposed "criminals representing a threat to the security of the state" had been put out of harm's way "to protect the people and the state," as a group of people of whom one could be absolutely certain that they would not engage in any seditious activities! Himmler saw them as ideal citizens of the Soviet Union and expected that their missionary zeal would give rise to a population who would out of principle offer no resistance.

Interestingly, Himmler wrote down his ideas for a Greater Germany which would make use of the teachings of the Bible Students to protect its future eastern border on the day after the assassination attempt on Adolf Hitler. Despite the fact that the fall of the National Socialist regime was becoming increasingly apparent, Himmler's thoughts still centered on absurd schemes which had no relation at all to reality.

Source: *Detlef Garbe, Zwischen Widerstand und Martyrium: Die Zeugen Jehovas im "Dritten Reich"* (Munich 1997).

INDEX OF PERSONS

REFERENCES

Wulff E. Brebeck/Karl Hüser, *Wewelsburg 1933-1945: Das Konzentrationslager* (Münster, 1998)

Brockhaus Encyclopedia (Mannheim, 1992, 19th edition)

DÖW, *Widerstand und Verfolgung in Oberösterreich 1934-1945, Vol. 2* (Vienna, 1982)

DÖW, *Widerstand und Verfolgung in Salzburg 1934-1945* (Vienna, 1991)

Ursula Floßmann/Oskar Lehner, *Geschichte* (Linz, 1990)

Detlef Garbe, *Zwischen Widerstand und Martyrium: Die Zeugen Jehovas im "Dritten Reich"* (Munich, 1997)

Gedenkstätte Buchenwald (Buchenwald Memorial Site), archives

Brigitte Hamann, *Elisabeth—The Reluctant Empress* (New York, 1986)

Heinrich Heine, *Gesammelte Gedichte und Verse* (Lechnerverlag, Switzerland, 1994)

Hans Hesse, *"Am mutigsten waren immer wieder die Zeugen Jehovas"—Verfolgung und Widerstand der Zeugen Jehovas im Nationalsozialismus* (Bremen, 1998)

Kirsten John, *Mein Vater wird gesucht* (Munich, 1998)

Guido Knopp, *Hitlers Helfer* (Munich, 1998)

Österreich Lexikon www.aeiou.at

Salzkammergut-Zeitung, Gmunden, 1918, 1936

Salzkammergut-Beobachter, Gmunden 1938

Rolf Steininger (ed.), *Vergessene Opfer des Nationalsozialismus* (Innsbruck, 2000)

Stiftung Brandenburgische Gedenkstätten/Mahn-und Gedenkstätte Ravensbrück (The Brandenburg Memorials Foundation/Ravensbrück Memorial Museum)

Alfred Vogel, *Der kleine Doktor* (Augsburg, 1993)

Weltbild Software 1998, CD-ROM, *Meilensteine des 20. Jahrhunderts: Widerstand und Verfolgung im III. Reich*

LIST OF ILLUSTRATIONS

SELECTED BIOGRAPHY

1. General Works

Wolfgang Benz/Walter H. Pehle (editors), *Lexikon des deutschen Widerstandes* (Frankfurt am Main, 1994), pp. 321-25

Detlef Garbe, *Zwischen Widerstand und Martyrium: Die Zeugen Jehovas im "Dritten Reich"* (Munich, 1997), definitive work with a extensive bibliography

Hans Hesse (editor), *"Am mutigsten waren immer wieder die Zeugen Jehovas"–Verfolgung und Widerstand der Zeugen Jehovas im Nationalsozialismus* (Bremen, 1998), extensive collection with bibliography

Michael H. Kater, *Die Ernsten Bibelforscher im 3. Reich*, in: Hans Rothfels/Theodor Eschenburg (editors), quarterly historical magazines (Stuttgart, 1969), 2nd edition, pp. 181-218

Watchtower Society, *Yearbook of the Jehovah's Witnesses 1974* (Watchtower Bible and Tract Society, Wiesbaden 1974), pp. 66-253

Friedrich Zipfel, *Kirchenkampf in Deutschland 1933-1945, Religionsverfolgung und Selbstbehauptung der Kirchen in der nationalsozialistischen Zeit* (Berlin, 1965), pp. 175-201, 352-58, 363-71, 411-17, and 527-33

Franz Zürcher, *Kreuzzug gegen das Christentum: Moderne Christenverfolgung, Eine Dokumentationensammlung* (Zurich/New York, 1938)

Andreas Maislinger (editor), in Fred Parkinson, *Conquering the past: Austrian Nazism yesterday and today* (Wayne State University Press, Detroit 1989) pp. 177-89

Rolf Steininger (editor), *Vergessene Opfer des Nationalsozialismus* (Innsbruck, 2000)

2. Local Studies

Martin Broszat/Elke Fröhlich/Anton Grossmann, *Bayern in der NS-Zeit, Vol. 4, Herrschaft und Gesellschaft im Konflikt, Section C* (Munich, 1983), pp. 621-43

Andreas Maislinger, *Die Zeugen Jehovas (Ernste Bibelforscher)*, in *Widerstand und Verfolgung in Tirol Vol. 2*, (Vienna, 1984), published by the Documentation Centre of Austrian Resistance, pp. 369-83, 623

Ch. Mitterrutzner, *Andere religiöse Gruppen*, in *Widerstand und Verfolgung in Niederösterreich 1934-1945 Vol. 2* (Vienna, 1987), published by the Documentation Centre of Austrian Resistance

Rudolf Zinnhobler, *Die Zeugen Jehovas (Ernste Bibelforscher)*, in *Widerstand und Verfolgung in Oberösterreich, Vol. 2* (Vienna, 1982), published by the Documentation Centre of Austrian Resistance, pp. 199-210

3. Biographies

Max Hollweg, *Es ist unmöglich von dem zu schweigen, was ich erlebt habe: Zivilcourage im Dritten Reich* (Bielefeld, 1997)

Vinzenz Jobst, *Anton Uran: Verfolgt – vergessen –
hingerichtet* (Klagenfurt, 1997)
Hans-Werner Kusserow, *Der lila Winkel: Die Familie
Kusserow – Zeugen Jehovas unter der
Nazidiktatur* (Bonn, 1998)

4. Franz Jägerstätter

Gordon C. Zahn, *In Solitary Witness. The Life and
Death of Franz Jägerstätter* (Springfield:
Illinois, 1964)
G. Bergmann, *Franz Jägerstätter: Ein Leben vom
Gewissen entschieden* (Stein am Rhein, 1980)
Andreas Maislinger, *Der Fall Jägerstätter*, in *Yearbook
1991, Vol. 2*, published by the
Documentation Centre of Austrian
Resistance, pp. 20-32
Erna Putz, *Franz Jägerstätter: "...besser die Hände als
der Wille gefesselt"* (Linz, 1985)
Erna Putz, *Gefängnisbriefe und Aufzeichnungen – Franz
Jägerstätter verweigert 1943 den Wehrdienst*
(Linz, 1987)
Alfons Riedl/Josef Schwabeneder (editors), *Franz
Jägerstätter – Christlicher Glaube und
politisches Gewissen* (Thaur, 1997)

INDEX

BERNHARD RAMMERSTORFER was born in 1968 in Neiderwaldkirchen, Austria. He worked for the provincial government in Upper Austria while pursuing his law studies at Linz University. In 1999, Rammerstorfer authored *Unbroken Will: The Extraordinary Courage of an Ordinary Man* (in German: *Nein statt Ja und Amen*) and produced a film documentary of the life of Leopold Engleitner, Austrian concentration camp survivor.

Rammerstorfer and Engleitner have lectured at universities, schools, and memorial sites in Austria, Switzerland, Germany, and Italy. In January 2003, Rammerstorfer presented the Italian version of the film at Castello Sforzesco in Milan. The film won the Golden Bear award at the 31st Festival of Nations For Film and Video in 2003. Rammerstorer's extraordinary commitment has brought Engleitner widespread recognition as his story has resonated far beyond the borders of Austria.